Waters of Promise

Waters of Promise
Finding Meaning in Believer Baptism

Brandon C. Jones

☙PICKWICK *Publications* · Eugene, Oregon

WATERS OF PROMISE
Finding Meaning in Believer Baptism

Copyright © 2012 Brandon C. Jones. All rights reserved. Except for brief quotations in critical publications or reviews, no part of this book may be reproduced in any manner without prior written permission from the publisher. Write: Permissions, Wipf and Stock Publishers, 199 W. 8th Ave., Suite 3, Eugene, OR 97401.

Pickwick Publications
An Imprint of Wipf and Stock Publishers
199 W. 8th Ave., Suite 3
Eugene, OR 97401

www.wipfandstock.com

ISBN 13: 978-1-61097-628-2

Cataloguing-in-Publication data:

Jones, Brandon C.

    Waters of promise : finding meaning in believer baptism / Brandon C. Jones.

    viii + 170 pp. ; 23 cm. Includes bibliographical references.

    ISBN 13: 978-1-61097-628-2

    1. Baptism—Baptists. 2. Covenant theology. 3. Sacraments—Baptists. I. Title.

BV811.2 J65 2012

Manufactured in the U.S.A.

Contents

Acknowledgments / vii

1. The Search for the Meaning of Believer Baptism / 1
2. Baptist Sacramentalism in the Twentieth Century / 9
3. A Resurgence in Baptist Sacramentalism / 26
4. Recovering Sacramentalism in the Baptist Tradition / 50
5. Covenant Theology in the Baptist Tradition / 73
6. Covenant Ecclesiology in the Baptist Tradition / 102
7. A Historic Link between Covenant and Sacrament / 115
8. A Covenantal View of Baptism / 132
9. Beyond the Waters of Promise / 154

Bibliography / 157

Acknowledgments

I AM INDEBTED TO several people who have helped me write this book, especially the members of my dissertation committee, Ronald J. Feenstra, John J. Bolt, Richard A. Muller, and Stanley K. Fowler. They all had a hand in sharpening my argument and their feedback was invaluable. Anthony R. Cross was also instrumental in providing crucial resources as well as being a helpful partner in my research. Most of all, I am grateful to my family, who first introduced me to the gospel of Jesus Christ as well as my heritage as a Baptist. Much thanks also go to my wife, Marci. She has been my most important resource for this book, providing a loving home for our children and constant support and encouragement to me throughout the writing of this book. I dedicate this book to her.

1

The Search for the Meaning of Believer Baptism

THE BAPTIST OPPOSITION TO infant baptism, expressed in exclusively baptizing disciples, is the main thing that distinguishes Baptists from many other Christian traditions. Baptists have said much about who should *not* be baptized, what baptism does *not* accomplish, and what modes are *not* acceptable, but they have said little about the meaning of baptism. Despite the lack of discussion about the meaning of baptism, most Baptists today, hereafter referred to as "ordinance-only Baptists," think baptism is an ordinance, or the uniquely God-ordained means through which a believer, by performing the outward physical act of baptism, obediently commemorates his or her prior inward change that has arisen through faith in the gospel. In contrast, some Baptists today, hereafter referred to as "sacramentalists," think baptism is a sacrament, or a means of grace through which God normatively confirms the union a believer has with Christ and his church by bestowing a deeper consciousness of that union. Ordinance-only Baptists think sacramentalists make too much of baptism, while sacramentalists think ordinance-only Baptists make too little. As a result, the search for the meaning of baptism continues.

Despite an abundance of literature that has presented the biblical case for sacramentalism most Baptists reject this understanding. If sacramentalists want to make a larger impression on their fellow Baptists they must address the heart of the divide between ordinance-only Baptists and sacramentalists that is rooted in these groups' different conceptions of how God works in and through the world generally and in salvation specifically. Such a task requires clearer and more coherent explanations of the sacramentalist understanding of the meaning of baptism that answer ordinance-only Baptist objections directly. Until sacramentalists adequately address these objections, they can continue to expect fellow Baptists to dismiss their views.

THREE OBJECTIONS TO BAPTIST SACRAMENTAL THEOLOGY

Sacramentalism Teaches Baptismal Regeneration

Ordinance-only Baptists' first major objection to sacramentalism is that it entails baptismal regeneration. This objection is part of a greater debate in Baptist circles about the place of sacramental terminology (or the lack thereof) in Baptist theology. Baptist sacramentalists use sacramental terminology to refer to their belief that God ordains certain acts of faith that involve physical things as means of his grace to believers. Ordinance-only Baptists claim that the use of sacramental terminology is inherently tied to how other Christian traditions conceive of such rites as baptism and the Lord's Supper. For instance, Thomas R. Schreiner and Shawn D. Wright choose not to use sacramental terminology in a book they edited on baptism because it is "liable to a number of different interpretations," and they claim "sacramental theology clearly compromises the gospel since it teaches that infants enter God's kingdom by virtue of the sacramental action."[1] For Schreiner, Wright, and many other ordinance-only Baptists, the sacramental theology of other Christian traditions links salvific grace with physical acts such as baptism. In their opinion, claiming that baptism is a sacrament also implies claiming some form of baptismal regeneration and thereby undermining the doctrine of salvation by grace through faith in Christ alone.[2] They further claim that sacramentalists misuse sacramental terminology, rendering the sacramentalist view of baptism to be vague at best—which leads to their third objection below.[3]

To be sure, some Christian accounts of sacramentalism tie baptism to salvific grace. But Baptist sacramentalists use the term *sacrament* to describe a more modest concept. In their use, acts of faith that involve

---

1. Schreiner and Wright, introduction to *Believer's Baptism*, 2n4.
2. Nettles, *The Baptists*, 3:311.
3. Schreiner and Wright, introduction to *Believer's Baptism*, 2n4.

physical things, such as baptism and the Lord's Supper, are indeed means of grace, but not means of salvific grace. They use the term *sacrament* to refer to the concept that baptism and the Lord's Supper are unique means of divine-human encounters in which God deepens his relationship with believers. The sacrament does not signify the beginning of a relationship with God as this is seen as a separate event in a believer's life. In this way, sacramentalism does not have to entail baptismal regeneration as it is faith and not any sacrament that begins the relationship between God and a believer. To avoid being misunderstood, some sacramentalists see baptism as an ordinance while conceiving of it as a means of grace, or they avoid using such terms as *sacrament* or *ordinance* altogether when discussing baptism. While the meaning of baptism matters more than the terms used in reference, there is no better term than *sacrament* for any view that presents baptism as a means of grace. Thus, this book will refer to baptism as a sacrament, even if its understanding of the term differs from that of other Christian traditions. If Baptists can have their own understanding of the term *baptism*, they can also have their own understanding of the term *sacrament* and conceiving baptism as a means of grace is closer to what most religious traditions, Baptist or otherwise, mean by the term *sacrament* rather than by the term *ordinance*.[4]

---

4. Cross and Thompson discuss how Baptists use the term *sacrament* in introduction to *Baptist Sacramentalism*, 3–7. To be sure, one risks being misunderstood or dismissed by using sacramental terminology, but keeping the terminology and specifically defining the concept it refers to follows Clark's warning that one should not let broad theologies of the sacraments dictate how one specifically understands baptism and the Lord's Supper (*Approach*, 71). This is not just special pleading from Baptist sacramentalists. For example, Heron, a Reformed theologian, cautions against letting "the specific nature and character of particular 'sacraments'" be dominated by the discussion of a "general conception of what a sacrament is or ought to be. However the idea of a sacrament is defined and applied, it must be used in a way that permits the things which are called 'sacraments' to stand out and be recognised in their own colours and with their own distinctive shape and meaning," (*Table and Tradition*, 56). Heron also has a helpful discussion of the development of sacramental terminology in the early church and beyond, (ibid., 59–107). Cf. Grenz's summary of Heron's discussion in "Baptism and the Lord's Supper," 77–79. Schmemann makes a similar point for Eastern Orthodox theology, but he is more concerned with drawing materials for sacramental theology from the Divine Liturgy rather than from Scripture (*Introduction to Liturgical Theology*). Cf. Ellis, "Embodied Grace," 4–5.

Sacramentalism Is Not a Baptist Doctrine

Ordinance-only Baptists' second objection against sacramentalism is that it is not a genuine Baptist position. Rather, they argue that what motivates sacramentalism are issues that lie outside the Baptist tradition, such as the ecumenical movement. These issues, and not biblical concerns or Baptist commitments, are really responsible for an increase of interest in sacramentalism among Baptists during the past fifteen years. One ordinance-only Baptist, Christopher Bryan Moody, even argues that sacramentalism is more prevalent among British Baptists than North American Baptists because ecumenical concerns from fifty years ago have fueled the doctrine rather than genuine Baptist concerns.[5] While it is true that sacramentalism is more popular among British Baptists than their North American counterparts, that is no reason to reject sacramentalism itself. However, if sacramentalism has never been part of the Baptist tradition, then most Baptists should rightly question its place in Baptist theology today.

Unfortunately, ordinance-only Baptists often assume rather than prove their claim that genuine Baptist theology, both past and present,

---

5. Moody has two other critiques against sacramentalism: it looks too much like Stone-Campbell theology (and thus is not genuinely Baptist), and it is provincial, because it looks only at British Baptist sources instead of including North American ones ("American Baptist Sacramentalism?" 129. We will reference Moody's unpublished dissertation, which is also available in print under the title *American Baptist Sacramentalism?*). Regarding provincialism, Moody specifically charges Fowler and Cross with being too provincial in their research, but both authors explicitly limit their studies to British Baptists in the titles and introductions of their books. Fowler argues that there is nothing "uniquely British about" the content of sacramentalism, so it "might well serve as a new paradigm for Baptist thought on a wider scale," (*More Than a Symbol*, 4). Yet he never claims to present anything other than British Baptist views in his book; the full title of his book is *More Than a Symbol: The British Baptist Recovery of Baptismal Sacramentalism*. The full title of Cross's book, *Baptism and the Baptists: Theology and Practice in Twentieth-Century Britain*, likewise clues the reader to the limits of his research. Moreover, Cross's expanded conclusions from his research come in an article entitled "Baptists and Baptism." Moody critiques Fowler and Cross for failing to do what neither of them ever claims to do, namely present North American or even global Baptist baptismal theology. Such research would be helpful, and Moody provides some of it when he surveys North American Baptist baptismal theology. This book will also interact with some North American sources, but it will focus on British Baptist theologians, agreeing with Fowler that, while social and historical factors rather than theological ones may be decisive for sacramentalism's greater *popularity* in Britain than in North America, there is nothing uniquely British about the theology *itself*. Cross summarizes some social and historical factors for British Baptist acceptance of sacramentalism in "Baptists and Baptism," 113–16.

opposes sacramental theology. In doing so, they have dismissed several works that demonstrate how the turn to sacramentalism among Baptists fifty years ago was a recovery of a much older Baptist view rather than an unprecedented infusion of ecumenism into the Baptist tradition.[6] To be sure, many twentieth-century Baptist sacramentalists spoke of their desire to unite in some visible way with other Christian traditions. However, that desire did not go against the Baptist tradition, neither did it override the presence of sacramentalism among Baptists centuries ago. Sacramentalism, even if it is a minority position today, is a genuine part of both historic and contemporary Baptist theology.

Sacramentalism Is Vague

Ordinance-only Baptists' third objection against sacramentalism is that it is at worst an unbiblical concept and at best vague. This objection is not new because for decades the main issue was—and in many ways still is—whether sacramentalism is biblically defensible. Most works on sacramentalism present and defend it from the perspective of biblical theology, providing arguments based in Scripture that support sacramentalism.[7] These works do not prove the biblical case for sacramentalism beyond a shadow of a doubt, but they have enough exegetical analysis of the pertinent baptismal passages in the NT to meet the objection that sacramentalism is an unbiblical concept. There is no need here to present arguments that can already be found in works such as G. R. Beasley-Murray's *Baptism in the New Testament*, but there is room for further discussion as many biblical defenses of sacramentalism do not build on the exegetical foundation of sacramentalism by also demonstrating clearly what the sacramental meaning of baptism is. Readers of these works are expected to figure out on their own how a sacramental view of baptism coheres with broader doctrines such as salvation and sanctification, rightly exposing sacramentalism to misunderstandings about what it is and is not.

6. Such works include Fowler, *More Than a Symbol*; Cross, "Myth," 128–62; and Thompson, "Re-envisioning Baptist Identity," 287–302. Moody follows the lead of Garrett by appealing to Baptist confessions in response to sacramentalists' historical arguments rather than doing his own research in the primary sources to substantiate his claims, ("American Baptist Sacramentalism?" 168–72).

7. Examples of this approach include Robinson, *Life and Faith*; Robinson, *Baptist Principles*, Clark, *Approach*; Gilmore, ed., *Christian Baptism*; White, *Biblical Doctrine*; Beasley-Murray, *Baptism in the New Testament*; Beasley-Murray, *Baptism Today and Tomorrow*; and Gilmore, *Baptism and Christian Unity*.

For example, according to H. Wheeler Robinson, baptism is for believers alone, but it also implies the cleansing of sin, is linked to the gift of the Holy Spirit, and is a means of an experimental union with Christ in his redeeming acts.[8] Similarly, G. R. Beasley-Murray says it is "axiomatic that conversion and baptism are inseparable, if not indistinguishable. In the primitive apostolic Church baptism was 'conversion-baptism.'"[9] The face value of these claims renders the earlier objection—that Baptist sacramentalism really is another form of baptismal regeneration—somewhat compelling. Sacramentalists elsewhere insist that they affirm the primary role of faith in justification rather than that of baptism, thus acknowledging some tension within their view. They say this tension derives from the biblical witness itself rather than their own baptismal theology, and there is no need for people to demand more coherence or detail than the texts themselves allow. The rejoinder from ordinance-only Baptists is that these tensions stem from sacramentalist formulations of the texts (or the lack thereof) rather than from the texts themselves, making sacramentalism either vague or misleading.

Sacramentalists rightly appeal to tensions within Scripture to account for some level of vagueness in their views. For example, Beasley-Murray argues that after one considers the variety of ways in which God gives the Spirit to people in the book of Acts, "it becomes apparent that while a normative doctrine can be gleaned, life is more complicated than any formulations of doctrine; moreover, the Lord is able to take care of the conditions that fall outside the formulas!"[10] If the criterion for judging a position to be vague is that it fails to account for every possible practical scenario, then most, if not all, theologies of baptism are vague. However, many sacramentalist views truly are vague in another sense because they do not clearly explain the theological relationship between baptism, faith, and conversion in light of the teachings of Scripture.

THE NEED FOR A NEW APPROACH

Sacramentalists have responded to these ordinance-only Baptist objections but the debate between the two groups has become circular. Sacramentalists begin by placing baptism within the broader realm of sal-

---

8. Robinson, *Baptist Principles*, 13–14.
9. Beasley-Murray, *Baptism Today and Tomorrow*, 37. Cf. Clark, *Approach*, 84.
10. Beasley-Murray, *Baptism Today and Tomorrow*, 39–40.

vation (and, more narrowly, of sanctification) and then go on to explain what that does *not* mean for baptism, rather than saying clearly what it does mean. Ordinance-only Baptists often respond to this negative presentation of sacramentalism by just repeating their own objections. In return, sacramentalists often just repeat the exegetical and historical case for their position rather than present and defend their view in a more compelling way that meets ordinance-only Baptist objections.

What is needed from sacramentalists is a clearer presentation and defense of sacramentalism that no longer tries to offer results from exegesis and biblical theology alone as sufficient responses to systematic concerns such as the relationship between faith, baptism, and salvation. Such a defense would build on the exegetical work that has been laid out already and seek to clarify it, making sacramentalism less prone to misunderstanding. Such a defense would also show how sacramentalism benefits several practical issues in Baptist baptismal theology today, such as the proper relationship between baptism and church membership, the proper age at which to baptize youth within the church community, and the proper reason to rebaptize prospective members of Baptist churches. Such a defense, perhaps to Beasley-Murray's dismay, would culminate in the realm of systematic theology, formulas and all.

Therefore, this book offers a theological defense of sacramentalism by arguing that covenant theology, as held by seventeenth-century Baptists, is a helpful framework in which to place a sacramental view of baptism. Covenant theology is helpful because a covenantal view of sacramentalism clarifies baptism's meaning, allows it to cohere with other key doctrines, and has communal aspects that address several practical concerns. The covenantal view transforms the waters of baptism into waters of promise between God, his covenant community, and the baptizand. As a result, the covenantal view, by responding to the most common objections to sacramentalism, may help end the search for the meaning of baptism.

THE COVENANTAL VIEW OF BAPTISM

The covenantal view of baptism states that the Spirit graciously uses baptism as a confirming sign and seal of a believer's initiation into the new covenant, thereby strengthening his or her consciousness of salvation. In baptism, God, through his Spirit and his covenant community, confirms that he has covenanted with the believer. Likewise, in baptism, the believer faithfully takes hold of God's covenant by consciously receiving its blessings and by pledging to fulfill its duties—both of which are tied to God's new covenant community, the church. What follows is a defense of this view that argues for its biblical grounding, systematic coherence, historical roots, and practical benefits.

2

Baptist Sacramentalism in the Twentieth Century

BAPTISTS HAVE FOCUSED ON different doctrines throughout their history, and the twentieth century brought a renewed focus on the meaning of baptism. Culminating in the middle of the twentieth century, a group of sacramentalist authors produced several works that defended a radically different understanding of the meaning of baptism than the status quo. While some ordinance-only Baptists outright rejected these works, most Baptists were indifferent to them. By the late 1960s sacramentalist authors turned to different subjects and whatever momentum the movement had appeared to completely stop. One reason why sacramentalism did not gain a larger foothold among Baptists during the twentieth century is that most works on the subject kept the same focus on the individual believer that the ordinance-only view already offered. For all the sacramentalist claims about how different their view of baptism was, its effect on the actual practice of baptism was minimal. This is an area in which the covenantal view can build on previous sacramentalist works, beginning with the author who first started focusing on sacramentalism—H. Wheeler Robinson.

H. WHEELER ROBINSON

Robinson began publishing works that deal with baptism in the 1920s.[1] He claims baptism is an ethical sacrament in which the believer makes a

---

1. These works include "Place of Baptism"; *Baptist Principles*; *Christian Experience*; "Believers' Baptism"; and "Five Points." Robinson also wrote *Redemption and Revelation*,

moral commitment to Christ, but he also argues that the NT closely links the gift of the Spirit to baptism, making it a means of grace as well. He defends this view against the charge of baptismal regeneration by claiming that baptism's efficacy, as a moral and ethical act, arises from internal conditions such as faith:

> There are two distinct ways of representing the operation of the Spirit of God in regard to baptism. We may think of the external act, and the material means, as the prescribed channel of the work of the Spirit, and then the result is what is commonly known as sacramentarianism. Or we may think of the internal conditions, the personal faith and conversion emphasized in Believers' Baptism, and see in them the true realm of the Spirit's activity. . . . In fact, when we speak of Believers' Baptism, we mean that baptism in the Spirit of God, of which water baptism is the expression.[2]

Robinson successfully avoids baptismal regeneration here, but his answer lacks clarity on how baptism emphasizes faith and conversion. Does it emphasize one's consciousness of having the gift of the Spirit or does it emphasize faith and conversion by mediating the gift itself, making baptism an integral part of the conversion process? Unfortunately, this is a question that sacramentalists rarely answer. Robinson's works started a welcome trend of drawing from often overlooked biblical passages for one's doctrine of baptism, but the meaning of baptism he presents in these works often raises more questions about sacramentalism than it answers, because he does not explore how baptism coheres with other doctrines.

CHRISTIAN BAPTISM (1959)

By 1955, members of the ecumenical movement were focusing on doctrines such as baptism, but there were only a few Baptist treatments of it

---

which served to complete a trilogy that began with *Christian Doctrine of Man* and continued with *Christian Experience*. All three books emphasize the psychology of religion, approaching it from what Robinson calls "the actuality of history," (*Redemption and Revelation*, x).

2. Robinson, *Baptist Principles*, 24–25. Cf. Robinson, *Redemption and Revelation*, 105–6. Underwood also adopted the phrase "ethical sacramentalism" with this understanding in mind, "Baptism and Regeneration." Underwood's ethical sacramentalism separates conversion from baptism, making the latter a "new, thrilling unforgettable experience, which brought them [believers] closer to Christ, Who Himself met them in it in response to their faith and love. . . . [It gave them] further divine power to walk in the newness of life," ("Views of Modern Churches," 228).

at that time. Moreover, according to Ernest A. Payne, those few Baptist treatments lacked agreement and authority in representing a proper apologetic for believer baptism.[3] Thus, a group of British Baptist scholars, including Neville Clark, G. R. Beasley-Murray, R. E. O. White, and Alec Gilmore, worked on a reexamination of baptism in light of recent scholarship from biblical, historical, and systematic angles. In 1959, they published *Christian Baptism*, which, among other things, incited controversy for its sacramental arguments. While most chapters in *Christian Baptism* focus on biblical exegesis of baptismal texts rather than history or systematic theology, Neville Clark's chapter, "The Theology of Baptism," elicited the strongest responses from ordinance-only Baptists because of his sacramental claims.[4]

In "The Theology of Baptism," Clark speaks of the relationship between baptism, faith, and conversion more explicitly than Robinson ever does. He argues that Christ's life and work must influence the meaning of baptism, grounding his view of baptism in Christ's atoning work. Clark then argues that baptism into Christ is baptism into his own death, resurrection, ascension, and future glory. For Clark, "baptism effects initiation into the life of the blessed Trinity and all the blessings of the new 'age', and so embodies the wholeness of redemption."[5] Of course, there is a tension in this age between the already and the not-yet effects of Christ's work, making a baptized believer forgiven of sins but still a sinner awaiting his or her inheritance. Clark emphasizes divine action in baptism but notes there is an interdependence of divine and human factors in baptism just as there was in the life of Christ. This is not to say that Christ was at odds with the will of the Father, as Clark argues: God does not work "outside of, apart from, [or] over the head of man. To deny this would be to deny both the principle of incarnation and the pattern of the life and death of the incarnate Son. But just as the baptism unto death of the Lord is constituted by the conjunction of divine action and human response, so the baptism into His death of His followers demands for its reality their ratification of His response, in obedience to the word proclaimed to them."[6] In other words, if Christ's life and work directly influences the meaning of

---

3. Payne, "Believers' Baptism," 39.

4. Clark, "Theology of Baptism," 306–26. Clark's previous work, *An Approach*, gives a more detailed account of his sacramental theology.

5. Clark, "Theology of Baptism," 309.

6. Ibid., 313–14.

baptism, then one must emphasize both God's work and the free human response in baptism.

One upshot of Clark's emphasis on Christ's crucifixion and resurrection for baptism is that it disturbs the paedobaptist continuity between the old and new covenants, including the link between circumcision and baptism. Clark critiques paedobaptists for linking the covenants together too much and argues that, in the process, Christ's work is ignored. He also critiques Baptists for severing the old and new covenants too much, leading to overly individualistic tendencies in typical Baptist accounts of salvation.[7] Clark's theology avoids these extremes by letting the Christ event govern his interpretation of the covenants and their continuity or lack thereof. However, it is debatable how unique his approach is as a third way since most other Baptists would also make this claim.

With his placement of baptism within the theological framework of the Christ event, Clark may be somewhat unique as far as sacramentalists go, but his baptismal theology retains a common tension between the roles of the Spirit and of faith in baptism. In some places Clark emphasizes God's role over the role of faith: "Baptism is a sacrament of the Gospel, not of our experience of it; of God's faithfulness, not of our faithful response to Him; and any theological formulation which lends itself so readily to an interpretation of the rite primarily in terms of a public confession of faith must at once be suspect."[8] One's faith may not give baptism either its efficacy or significance, but "it is the response to the Word which the Spirit empowers that makes baptism Christologically congruous and ethically meaningful."[9] In other words, God always works in accordance with human freedom, and baptism is no different, even in a sacramental understanding of baptism in which God's activity and promises are dominant. Clark may have clearly presented the major tenets and influences of his baptismal theology, but he was less clear on how it addresses systematic issues and practical concerns that surround baptismal theology in general. The covenantal view also emphasizes both the promise God makes to the believer and the commitment the believer makes to God and the church through baptism, so it will build somewhat

---

7. Ibid., 316–17.
8. Ibid., 316.
9. Ibid., 324.

on Clark's understanding without placing baptism within the realm of Christology as Clark does.

Clark's lack of clarity on how sacramentalism relates to salvation in general prompted many criticisms from other Baptists that the sacramentalism espoused by Clark and others in *Christian Baptism* denies *sola fide*, affirms baptismal regeneration, misinterprets key biblical texts that could have non-sacramental readings, excludes the unbaptized from salvation and the church, and runs contrary to historic Baptist theology.[10] Beasley-Murray responds to these criticisms in two articles in *The Baptist Times*, in which he says the exegetical portions of *Christian Baptism* were more concerned with presenting baptismal theology in "the Church of the Apostles" rather than formulating how baptism can or should be performed today.[11] Beasley-Murray goes on in these articles to present needed arguments on a sacramental theology of baptism that Clark's chapter lacks. Beasley-Murray clarifies the role of faith in sacramentalism, supports exegetical decisions on key texts that argue in favor of it, distinguishes how it makes baptism normative for salvation (acknowledging God's freedom to work outside baptism) rather than absolute, and gives criteria for a view to be genuinely Baptist. Beasley-Murray may have clarified the sacramentalist view, but his responses did not stop the debate that ensued after *Christian Baptism* was published.

Such debate prompted Beasley-Murray and other contributors to *Christian Baptism* to write more in the following decades, and R. E. O. White was the first among them when his *The Biblical Doctrine of Christian Initiation* was published in 1960.

R. E. O. WHITE

In *The Biblical Doctrine of Christian Initiation*, White presents many of the same exegetical arguments for a sacramental view of baptism that *Christian Baptism* has, but he also complements his biblical treatment with some theological aspects of sacramentalism. Among these aspects is his treatment of covenant theology, although he never develops what is presented in this book as the covenantal view of baptism. Rather, he uses

---

10. These are the five chief criticisms Fowler identifies after researching the reception of *Christian Baptism* in *The Baptist Times* in 1959–60, ("Is 'Baptist Sacramentalism' an Oxymoron?" 140–47).

11. Beasley-Murray, "The Spirit Is There." His other article is "Baptism and the Sacramental View."

his understanding of covenant theology to reinforce baptism as a rite God designed with an individual, rather than a community, in mind.

White builds his understanding of baptism on a theology of divine-human covenant that is expressed through baptism's predecessors: circumcision, proselyte baptism, and Johannine baptism. These considerations lead to his discussion of covenant theology in which he says the OT reveals a unique divine-human relationship between God and his people that is neither natural nor unchangeable. White says the "initiative was with God, who offered the covenant, and who redeemed Israel from Egypt that they might be His people. Israel's response was an equally free, deliberate, moral act; the gratitude and loyalty which their redemption evoked were entirely unforced."[12] White's account is a bilateral covenant, but because it has divine origins and terms it is a loving extension of God's grace rather than some sort of "bargain" between equals.[13] White carries this bilateral concept further with his Arminian soteriology, the key to which is man's free "response to a divine initiative of grace in history, upon terms which are in no sense agreed between God and man, but presented by God for man's unforced acceptance or rejection, for his weal or woe."[14]

While God always honors human freedom, there are important distinctions between God's relations with Israel and the church. For example, God made the old covenant with a people rather than individuals, so the community as a whole could either disobediently break it or obediently restore it. Unlike most accounts of covenant theology, White is not willing to uplift circumcision as a rite that is necessarily tied to initiation into the old covenant. Instead, he argues that it was merely a "tribal mark, shared among many others by that Israelite community with whom Yahweh chose to make covenant."[15] He supports this claim by citing the OT prophetic call for a personal religion complete with personal responsibility to obey God's commands as the mark of covenant fidelity rather than circumcision.

Unfortunately, White does not address the common claim that circumcision was a sign and seal of covenant fidelity. He also does not

---

12. White, *Biblical Doctrine*, 15.
13. Ibid.
14. Ibid., 17. Cf. Robinson, *Redemption and Revelation*, 226–27.
15. White, *Biblical Doctrine*, 25.

pursue the possibility that the prophetic calls for personal responsibility included or implied appeals to the purpose of the sign of covenant initiation. His failure to address these concerns leads him to make too little of circumcision and as a result limits his sacramental theology in general. If circumcision has no relation to any OT covenant for White, then his linking of baptism to the new covenant as its sacrament of initiation may look like special pleading, for his treatment of the new covenant builds on his understanding of the old.

White considers it important that the OT prophets say the new covenant will have different terms (one of them being the exclusion of circumcision) and include different people than the old covenant did. According to these prophets, pure and righteous people will constitute the new covenant community, regardless of race and heritage. While the individuals in this community will stand in succession with Abraham, any communal concerns within the covenant will be secondary to individualistic ones, such as "enlightenment, repentance, purification, faith, obedience, possession of the Spirit, [and] knowledge of Yahweh. . . . *The elect community is thus a community of duly qualified individuals, and the qualifications are neither racial nor ritual but moral and spiritual.*"[16] The OT prophets tied this new covenant community to a remnant of Israel, but they also recognized that it was for all peoples of the earth. White goes on to say that the NT authors followed the best in OT covenantal teaching when they spoke of initiation into the new covenant with the understanding that baptism serves a different purpose than circumcision. Such NT covenantal teaching, according to White, should prompt Christians to conceive of baptism as an objectification of faith.

G. R. BEASLEY-MURRAY

Beasley-Murray started writing on baptism in 1948 and continued to publish on it throughout his life.[17] In these writings he presents and defends a biblical theology of baptism that is rooted in NT exegesis rather than

---

16. Ibid., 40, emphasis his.

17. Beasley-Murray, "Sacraments." This article is a response to Read, "Ordinances," 8–10, which expresses Read's concerns with trends in Baptist theology to use the word *sacrament* and to speak of baptism and Communion as "means of grace." Other works by Beasley-Murray that deal with baptism are "Baptism in the Epistles of Paul," "The Spirit is There," "Baptism and the Sacramental View," "Baptism in the New Testament," *Baptism Today and Tomorrow*, *Baptism in the New Testament*, "Church and Child," "Holy Spirit,"

in the Baptist tradition (understood by Beasley-Murray as an ordinance-only tradition). Beasley-Murray found that Baptists were quick to use the NT when they critiqued paedobaptist accounts, but they often failed to let key baptismal texts shape their own theologies of baptism.[18] In response, his chief work on baptism, 1962's *Baptism in the New Testament*, remains one of the most complete defenses of sacramentalism due to the scope of its exegetical arguments from the NT and responses to common objections. In that work, Beasley-Murray focuses on the connection between faith and baptism more than his fellow contributors to *Christian Baptism*. He argues that the NT so closely links baptism to faith that they are two divine-human encounters that together form one event: faith-baptism, or conversion-baptism. He explains this concept when reflecting on Galatians 3:26–27: "In this passage the exegetes frequently either exalt baptism at the expense of faith or faith at the expense of baptism. . . . If Paul were pressed to define the relationship of the two statements in vv. 26–27, I cannot see how he could preserve the force of both sentences apart from affirming that baptism is the moment of faith in which the adoption is realized—in the dual sense of effected by God and grasped by man—which is the same as saying that in baptism faith receives the Christ in whom the adoption is effected."[19] For Beasley-Murray, one cannot separate faith from baptism or baptism from faith because one expresses his or her faith *in* baptism. The NT writers associate the gift of salvation in Christ with both faith and baptism for God does not bestow this gift partly to faith and partly to baptism, but God gives "*all* in baptism and *all* to faith."[20]

Beasley-Murray also argues that water baptism is a baptism in the Spirit that brings regeneration (understood as the washing and forgiveness of sins), an empowered call to a holy life, and the hope of a new creation and resurrection to come, but, unlike faith, it is not absolutely necessary for salvation. For Beasley-Murray, the apostolic NT doctrine of baptism inherently links faith to a baptism that paedobaptist and credo-

---

"I Still Find," "Second Chapter of Colossians," "Authority," "Faith in the New Testament," "Theology of the Child," and "Problem of Infant Baptism."

18. Beasley-Murray, "Sacraments," 3. Cf. Beasley-Murray, *Baptism in the New Testament*, 263.

19. Beasley-Murray, *Baptism in the New Testament*, 151.

20. Beasley-Murray, *Baptism Today and Tomorrow*, 39. Cross has a helpful chart of the gifts promised to faith and to baptism in the NT, "Faith-Baptism," 16–17.

baptist churches alike do not practice today because they both separate faith from baptism. One of his hopes for his writings was that churches would respond to the doctrine of conversion-baptism by gratefully receiving it as God's gift rather than wrongly insisting that it makes baptism absolutely necessary for salvation. After all, Paul taught that "faith in God manifested in Christ is *prior* to baptism, and faith receives the gift of God *in* baptism, and faith in God is the constitutive principle of the Christian life *after* baptism. Paul's writings do not justify a reversal of this emphasis in the relationship between the two."[21] Given his emphasis on faith, even Beasley-Murray's conversion-baptism does not entail baptismal regeneration.

Beasley-Murray devotes a lengthy chapter in *Baptism in the New Testament* to the rise and significance of infant baptism, complete with several areas of arguments against the practice. The main area of interest for the covenantal view of baptism is the section, "The Covenant, Circumcision and Baptism," in which Beasley-Murray interacts with Pierre Marcel and Oscar Cullmann. Beasley-Murray focuses his discussion on Marcel, not because he considers Marcel's work to be a satisfactory defense of infant baptism, but because Marcel is so strenuously exuberant in expounding his doctrine.[22] Marcel's defense of infant baptism is more extreme than Cullmann's, but Beasley-Murray thinks their arguments essentially agree with one another and together faithfully represent the Reformed tradition on covenant theology, circumcision, and baptism.[23] In short, the argument from Marcel and Cullmann focuses on one covenant of grace, one gospel, one condition of receiving salvation, one church, and one significance for sacraments—making circumcision and baptism virtually equivalent.

Beasley-Murray recognizes some truth in their account, but he thinks Marcel's and Cullmann's interpretation of Scripture is nothing short of unacceptable:

> The major mistake of the writers of this school is their one-sided stressing of the elements of unity in the Covenant, Gospel and Church of both dispensations, and their ignoring of the equally clear elements of discontinuity, elements which, in fact, often

---

21. Beasley-Murray, *Baptism in the New Testament*, 304, emphasis his.
22. Ibid., 334n3.
23. Ibid., 336.

> take the attention of the New Testament writers more than the elements of unity because they are so overwhelming.... This attempt to reduce to uniformity the old and new covenants and their respective sacraments belongs to an unrealistic mode of exegesis that fails to distinguish between shadow and substance, that fails to understand New Testament eschatology and that fails to take into account the significance of Christ and the coming of the Holy Spirit.[24]

While Marcel and Cullmann may fail to make some of the distinctions Beasley-Murray mentions above, theologians on both sides of the paedobaptist/credobaptist divide recognize continuities as well as discontinuities between the old and new covenants. Beasley-Murray makes sweeping arguments against paedobaptism in general, especially Marcel's version of it, without also presenting his own understanding of the relationship between the old and new covenants. As a result, Beasley-Murray's defense of credobaptism is incomplete, because he addresses neither the continuity between the covenants nor the role of circumcision for OT saints. He comes close to developing his own covenant theology when he associates law, death, and flesh with the old covenant; and gospel, life, and Spirit with the new covenant.[25] But these associations only reveal that Beasley-Murray's position does not account for the complex relationship between the covenants found in the NT.

Beasley-Murray's chapter on infant baptism moves from greater theological concerns to specific exegetical ones when he argues that Marcel's and Cullmann's views are not "reconcilable with the teaching of Paul on the covenant in Galatians 3."[26] According to Beasley-Murray, Paul demonstrates in this passage who the true sons of Abraham are and how they enter into Abraham's covenant. God made a covenant with Abraham and his seed, Christ (Beasley-Murray includes Christ's people here in Christ). In this covenant, God works a redemption that is for the Gentiles too, that they may also receive Abraham's blessing. Thus, only Christ rather than the Law, or the old covenant, can fulfill this covenant. One can be brought into this covenant by having the same kind of faith Abraham had with the clarification that Abraham's faith was in a promise that would one day be realized, while one's faith today is in the promise

24. Ibid., 337–38.
25. Ibid., 338.
26. Ibid., 339.

actualized in Christ. Paul concludes this chapter by stating that the promise today is for those baptized in Christ in faith, who now belong to Christ and as such are Abraham's children and heirs according to the promise. Thus, the covenant in Christ does not operate on a hereditary basis, and baptism does not replace circumcision as the sacrament of the covenant.[27] Beasley-Murray's explanation of this text falls short of adequately explaining the relationship between the old covenant and circumcision as well as that between the new covenant and baptism, and so it also falls short of demonstrating that Marcel's and Cullmann's baptismal theology cannot account for this text.

Beasley-Murray attempts to explain the relationship between circumcision and the old covenant by focusing on proselyte baptism in the NT rather than addressing the institution of circumcision in Genesis 17. He argues that the early NT church, especially the Jerusalem church, did not consider the rite of circumcision to be the same as the "circumcision of the heart" that Paul mentions in Romans 2:29, because the rite of circumcision "was administered to every male child in Israel as a sign of his membership in the covenant people and had no relation to moral renewal; the prophetic call for heart circumcision is an application of the rite in symbol, not an exposition of the rite itself."[28] So much for the link between circumcision and "heart circumcision," but Beasley-Murray is still missing an explanation of what it means to be a member of God's covenant people and whether people rightly apply circumcision as a symbol of inclusion in that covenant.

Beasley-Murray's underdeveloped covenant theology limits some of the effectiveness of his defense of credobaptism. For instance, Beasley-Murray does not explain the relationship between the covenant with Abraham and the covenant of grace, if he even believes in such a covenant or the relationship between the institution of circumcision and the covenant with Abraham. Nor does he indicate whether there is more than one covenant with Abraham in Genesis. In fairness, Paul does not explain such things in Galatians 3 or Romans 2 either, but any defense of credobaptism that uses these passages should delve into such subjects. For example, Baptists who espoused covenant theology in the past address such issues.[29] To be sure, Beasley-Murray falls short of having a

27. Ibid., 399–40.
28. Ibid., 341.
29. One example is Coxe, *Discourse*.

covenantal view of baptism in part because that is something he never purports to attempt. However, he would have strengthened his defense of credobaptism against paedobaptist arguments and provided firmer support for the communal aspects of baptism had he developed his covenant theology more. Whereas covenant theology focuses on God's actions to form and sustain a community in which baptism is a sign and seal of one's experience of God's grace and entrance into this covenant community, Beasley-Murray's account of baptism focuses on God's dealings with individual believers who have come to faith. Nonetheless, he at least stresses the significance of baptism for these individuals in ways that ordinance-only Baptists usually do not.

Beasley-Murray concludes *Baptism in the New Testament* with a call for churches to reform their current practices so that they can make baptism integral to the gospel, conversion, and church membership.[30] Preachers and hearers of the gospel should give baptism its proper emphasis so that "whether the time between baptism and conversion be little or much, baptism should be regarded as the ultimate and unreserved ratification of the individual's turning to God and of God's gracious turning to the individual, with all that means of dedication on the one hand and of grace on the other."[31] Beasley-Murray recognized that practical issues will always be barriers to reform, such as when to baptize youth in the church, whether to rebaptize people who want to join a Baptist church but were baptized as infants, or the amount of time it takes a church to verify one's faith before baptizing him or her. However, he argues that churches can still address these issues while also striving for the ideal theology and practice of baptism rooted in the NT, which is conversion-baptism.[32] Despite its shortcomings, *Baptism in the New Testament* has for good reason withstood the test of time as the best Baptist work on baptism from the last century, even garnering some respect outside Baptist circles.

ALEC GILMORE

Alec Gilmore edited *Christian Baptism* and wrote the chapter in it entitled "Jewish Antecedents," but he did not give an account of his own

---

30. Beasley-Murray, *Baptism in the New Testament*, 393–95. Cf. Cross, "Faith-Baptism," 18–20.

31. Beasley-Murray, *Baptism in the New Testament*, 394.

32. Beasley-Murray deals with such matters in a few places in his works: ibid., 387–95; *Baptism Today and Tomorrow*, 98–108; and "Problem of Infant Baptism."

theology of baptism until he published *Baptism and Christian Unity* several years later. In that work, he investigates the meaning of baptism and some practical issues surrounding it with the goal of bringing Baptists and Anglicans together.[33] He spends much of his first chapter, "Faith and Baptism," dealing with the issue of faith for paedobaptist denominations before focusing on Baptists in his second chapter, "The Material, the Spiritual, and the Sacramental." He challenges Baptists to produce a theology of the sacraments that seriously considers other Christian positions and the Bible with an open mind.[34] Gilmore believes such a theology is needed because Baptists develop their theology of baptism and the Lord's Supper by driving a wedge between the spiritual and material worlds. Gilmore wants to remove this wedge since science, medicine, psychiatry, and contemporary biblical theology do not support placing it there in the first place.

The last item in that list, contemporary biblical theology, is the area in which Gilmore makes his most interesting claims for Baptist sacramental theology. Gilmore notes that in both the OT and NT there is not a clean distinction between what is ritual and what is spiritual, which creates space for sacramental theology. Gilmore argues that Paul shares the OT idea of "corporate personality . . . in which his mind moves freely from Christ to the Church and back again to Christ. . . . Similarly, it is equally difficult to see where Paul distinguishes between the spiritual and the material, because this too is a distinction that he does not draw. Salvation, for Paul, comes neither by faith nor by baptism, but by faith *and* baptism."[35] Gilmore does not utilize covenant theology here. Rather, he emphasizes the covenantal theme of unity in Scripture, making room for the OT and NT to agree on many things, including the role of rituals as organs of the Spirit. If baptism can act as a vehicle of the Spirit, then Baptists need to "stop trying to drive a wedge between matter and spirit by asking whether salvation came by baptism or by faith, and then to make a new effort to realize that it comes by both. The gateway to church

---

33. Gilmore, *Baptism and Christian Unity*, 16. The 1960s movement to form a united church in England that practiced both infant and believer baptism fueled Gilmore's ecumenical hope.

34. Ibid., 42.

35. Ibid., 56, emphasis his.

membership would then be one that was concerned with *both* faith *and* baptism."[36]

Gilmore believes that if Baptists approached baptism and church membership in this new way, the door would open for "sound headway in ecumenical relationships."[37] He longs for a time when Baptists will recognize the validity of infant baptisms performed within a godly family and later confirmed by faith. In this way, both communion and membership in churches would be open only to baptized believers regardless of whether they were baptized before or after they came to faith. In Gilmore's view, Baptists should not rebaptize believers who were baptized as infants, although believer baptism should be the normative practice for Baptist churches.

Gilmore ends his book with a consideration of Baptist infant dedications. He would not mind eradicating the practice, but he knows that most churches would reject such a notion. Instead, he offers a new order of service for infant dedications that focuses on thanksgiving for the new child, declaring God's involvement with the child as one who grows up in a church with Christian parents, praying that God will "enable the child to realize to the full the special benefits and blessings with which he has been endowed" and that the parents and the church will respond in trust that God will bring to completion what he has started in this new life.[38] Gilmore's second focus raises the issue of children in the covenant community. This is not a new topic since Neville Clark's chapter in *Christian Baptism* anchors the relationship between children of believers and God in Christian marriage itself.[39] However, Gilmore disagrees with Clark and insists that all children should be dedicated to God, not just those from a Christian home. Infant dedication asserts what God has done, is doing, and will do in the life of a child, so there is no reason to bar any child from this rite. If the infant's parents are not part of the church, then some members of the church should "adopt" this infant to maintain God's relationship with him or her.[40] Thus, the parents' faith, or lack thereof, is not decisive for Gilmore when it comes to observing infant dedications.

---

36. Ibid., 60, emphasis his.
37. Ibid.
38. Ibid., 98.
39. Clark, "Theology of Baptism," 322.
40. Gilmore, *Baptism and Christian Unity*, 101–2.

Gilmore focuses so much on practical issues that it is difficult to discern his underlying theology of baptism. The chapter "Faith and Baptism" implies that it will include a discussion of how baptism relates to faith, but it concludes without Gilmore explaining his view of either faith or baptism. For example, Gilmore discusses how the Roman Catholic scholar, Alfred Wikenhauser, understands Paul's sacramentalism, noting that faith does not establish union with Christ alone, but rather it is the "indispensable condition for the establishment of this union" that comes at baptism.[41] Fowler notes that Gilmore seems to affirm Wikenhauser's view, but at face value this short quote differs from the sacramentalism of both White and Beasley-Murray. Here, Gilmore implies that faith is merely a precondition of baptism and baptism itself unites one to Christ, while White and Beasley-Murray argue that it is "the faith which is objectified in baptism that establishes union with Christ."[42] Gilmore notes that Wikenhauser goes on to explain his view of faith in ways that affirm Gilmore's own chapter on baptism and faith, but the reader will have to take Gilmore's word for it because he never really explains his view of faith. If Wikenhauser's view is the same as Gilmore's, then Wikenhauser's explanation of faith may clarify Gilmore's theology.

Wikenhauser makes such statements as "Faith is the necessary condition for receiving Baptism, which establishes union with Christ"; Paul's understanding of faith is "the agreement of the intellect with the content of the Gospel message, in other words the voluntary acceptance of the message of salvation as divine truth"; and "Faith necessarily leads to Baptism," so "if it does not lead to Baptism it is not genuine faith."[43] Wikenhauser summarizes his view in this way: "Faith for Paul was . . . the acceptance of the message of salvation which God had wrought through Christ, and therefore profession of the Christian religion. But the man who accepts this message with faith, is not thereby united mystically to Christ. This union is produced only by Baptism."[44] In light of these remarks, it is fair to say that Wikenhauser and Gilmore consider genuine faith to be the necessary precondition for baptism, inherently tying together genuine faith and baptism. Wikenhauser and Gilmore are not as explicit as White

---

41. Wikenhauser, *Pauline Mysticism*, 129.
42. Fowler, *More Than a Symbol*, 147.
43. Wikenhauser, *Pauline Mysticism*, 129–31.
44. Ibid., 132.

and Beasley-Murray are in attributing the benefits of baptism to faith, and Wikenhauser is careful not to attribute the believer's union to Christ to any means other than baptism, but he does say genuine faith necessarily leads to baptism. Thus, Fowler is right that this is a subtly different sacramentalism than that of White and Beasley-Murray. For Gilmore, there is a division of labor between faith and baptism because both are instrumental means of salvation. While faith and baptism may be inherently tied together, there is no primary place for faith over baptism in Gilmore's account as there is in Beasley-Murray's sacramentalism.

Given his focus on practical issues, Gilmore's book did not push Baptist sacramental theology much further. However, there was much reaction to his discussion of the problems with and solutions to the practical issues surrounding sacramental theology. One particular criticism focused on Gilmore's advocacy of the validity of infant baptism for Baptists. Beasley-Murray rejected this notion, arguing that paedobaptism and credobaptism are two different things and that Gilmore erred by trying to make them one.[45] Gilmore's practical concerns stemmed from a deeper desire for ecumenical relations. He offered some possible solutions for ecumenical tensions at the practical level, but he did not give clear theological support for his recommendations. Nonetheless, Gilmore's focus on practical issues and ecumenical concerns in the late 1960s signifies the closing of the period in which the first generation of Baptist sacramentalists produced their chief works.

CONCLUSION

In the twentieth century, Baptist sacramentalists produced many works to support their views. Primarily British Baptists produced these works and their influence was minimal among grassroots Baptists on both sides of the Atlantic due in part to their reliance on purely exegetical defenses of sacramentalism and their retaining an individualistic understanding of baptism.

Purely exegetical defenses of sacramentalism allowed sacramentalists to continue using vague or even misleading language when describing their views, which fueled rather than answered ordinance-only Baptist objections. Theological defenses of sacramentalism would have added

---

45. Cross, *Baptism and the Baptists*, 208–9. Cf. Beasley-Murray, *Baptism Today and Tomorrow*, 145–60.

clarity and coherence to the position, fostering more open debate rather than garnering suspicion from ordinance-only Baptists. Purely exegetical defenses of sacramentalism also tacitly conceded the historical aspect of the debate with ordinance-only Baptists, implying that sacramentalism was never part of the Baptist tradition.

The literature's lack of emphasis on the communal aspects of sacramentalism limited its impact on ordinance-only Baptists because it minimized the contrast between its understanding of baptism and ordinance-only views that were just as individualistic. This is not to say that sacramentalists and ordinance-only Baptists during this period shared the same underlying theology of the meaning of baptism. Rather, sacramentalists did not adequately show the implications of their view for the practical issues surrounding baptism, giving others fewer reasons to accept it beyond its exegetical support alone.

Despite these two weaknesses, the sacramental works from this period had many lasting results. They started a discussion on the meaning of baptism among Baptists that had been dormant for over a century. Exegetical defenses of sacramentalism warranted serious consideration from other Baptists, even if those same Baptists held sacramentalism at arm's length for some of the reasons above.[46] Another lasting result is the ongoing relationship between Baptist baptismal theology and ecumenical concerns, in which the latter pushed Baptists to develop their understanding of the former. After a downturn in sacramental literature for a few decades, the close of the twentieth century brought a renewed interest in sacramentalism that ushered in new discoveries in the search for the meaning of baptism.

---

46. Fowler discusses some of these receptions to Beasley-Murray's work in *More Than a Symbol*, 174–78. Among these receptions, Hull accepts Beasley-Murray's exegesis, but rejects his theological conclusions, "Baptism in the New Testament."

3

A Resurgence in Baptist Sacramentalism

THE DOWNTURN IN SACRAMENTALISM FROM 1967 TO 1996

Beasley-Murray, White, and Clark continued to publish on baptism after the 1960s. Beasley-Murray eventually softened his stance on how Baptists should approach infant baptism in his writings in the 1990s.[1] Despite some works here and there, the overall intensity of scholarship on sacramentalism declined from the late 1960s until the dawn of the twenty-first century. According to Anthony R. Cross, 1967–99 was an era that focused on ecumenical developments in which baptism played an important role, but "attention moved away from baptism to the wider discussion of the ecumenical developments taking place."[2]

---

1. In one of his last published articles, Beasley-Murray says Baptists should acknowledge "the legitimacy of infant baptism, and allow members in Paedobaptist churches the right to interpret it according to their consciences," ("Problem of Infant Baptism," 13–14). Works on sacramental theology from members of the first generation of sacramentalists during this period include White, *Christian Baptism*; and Clark, "Initiation and Eschatology."

2. Cross, *Baptism and the Baptists*, 454. Porter and Cross elaborate on this point and provide a summary of the relevant literature from this period in "Introduction: Baptism in Recent Debate." Cross has an expanded treatment of the period in *Baptism and the Baptists*, 244–318. He later concludes that the other matters British Baptists considered to be more important than baptism during this time include the "charismatic movements in their various expressions, issues of worship, the place of the child in the church, matters concerning change within the church and questions of the survival of the local church in the midst of the decline of church attendance across all denominations," (*Baptism and the Baptists*, 460–61).

Ecumenically minded Baptists during the middle of the twentieth century could not produce any substantially visible unity between Baptist and non-Baptist churches, so the last few decades has brought a shift in approach to ecumenical relations. Whereas the World Council of Churches sought unity partly through having its member churches mutually recognize each other's baptisms as valid, ecumenically minded Baptists now argue that unity should come chiefly through member churches recognizing a shared union with Christ through faith in his gospel. Their hope is that visible unity between churches would no longer depend in part on member churches adopting a common water baptism.[3] According to Christopher J. Ellis, this shift allows for an ecumenical theology that "is founded on the greatness of God, the awareness of our own limitations as finite and sinful creatures, and the invitation of the life-giving Spirit to follow Christ and live a life of faith. This faith is not so much doctrinal assent as an *openness of being* which searches out the glory and refuses to capture it in a single set of words or concepts."[4] Ellis argues that sustained diversity throughout church history shows that all branches of Christianity

---

3. *Believing and Being Baptized*, secs. 19, 29–31. Cf. Cross, *Baptism and the Baptists*, 358–64. Two examples for how this approach specifically applies to baptism are Haymes, "Making Too Little?"; and Kidd, "Baptism and Identity." In ways that anticipate developments after him, Yoder called for Southern Baptists to embrace this approach in 1970, but they and most other North American Baptists still do not adopt this approach today, mainly because they are uninterested in ecumenical discussions, ("Non-Baptist View").

4. Ellis, *Together on the Way*, 93, emphasis his. Cross thinks Ellis is accepting a common water baptism when Ellis writes, "In facing the claims of its Lord, the church is encouraged to seek the unity which comes from sharing a common baptism in a common Lord," (ibid., 22). Cf. Cross, *Baptism and the Baptists*, 358–59. However, Ellis elaborates on this in the next paragraph, noting that the Society of Friends and the Salvation Army, which do not practice water baptism, do recognize the lordship of Christ, so "their living the Lordship of Christ can be seen to be a baptism in the one Lord, and therefore something which binds them to other parts of the church," (*Together on the Way*, 22). Such a claim implies that the lordship of Christ, expressed through Spirit baptism, is what Ellis believes constitutes "common baptism." Ellis leaves it unclear here, but later he is involved in the committee that writes *Believing and Being Baptized*, which explicitly argues, "There is one immersion into the death and resurrection of Jesus through the Spirit. . . . It is in accord with Jesus' portrayal of his crucifixion as a baptism, as immersion into the dark waters of death (Mark 10:38–39); this is the baptism in which we share in union with Christ. There is therefore, we believe, one baptism despite diversity of practice, and this need not be reduced to a notion of 'common baptism,'" (*Believing and Being Baptized*, sec. 29). Thus, Cross is too hasty to claim that Ellis accepts a common baptism, understood as a common water baptism, in his ecumenical theology. Cf. Ellis's argument that the lordship of Christ undergirds baptism because of texts such as Mark 10:38–39, (*Together on the Way*, 27n15).

contain fellow pilgrims who can learn from one another *in* their diversity while also striving to achieve visible unity rather than maintain divisions. Such an ecumenical theology calls for Baptists to contribute to ecumenical discussions by emphasizing what makes their view of baptism unique, while also humbly learning from other traditions. This shift in ecumenical relations is not unique to Baptists because recent ecumenical dialogue and discussions have led to what is now called "receptive ecumenism," in which churches identify and keep their own distinctions and offer them to other churches. This is done with postures that focus on what each church tradition can learn from the other ones rather than with postures that presume other church traditions should learn from them.[5]

Once Baptists considered their theology of baptism to be a unique gift to the diversity of Christian traditions, they resumed their search for its meaning. 1996 marked a resurgence of works on sacramentalism with three works in particular that carried the discussion from previous decades further into the realm of systematic theology.

BELIEVING AND BEING BAPTIZED

Believing and Being Baptized is the result of three years of labor by the Doctrine and Worship Committee of the Baptist Union of Great Britain. It functions as the Baptist contribution to the Churches Together in England commission's report, "Christian Initiation and Church Membership," later published under the title *Called to Be One*.[6] *Believing and Being Baptized* presents baptism "as a place of special encounter with God along the road of salvation, or as a high point on the journey of increasing wholeness."[7] Thus, God graciously works through baptism but baptism is only valid when it points to an underlying spiritual reality of faith, whether the faith of a new convert from outside the community of faith or that of a child within the community of faith.[8] The majority of the document discusses the relationship between believer baptism and infant baptism and its implications for Baptist theology and practice. Committee members

---

5. Murray edited a helpful introduction to this movement, *Receptive Ecumenism*. Baptist contributions to this movement include Harmon, *Ecumenism Means You, Too*; and Fiddes, "Learning from Others."

6. *Believing and Being Baptized*, sec. 4. The report was later published as *Called to Be One*.

7. *Believing and Being Baptized*, sec. 10.

8. Ibid., sec. 8.

differed over how Baptists should recognize infant baptism, but all agreed that, for Baptists, infant baptism is not baptism and that the concept of a common water baptism, often pushed by ecumenical discussions in the past, is thus unhelpful.[9] The committee members go on to outline their reasons for not considering infant baptism and believer baptism to be baptism in the same sense, but of more relevant interest to the covenantal view of baptism is how the committee members espouse a sacramental view of believer baptism. They write, "in baptism, God takes an element in his creation—water—and uses it as a place where he meets us with his grace. The drama of believers' baptism is a multi-media event, engaging all the senses and involving the person as a whole. To call something a 'sacrament' means that God uses some material stuff of creation (water, bread, wine) as a means of grace, that is as a way of deepening his relationship with us."[10] Likewise, baptism is "the seal of the Spirit for a believing and obedient disciple."[11] The committee clearly affirms baptism's role as a means of confirming or strengthening God's relationship with a believer, and they connect the Spirit's work in baptism to that effect.

While they are clear on baptism's instrumental role as a means of grace, the committee members follow Beasley-Murray on the tension held between faith and baptism. They stress that personal faith in Christ is essential for being a Christian, and therefore "this takes priority over all symbolic acts, however much these acts are vehicles of grace."[12] Thus, baptism is not absolutely necessary for being a Christian, but this does

---

9. Ibid., sec. 12. This is not to say that the committee thought infant baptism had no spiritual realities associated with it. They later affirm that Baptists can and should "share in a *mutual recognition of others as being members of the Body of Christ*, regardless of the mode of initiation in their church tradition. . . . Baptists should also be able to share, at least partly, in a mutual recognition of *what is happening*, in and through the act that is called baptism by different churches. That is, we can as Baptists recognize that the rite called infant baptism involves and expresses *some* aspects of both the grace of God and human faith. We should also be able to recognize that the *whole process* of infant baptism followed by confirmation, as a sign of personal faith, marks initiation into Christian life and membership in the church as Christ's Body. . . . Baptists can recognize the reality of Christian ministry in other Christian churches, including the ministry exercised at the Lord's Supper/Eucharist, and can embrace a common participation in the Eucharist, without having to validate all this through a 'common baptism,'" (ibid., sec. 18, emphasis in the original).

10. Ibid., sec. 16.

11. Ibid., sec. 19.

12. Ibid., sec. 27.

not make it "an optional extra for a believer" either, because "it is 'necessary' in the sense of being a part of *genuine discipleship*."[13] Thus, baptism carries a prominent place within the context of salvation, even if it is not absolutely necessary for salvation. Baptism is "a *rendez-vous* that God has himself provided for the deepening of relationship with him. To this place of meeting he calls his disciples, to encounter their Saviour in a special way, at whatever stage in life it happens. Thus, even if conversion has been a long time before, baptism can still be a moment of renewal and growth in the Christian life."[14]

The committee members' rejection of a common water baptism leads to the issue of how this stance applies to the claim of biblical texts, such as Ephesians 4:5, that mention "one baptism" and the Nicene Creed, which speaks of "one baptism for the remission of sins." The committee members argue that despite different practices of baptism, "there is still one immersion into the death and resurrection of Jesus through the Spirit," so "this is the baptism in which we share in union with Christ."[15] Thus, all can be united in this baptism through the Spirit, even if they practice different kinds of water baptisms.

The last issue the committee members discuss is the relationship of children and the church—a topic most Baptist works neglect. Baptists often do not baptize young children, because baptism should mark "a clear divide in a person's life in which personal faith plays a critical part. This has not been seen as appropriate for young children, partly because of a feeling—often ill-expressed—among Baptists that children are not in the *same kind of state* before God as a person who has reached an age of moral responsibility and moral choice."[16] Baptists differ on what this state is as well as on what the proper age of moral responsibility is: some deny original guilt (as opposed to original sin),[17] and others do not reflect on the state of children who are old enough to choose sin but too young

---

13. Ibid., sec. 28, emphasis in the original.
14. Ibid., sec. 28.
15. Ibid., sec. 29.
16. Ibid., sec. 33, emphasis in the original.

17. Ibid., sec. 33. Those who accept original sin but deny original guilt believe that "while children share the fallen and sinful *condition* of all human beings they are not reckoned by God to be *guilty* of sin until they reach an age when they can make truly moral decisions for themselves," (ibid., sec. 33, emphasis in the original).

to appreciate the fullness of the obligations of discipleship—leaving such matters in the hands of a holy and loving God.

Baptists as a whole do not usually appeal to a covenantal understanding of households to address this issue, but they do recognize the many benefits a Christian home has for its children, and many Baptists express belief in these benefits through infant blessing/dedication services.[18] Baptists usually reason that children cannot properly join a church until they have confirmed their personal faith by accepting not only the privileges but also the obligations of being a member of the covenant community, because the new covenant community, which for Baptists is nearly synonymous with the church, comprises only believers in Christ. To be sure, Baptists think young children can have genuine faith in Christ, but the decision to be baptized entails "the burden of responsible discipleship, at a point in development when they [children] are able meaningfully to say 'no' as well as 'yes' to the invitation to be a disciple."[19]

The committee members want to recognize the place of children who are in the church and have faith but who are not yet old enough to confirm their faith by accepting discipleship, so they propose that these children are to be considered in the body, or church, in the sense of being embraced by it rather than being active members within it.[20] Such an understanding allows the church to recognize the place of children within it while limiting membership to those baptized for discipleship.

Believing and Being Baptized offers several practical recommendations for Baptist churches regarding such issues as when it is proper to rebaptize believers and the proper age to baptize children. This last issue is interesting since the committee espouses a sacramental view of baptism, making it a high point of the process of being saved, only to argue that children should wait to experience it until they can better appreciate the cost of discipleship baptism expresses. In this way, the committee borders on stressing covenant obligations in baptism at the expense of

18. Ibid., sec. 40.

19. Ibid., sec. 8. Cross claims the proper age to baptize is currently an open issue for British Baptists, with different calls for baptizing at early, middle, or late adolescence, but he claims the "normal practice" is to baptize people between the ages of eight and fifteen, (*Baptism and the Baptists*, 392–95). The typical age for baptism among North American Baptists has become younger during the last century, and Dever has cautioned North American Baptists against baptizing young children, especially under the age of eight; his article has helpful resources on this issue, (see "Baptism in Context").

20. *Believing and Being Baptized*, sec. 36.

the covenant blessings it also has to offer, since baptism is in many ways the commencement of one's discipleship rather than its culmination. *Believing and Being Baptized* reveals that any covenantal view of sacramentalism will also have to wrestle with how to balance the reception of God's covenant blessings and the reception of God's covenant obligations in baptism.

Believing and Being Baptized provides practical rather than theological reasons for its advice on when and whether to baptize. As a result, it leaves unanswered many questions about the meaning of baptism. In fairness, the committee appeals to covenantal burdens and obligations for its rationale on suggesting the proper age at which to baptize youth, but it does not explicitly base these suggestions on a greater theology of baptism's meaning. Although there is no perfect answer to some of these knotty practical issues in Baptist baptismal theology and practice, the answers in *Believing and Being Baptized* are shallow. Nonetheless, its extended discussion of children in the church is a welcome addition to sacramentalism.

SOMETHING TO DECLARE

Something to Declare is the joint product of four Principals of English Baptist colleges who wanted to offer some expository thoughts on the Baptist Union of Great Britain's three-paragraph *Declaration of Principle*, which was up for discussion at a Baptist Union meeting in 1996.[21] The authors begin by defending the Baptist Union's use of a covenant that binds together its members, because biblical covenants are both vertical and horizontal in that they bind believers not only to God but also to each other:

> The goal of God's initiative in making covenant is the formation of a *people*; indeed, of a people covenanted together, as in the making of Israel. . . . God's initiative in gracious love is the basis, the very possibility and vitality, of their relationships one with another, as well as of their direct relationship with God. When it comes, then, to the making of a 'new covenant' through Christ, it is not at all surprising that the context in which this gains clearest expression is that of the communion meal, in which the 'vertical' initiative of

---

21. Kidd (ed.), *Something to Declare*.

God and the 'horizontal' bonds of fellowship are also *both* sharply in focus.[22]

The authors support this notion by arguing that seventeenth-century Baptists used this twofold covenant concept as a line of demarcation between their form of church government and others that were either hierarchical or purely congregational as found among Anglicans and Quakers respectively.

What is of interest for the covenantal view of baptism is how the authors stress the role of the covenant community in the Lord's Supper, but they do not explore how it also relates to baptism, the very rite through which God confirms a believer's initiation into the covenant community itself. This could be because, according to Cross, most contemporary Baptist works that discuss covenant theology do not also discuss baptism.[23] But Cross does not explain why contemporary Baptist works do not tie baptism to covenant theology. A reasonable explanation could be that covenant theology is so entrenched in the Reformed conception of infant baptism that Baptists do not think it can apply to believer baptism. *Something to Declare* is a case in point: it mentions the communion meal alone as the clearest expression of the new covenant's vertical and horizontal relationships, but excludes baptism from the discussion for no apparent reason.

When the authors later discuss baptism in *Something to Declare*, they speak of "those who would define Christian baptism in a wider biblical context, especially in their understandings of the Old Testament circumcision and covenant traditions" as if there were currently no Baptist covenantal understandings of believer baptism as well.[24] This is not to say that the authors do not recognize any communal aspect of baptism. The Baptist Union's *Declaration of Principle* states, "Christian Baptism is the immersion in water into the Name of the Father, the Son, and the Holy Ghost,"[25] and the authors comment that this clause expresses "how much Christian baptism is a personal movement with dynamic incorporation into fresh commitment. The very word *into* strongly suggests a 'coming-into-relationship-with.' Something powerful is happening both to the

22. Ibid., 12–13, emphasis in the original.
23. Cross, *Baptism and the Baptists*, 378n239.
24. Kidd (ed.), *Something to Declare*, 38.
25. Ibid., 37.

individual concerned, but also to the whole community which itself belongs to the Name. This extraordinary move from being outside of a living relationship to living within the community of faith needs an emphatic immersion in water to begin to do it justice."[26] The authors recognize that the communal aspect of baptism emphasizes God's relationship with his people, and covenant theology is not far from this conception. However, the authors keep any covenantal aspects of baptism at arm's length as if such things are coextensive with a paedobaptist understanding of baptism.

The authors go on to speak of baptism in ways reminiscent of the writings of the earlier generation of sacramentalists. The authors see an ethical dimension in baptism, because believers come to baptism renouncing their previous lifestyles. They also see baptism as a divine-human encounter in which God meets "the believer in the fullness of his work as faith responds to grace."[27] They argue, as does the committee for *Believing and Being Baptized*, that baptism is a symbol, as opposed to merely a sign, that enables believers to participate in the spiritual reality it represents. They also affirm an understanding of salvation as a journey with three tenses of salvation: have been saved, are being saved, and shall be saved. They even agree with the committee that produced *Believing and Being Baptized*, saying, "baptism is the decisive moment in the process of being saved."[28] In these ways, *Something to Declare* does not push Baptist sacramental theology much further than other documents, but it does provide some helpful statements on the communal aspects of baptism and the covenantal aspects of churches—even if it does not connect them together in ways that the covenantal view of baptism offers.

REFLECTIONS ON THE WATER

The last major work on Baptist sacramental theology from 1996 is *Reflections on the Water*, which contains six chapters written by several Baptist authors on different aspects of baptism, followed by an Anglican response to all the chapters. Cross goes so far as to say that it is a "radical departure" from most previous Baptist works on baptism, because it is

---

26. Ibid., 41, emphasis in the original.
27. Ibid., 43.
28. Ibid., 45.

"deliberately less biblical and more theological in its approach."[29] The next three sections will present the essays of Ellis, Fiddes, and Brian Haymes, using their discussions in *Reflections* as a starting point to discuss their subsequent writings on Baptist sacramental theology.

Christopher J. Ellis

Ellis's essay in *Reflections on the Water*, "Baptism and the Sacramental Freedom of God," is mostly a theological defense of Baptist sacramental theology. Rather than define sacrament, Ellis expounds the meaning of sacraments by focusing on the truths they express. These truths include what he calls "continuing incarnation," or "the use of the material [water, bread, and wine] as sign and symbol" to express "the embodiedness of the sacraments."[30] He links these truths to the incarnation of Christ, the mission of disciples to live their faith in the world, and "the eschatological hope whereby the sacramental use of material things might prefigure the redemption of all things. Here is a link between creation and redemption, where the experience of God using water, bread, and wine provides a lens for seeing the world and God's activity in a new light."[31] A sacramental understanding of baptism must also acknowledge God's action and promises as well as a person's faith—a gift of grace itself—in baptism. Sacraments are also inherently tied to the church and salvation, but not in the sense that they effect salvation; rather, they embody the gospel in a communal way that focuses on Christ. Thus, baptism is done in obedience to Christ, but a more adequate explanation of baptism recognizes that it is more than that: "The person [being baptized] moves beyond following an example to being united with the risen Christ in the power of the Spirit—united with Christ in his baptism, in his death on the cross, and in the resurrection."[32]

Having expounded a sacramental understanding of baptism, Ellis then presents Baptist teaching on baptism. He notes that Baptists in the past have fought battles over the proper subjects and mode of baptism to the point where Baptists have become impoverished in their own theology of baptism. Such battles "reduce the possibility of a rich Baptist affirma-

---

29. Cross, *Baptism and the Baptists*, 381.
30. Ellis, "Baptism and Sacramental Freedom," 24.
31. Ibid., 25.
32. Ibid., 27.

tion about the nature and meaning of baptism and short-change the rest of the church that consequently suffers from this lack of Baptist witness."[33] Of course, these common battles are the product of key Baptist concerns that usually stem from Baptist distinctives, or what most Baptists take to be the defining characteristics of Baptist churches. These include submission to Scripture alone, a church of disciples alone, a baptism of disciples alone, the norm of baptism by immersion, a suspicion of sacramentalism, an uneasiness with ritual, an uneasiness with sacramental terminology, and an emphasis on the freedom of God.

Ellis raises these concerns in order to demonstrate that sacramentalism does not threaten them as ordinance-only Baptists commonly object. Ellis thinks Baptist opposition to sacramental theology stems from the position of the radical Reformers who saw a connection between sacramental theology and the enabling of "church and state to control the dispensing of salvation."[34] Later opposition to sacramental theology in nineteenth-century England was "largely a reaction against the Oxford Movement," which offered a mechanistic view of sacraments rather than a Baptist sacramentalist view.[35] Baptists' uneasiness with ritual, Ellis explains, stems from the practice of "*abstract* worship," which, along with the emphasis of personal faith, leads Baptists to see baptism "through a lens that views actions in worship as unimportant and ritual as suspect."[36]

Throughout his description of Baptist concerns, Ellis recognizes the diversity found in past and present Baptist views regarding in what way baptism can be a means of grace and what are the precise manner and timing of God's actions in salvation. Despite these variations, no Baptist position, sacramental or otherwise, argues that baptism is the initial means of salvation. Sacramentalists sometimes need to be sympathetic to opposition as a reminder that "God is not restricted by the sacraments as the only means whereby He may graciously work in the lives of men and women. Any theology that is developed concerning baptism as a means of grace must make room for this inconvenient, yet gloriously inspired, belief in the freedom of God."[37]

---

33. Ibid., 27.
34. Ibid., 30.
35. Ibid., 30.
36. Ibid., 32, emphasis his.
37. Ibid., 35.

In light of these arguments, Ellis thinks Baptists can and should use the word *sacrament* without threatening the Baptist concerns above, and they should define it in a way that other Christians will easily recognize. Ellis proposes a working definition that "the term 'sacrament' suggests the power of symbols to link us to the depths of reality, and point us to the use by God of material means to mediate His saving action."[38] Such a definition still needs qualification, especially in its use of "symbols" and "saving action," but it suffices as a definition of *sacrament* that other Christians would recognize.

Ellis gives three observations about Baptist sacramentalism in general before giving his own theology of baptism. First, ecumenical studies in the late twentieth-century emphasize Christian initiation as a process rather than a distinct point in time. Ellis considers this to be important, "for it removes some of the historical pressure to identify the moment and the precise means of the divine activity."[39] Second, "our understanding of the freedom of God is clarified when His activity in baptism is seen as a pointer to His activity elsewhere, as well as an example of that wide-ranging saving activity," that is, when we see baptism as part of a greater process of salvation.[40] Third, retaining the word *sacrament* among Baptists helps strengthen the link between the objective word of God in baptism and one's subjective experience of it: "Unless water is given a magical value, part of the means of grace is the subjective reinforcement offered by the symbols of water, immersion, and rising again."[41] Having laid the groundwork above, Ellis then gives his theology of baptism as a sacrament of proclamation, partnership, presence, prophecy, and promise.

As a sacrament of proclamation, baptism proclaims, demonstrates, and enacts the gospel of Jesus Christ in a way that a vocal confession of faith cannot. Ellis draws from his description of continuing incarnation to support this claim: "Union with Jesus Christ is more than the following of an example; it becomes the proclamation of the gospel of Christ. It is meaningless to divide what God does from what the believer or the church does, for in this proclamation the Holy Spirit is working—in those who act and those who witness, in those who speak and those who hear. At the centre of it all, the Word of God made flesh is enfleshed again in

---

38. Ibid., 36.
39. Ibid.
40. Ibid.
41. Ibid., 37.

the fellowship of His people and the testimony of a new disciple."[42] For Ellis, God, the church, and the individual believer all contribute to the one baptismal act in which the Spirit does his work.

Baptism is a sacrament of partnership into which God enters "with the church and the person being baptized. The individual and the church also enter into partnership."[43] In the incarnation, the Spirit works in an embodied way that continues "in the life of discipleship as the Spirit beckons, stirs, cleanses, and inspires the faltering steps of one who would follow Christ. Between the incarnation and the life of faith lie the waters of baptism where the believer abandons the past and seeks a new life of partnership not only with other Christians but in union with Christ."[44] Ellis believes partnership carries much value for baptism's meaning because it points to things central to the Christian faith such as grace, intra-Trinitarian relationships, fellowship, worship, and obedient faith.

God comes to us in baptism, so it is also a sacrament of presence. Just as the incarnation unites creation and redemption in God's saving action, so too baptism offers an embodied form of "the *mysterion* of God's salvation . . . that defies simple, verbal explanation."[45] A link between baptism and incarnation recognizes that God "may come to us outside the church, mediated through substances and situations that make up His world. A recognition of God in the sacramental act of baptizing opens our eyes to the sacramental nature of reality. An affirmation of God's presence in the sacraments of the church only has meaning insofar as it points to His sacramental presence in the world Christ died to save."[46] Sacraments celebrate creation and proclaim hope that God will redeem his world; they are also enfleshed acts of obedient love that recognize and follow God's own act of obedient love enfleshed in Jesus.

As a sacrament of prophecy, baptism incorporates the believer into Christ's body and into his church, thereby linking the fate of the person baptized to that of the mission and witness of the church. Because God calls his church to prophetically witness God's kingdom in a fallen

---

42. Ibid., 38. Elsewhere, Ellis speaks of the influence of Roman Catholic theologian Schillebeeckx in developing this thought, ("Embodied Grace," 5–6). The most relevant work by Schillebeeckx on this point is *Christ the Sacrament*.

43. Ellis, "Baptism and Sacramental Freedom," 38–39.

44. Ibid., 39.

45. Ibid.

46. Ibid., 40.

world, "the sacraments are offered to the church as a means of enabling the church to be a sacrament of the Kingdom."[47] Ellis reminds Christians that baptism signifies not only Christ's resurrection but also his cross (cf. Mark 10:38), and "the prophetic witness of the church is not primarily the press release or even the political analysis, but the baptism and the martyrdom of the saints of God."[48]

As a sacrament of promise, baptism points to the consummation of all things. The gift of the Spirit in baptism is the gift of his indwelling presence for the believer as well as "the pledge of what is in store for us, the seal of God's promises, the inspirer of a hope that rocks us out of a complacent acceptance of the way things are."[49] This is not to say that baptism mechanically gives assurance and certainty of salvation, but it is the "sign and seal of God's covenant promises. . . . What is offered in baptism is not certainty of salvation, but union with one whose promises can be trusted."[50]

Ellis concludes his chapter in *Reflections on the Water* by acknowledging God's sovereign freedom, which cautions sacramentalists against saying that God only works through baptism. Rather, they should say, "God is here, therefore we can meet Him here and be equipped to meet Him elsewhere."[51] God is free to work through the means of grace that he ordained his church to obey, but he need not work only through these means alone. Sacramentalists do not have a mechanistic view of grace or of baptism, so they "approach baptism as an opportunity for celebration and fruitfulness where the Spirit moves powerfully amongst a praising and responsive people."[52] In sum, Sacramentalists believe God freely "promises to meet us both in the waters of baptism and in the world to which we are sent."[53]

Ellis's chapter in *Reflections on the Water* contributes to the discussion of Baptist sacramental theology in several ways. He demonstrates how Sacramentalists can embrace sacramental terminology in a way that

---

47. Ibid.
48. Ibid., 41.
49. Ellis, "Baptism and Sacramental Freedom," 41.
50. Ibid.
51. Ibid.
52. Ibid., 42.
53. Ibid.

keeps the essential concept of sacramentalism intact that other Christian traditions also believe, while making room for a Baptist understanding. Ellis addresses the main rift between sacramentalists and ordinance-only Baptists: different conceptions of how God works in and through the world generally and in salvation specifically. Ellis's approach of using the incarnation as a model of understanding how God works in baptism is helpful, and in some ways it stands as a forerunner of calls for the incarnational models of church ministry that have become popular in recent years. His approach may even influence ordinance-only Baptists who also value the incarnation in their theology but do not link it to baptism.

Theological defenders of sacramentalism still need to address one issue that Ellis does not mention: the relationship between faith and baptism in salvation. While Ellis is right that many regard Christian initiation as a process in which baptism is but one element, this point alone does not sufficiently explain what part a sacramental view of baptism plays in the greater process. To be sure, Ellis never claims that explaining salvation as a process is tantamount to explaining the particulars of the relationship between the elements within the process. But ordinance-only Baptists will not seriously consider sacramentalism until its defenders clearly explain how its meaning of baptism relates to faith. Nonetheless, Ellis's chapter in *Reflections on the Water* lays some of the groundwork for the covenantal view of baptism, which will build on his points about baptism as participation and promise, points that Ellis develops in a later work, *Gathering: A Theology and Spirituality of Worship in Free Church Tradition*.

In *Gathering*, while Ellis mainly explores the spirituality of baptism, he first gives more details about the relationship between faith, baptism, and salvation.[54] Drawing from seventeenth-century Baptist confessions, Ellis claims "the grace conferred [in baptism] is a gift of the Holy Spirit and, in the case of Baptists, assumes the presence already of saving faith."[55] This faith is more than merely mental assent because it is evidenced by a changed lifestyle, and it must precede both baptism and church membership. Ellis argues, "those who repented and believed would still need to be faithful to the divine ordinances—they would need to obey the command of Christ and be baptized and enter into a covenant relationship with others to form a society of saints, a visible manifestation of Christ's

---

54. Ellis, *Gathering*, 200–221.
55. Ibid., 216.

kingdom."[56] Under this view, Baptists consider baptism to be "a sign of that which was already accomplished in a person's life, an act of obedience and the conferring of blessing through a closer fellowship with Christ, made possible by that very obedience and by an identification with Christ in his death, burial, and resurrection."[57] Thus, baptism is only for those who have saving faith, but it is still tied to the Spirit as a means both of grace and of initiation into the church. Such a view, as Ellis argues in his earlier piece, does not entail either baptismal regeneration or a renunciation of common Baptist concerns.

According to Ellis, as initiation into the church, baptism has both individual and ecclesial functions: "It is not only directed towards the believer as incorporation into the Body of Christ, but it is also directed reflexively back to the Church itself.... The Church is patterned after Christ and its identity as a gospel community is made clear and made possible in baptism."[58] Elsewhere Ellis suggests that churches should emphasize the communal aspects of baptism by having candidates "be baptized and received into membership, with prayer and the laying on of hands, in the same service" to embody "the conviction that baptism is into Christ and that 'into Christ' includes the corporate reality of baptism into the body of Christ."[59] This communal emphasis offers a helpful corrective to overly individualistic baptismal practices of sacramentalists and ordinance-only Baptists alike.

Gathering expresses a clear theology of baptism in which faith and baptism are not on an equal footing, so baptism is more concerned with mediating one's experience of salvation rather than mediating elements of justification proper. It is possible to interpret Ellis's statements in *Gathering* as referring only to how seventeenth-century Baptists thought of baptism rather than indicating a shift in his own theology, because he does not always distinguish clearly between the historical positions he covers and his own position. However, if he wished to distance himself from the historical positions he presents, he probably would have made such a distinction clearer. Thus, his statements on baptism in *Gathering* most likely reflect his own baptismal theology as well.

56. Ibid., 217.
57. Ibid.
58. Ibid., 219. Ellis expands this argument in his essay "Baptism of Disciples."
59. Ellis, "Embodied Grace," 6–7.

Waters of Promise

Paul S. Fiddes

Fiddes's chapter in *Reflections on the Water*, "Baptism and Creation," focuses on the contribution of the baptismal waters themselves to the meaning of baptism.[60] Fiddes argues that sacraments "are pieces of matter that God takes and uses as special places of encounter with God's own self; grace transforms nature, and grace is nothing less than God's gracious coming to us and to the world."[61] Baptists typically downplay the importance of water in baptism in order to emphasize the role of an individual's testimony for the rite, but Fiddes thinks "the Baptist practice of believers' baptism *does* make possible a recovery of the sense of the baptismal water as an actual element of the *natural* world, as well as a metaphor of God's redemptive activity"; moreover, he thinks focusing on baptism in creation, or even on water itself, contributes both to "issues of Baptist self-identity and to the Baptist contribution to the ecumenical scene."[62]

Fiddes identifies five key motifs connected with water that should also be associated with baptism: birth, cleansing, conflict, journey, and refreshment. There is a longstanding relationship between water and birth both in Scripture and in history to demonstrate that baptism fittingly functions as a rebirth. Water relates to cleansing in the sense that people turn to it for washing and purification, in both a physical and an ethical sense. Water, especially when it builds up to a flood level, evokes senses of conflict and hostile power, and baptism by immersion portrays a death underwater, under its power, only to be raised up to new life in Christ—sharing his victory over such power. Waters typically form boundaries, so passing through them often marks stages of a journey or rites of passage. Everyone associates water with refreshment, so OT imagery of rushing, life-giving waters and NT imagery of the "pouring out" of the Spirit give a refreshing element to baptism.

In light of these motifs, the presence of the water itself in baptism is important if baptism is a means of grace, because "the water in baptism is not merely a *visual aid* to help us understand various spiritual concepts; in its sheer materiality or 'stuffness' it actually *communicates* the presence

---

60. Fiddes, "Baptism and Creation." This section will reference Fiddes's updated version of this essay in *Tracks and Traces*.

61. Fiddes, "Baptism and Creation," 107.

62. Ibid., 108, emphasis his.

A Resurgence in Baptist Sacramentalism

of the transcendent God. A created thing provides places and opportunities for a transforming encounter."[63] Scripture and the incarnation portray a relationship, or even a covenant, of mutual influence between God and the world in which God's redemptive acts for human beings impact the created world itself. Baptism allows Christians to focus on the greater relationship between God and creation in a specifically ordained way that involves water, so Christians "will be the more aware of the presence of God in other situations where water is involved in birth, conflict, cleansing, journey, or refreshment."[64]

Having expressed the relationship between baptism and creation, Fiddes encourages Baptists to "draw upon the whole range of water-symbolism, and enable the baptismal pool to be the focus for God's creative-redemptive process."[65] Baptism can be the focus of this process because salvation is a journey of growth and within that journey baptism stands as an element in which God draws near to someone in a special way. This is not to say that salvation is restricted to baptism; rather, salvation "can be 'focused' there in the moment when the Christian believer is made part of the covenant community of Christ's disciples."[66]

Fiddes believes baptism initiates one into the church, making baptism a significant event not just for the individual being baptized but also for the church as a whole. Elsewhere, Fiddes addresses the place of unbelieving and believing children in the covenant community, including practical concerns such as the proper age at which to baptize youth. Fiddes wrote the paragraphs in *Believing and Being Baptized* on children and the church, so there is no need to repeat what that document says about how Baptists should welcome children who are on the way to faith. Fiddes does goes further in "Baptism and Creation" than in his other publications by rightly distinguishing between children on the way to faith from children who truly believe the gospel, and he encourages churches to integrate the latter without baptizing them until they are older:

---

63. Ibid., 117, emphasis his. Fiddes develops this argument elsewhere by upholding a Baptist understanding of *ex opere operato*, ("*Ex Opere Operato*"). His book on the doctrine of the Trinity also includes a chapter on God's presence mediated through creation and the sacraments, *Participating in God*.

64. Fiddes, "Baptism and Creation," 119.

65. Ibid., 121.

66. Ibid., 120.

> Why then, it may be asked, should they not be baptized? Is it excluding such believing children from a means of grace if baptism is not offered to them until the age of—say—thirteen or fourteen? Baptist churches in the Southern United States baptize regularly at the age of eight, and in some congregations children have been baptized as early as four. If children can believe, why cannot they receive the baptism of believers? Here I believe that the tradition of English Baptist church life is right to ask children to wait until later. Baptism is not simply believers' baptism, but a 'disciples' baptism.' It is a moment for taking up the responsibilities of carrying out the cross, suffering opposition for the sake of Christ, and sharing in the mission of God in the world. It is an occasion when the Spirit gives gifts for ministry, and calls us to use them in some vocation in life. It is not right to impose these demands and burdens on a child, for whom the playfulness of childhood is something which anyway passes too quickly away.[67]

Fiddes goes on say that such believing, unbaptized children are truly saved and share in Christ's redemptive benefits. Delaying their baptism should be expected because Baptists always have a "gap between entering upon salvation (conversion) and baptism," and if one affirms that "believers are 'incorporated into Christ' through water-baptism, the 'beginning' of Christian life must therefore be an extended process not a single moment."[68] Fiddes makes conversion punctiliar, occurring at the point of faith, but makes initiation into the Christian life a process in which baptism is the key element, but not the only element of the process—a process that may take on different patterns.

Fiddes thinks Baptist churches should embrace believing, unbaptized children by recognizing their faith in the gospel, which makes them fellow members of the body of Christ, even if they have not yet covenanted with other church members by being commissioned for service as disciples through baptism. Churches should take these children seriously, listen to their voices, and even include them at the table of the Lord's Supper, because such a child "is not yet commissioned as a disciple to work in the world (by believer's baptism or some kind of confirmation), but is still a member of the body, contributing a feature to the face of Christ

---

67. Fiddes, "Believers' Baptism?" 136. This chapter includes some arguments from his earlier work, "Baptism and Process."

68. Fiddes, "Baptism and Creation," 137.

which stands out in the community, and is valued by other members."[69] Fiddes's theology of the church body seems a little confused on this point since baptism initiates one into the covenanted church community, but unbaptized children are still members of the church body. Perhaps Fiddes conceives of the blessings of baptism to be tied to the church and one's covenant with and obligations to it, but the blessings of the Lord's Supper are only tied to one's identification in Christ.

Despite this confusion on how baptism relates to the Lord's Supper, Fiddes's contribution to sacramentalism aids the covenantal view of baptism in a few ways. He gives needed clarity to Baptist sacramental theology by addressing some of these practical questions while making it clear, in ways that many others do not, that conversion, in the sense of justification, happens at faith prior to baptism. His practical recommendations on how churches should integrate believing children are also helpful, since they are rooted in theology more than other accounts. Fiddes's works present a promising way forward for sacramentalists in that they understand baptism to mediate one's experience of salvation by uniting a believer to the church and empowering that believer for a life of discipleship rather than understanding baptism to be on an equal footing with faith in the process of salvation.

Brian Haymes

In his chapter in *Reflections on the Water*, "Baptism as a Political Act," Brian Haymes argues that baptism has consequences for Christian personal and social ethics, making it a politically significant act. Baptists often overlook the social aspects of baptism when they focus only on what it means for the individual's Christian life. In contrast, the NT "affirms not only that God has done in Christ something for your life and mine, but that the salvation of God is of cosmic significance (Eph 1:20–23; Col 1:14–20)."[70] Instead of emphasizing the communal or even covenantal aspects of baptism early on in his essay, Haymes first develops Fiddes's notion of water representing conflict and relates baptism to Christ's overcoming of what Haymes calls "the Powers."

---

69. Fiddes, "Church as a Eucharistic Community," 184. West also has a helpful discussion on the relationship of children in Baptist churches, ("Child and the Church").

70. Haymes, "Baptism as a Political Act," 70.

The Powers Haymes has in mind are the principalities, powers, and forces the NT mentions (cf. Eph 6:12).[71] He sides with Hendrikus Berkhof and John Howard Yoder in identifying these Powers as structures and systems of the world that God created good, but are now corrupt as a consequence of humanity's fall.[72] As the Powers relate to baptism, Haymes notes that most Christian traditions, including many Baptist ones, ask baptismal candidates if they renounce the devil and all his ways, showing that the Powers and baptism have ancient ties. Like Fiddes, he claims the Baptist practice of immersion, burying the candidate completely under the water, acts as vivid imagery of how Christ frees one from the Powers, even death itself. Of course, baptism today only points to the consummation of Christ's freeing work that will come in the *eschaton*. The social ethical implication of baptism is that one confesses through it that Jesus, not the Powers, is Lord, so "our values and goals will be his, and not just those of the society and ethos that have their own power to form us."[73]

Haymes next turns to the communal aspects of baptism. Instead of talking about a covenant community like Fiddes does, Haymes is more interested in applying the communal aspects of baptism to Christian social ethics. Baptism joins people to a new community, and this new community as a whole serves a different Lord than the rest of the world, making it an alternative society. Such a society should help its members develop good moral behaviors and virtues, constituting what Stanley Hauerwas calls "a community of character."[74] Members of this community should also corporately engage the Powers by striving to transform not only individual people with the gospel, but also the fallen structures of the world.

It is outside the scope of this book to evaluate Haymes's social ethics, but his association of baptism with the Powers and the forming of an alternative society is helpful for developing a covenantal view of

---

71. Haymes specifically mentions Romans 8:38; 1 Corinthians 2:8; 15:24–26; Ephesians 1:20; 2:1; 6:12; Colossians 1:6; and 2:8–20, ("Baptism as a Political Act," 82n2).

72. Berkhof's view of the powers is in *Christ and Powers*. Yoder gives his view in *Politics of Jesus*, 134–61. Haymes also references Wink's works on the Powers, which are some of the most thorough treatments of this theme: Wink, *Naming the Powers*; *Unmasking the Powers*; and *Engaging the Powers*.

73. Haymes, "Baptism as a Political Act," 77.

74. Hauerwas explores this theme in *Community of Character*. Haymes has a more in-depth treatment of this in "Moral Miracle."

A Resurgence in Baptist Sacramentalism

baptism. Haymes clarifies the political consequences of baptism for the individual in that he or she is confessing a changed allegiance in baptism. This confession, shared by all members of the church, also has implications for where the church's true allegiance lies. Haymes is right that most baptismal liturgies already make this clear, but most Baptist theologies of baptism do not. While it may be overwhelming to ponder the political consequences of baptism that Haymes discusses, his discussion of community gives some comfort, because this change of allegiance from the Powers to the community of Christ always accompanies a change of community in which one can develop and thrive, so no one walks aimlessly or alone in his or her faith.

After his chapter in *Reflections on the Water*, Haymes wrote two essays that explore the communal aspect of baptism, including some practical issues surrounding baptism, such as the proper age at which to baptize youth and whether to rebaptize prospective members.[75] In "Baptism: A Question of Belief and Age?" Haymes analyzes why North American Baptists typically baptize younger children than English Baptists do. In ways similar to Fiddes, Haymes argues that baptism is an act of grave commitment on the part of God, the church, and the candidate. While English Baptists affirm that children who accept Christ as their savior are truly saved, they also affirm that children cannot know all that baptism entails until they are older. Likewise, if baptism inherently involves the church community, then the decision to baptize ultimately rests not on the individual but on the corporate body as a whole. Haymes goes on to suggest to both North American and English Baptists some practical methods for involving the church in the process, such as altering baptismal liturgy. He then addresses some theological concerns.

First, he believes Baptists are prone to a view of individualism in which a believer's "God-given relationship with Jesus is entirely personal and involves no other persons at all."[76] In response he thinks Baptists must stress the personal decision of faith, but they must also stress the place of the church in the Christian life. Second, since there is no salvation outside the church as Christ's body, Baptists must link baptism to church membership, because being in the church is not an "optional extra we

---

75. Haymes, "Baptism: A Question"; and "Making Too Much." The second essay mostly covers the same arguments as the first essay on this issue, so this survey will only discuss the first one.

76. Haymes, "Baptism: A Question," 129.

could choose after Christ."⁷⁷ Third, Baptists must stress baptism into the name of the Father, Son, and Holy Spirit. This is not to say that Baptists baptize people into other names, but Haymes argues that many Baptists overemphasize one divine Person over others. Instead, "we are called to be the church of God, the triune God, whose being finds expression only in relating and loving. . . . Just as we cannot love God without loving neighbor and the rest of God's creation, no more can we be saved without recognizing and loving our brothers and sisters."⁷⁸ If God commands that his people be baptized into the name of the Father, Son, *and* Holy Spirit, then his people should remember that their salvation links them to a *community* of persons rather than to what Haymes calls "a committee of individuals."⁷⁹ Members of the former group share an identity and are interdependent in a way that members of the latter group fail to experience.

Haymes's theology of the meaning of baptism is a foundation from which sound practical suggestions regarding baptism can spring. Haymes raises the same questions as Fiddes does regarding children and the church, but Haymes explicitly brings theology into his practical discussions, so his practical suggestions carry more weight than those of Gilmore and *Believing and Being Baptized* to the degree that one finds Haymes's theology to be more persuasive than these other accounts.

CONCLUSION

1996 marked a resurgence in works on sacramentalism that revisited the meaning of baptism after a shift in Baptist ecumenical relations, hoping to enrich the baptismal theology of other Christian traditions by way of deeper reflection on Baptist baptismal theology. These works also built on those of the previous generation by enhancing sacramentalism's exegetical support with theological arguments. As Baptist sacramental theology continued through the new millennium, works emerged that either developed these same topics in different contexts, such as North American Baptist theology, or extended the ecumenical implications of sacramental theology beyond ecclesiology to larger topics such as

---

77. Ibid.
78. Ibid.
79. Ibid.

tradition and hermeneutics.[80] Those contemporary developments in Baptist sacramental theology do not focus on baptism and are therefore outside the scope of this book. However, the new millennium also brought more works on sacramentalism from Philip E. Thompson, Stanley K. Fowler, and Anthony R. Cross, who add a historical dimension to the case for sacramentalism.

---

80. The former group's works include several essays in Cross and Thompson (eds.), *Baptist Sacramentalism*; and in *Baptist Sacramentalism 2*, especially the contributions of Grenz and Pinnock in the former volume. Other works in this group include many works by George such as "Reformed Doctrine." Cross discusses Pinnock's sacramental theology in "Being Open." The latter group's works include Harvey, *Can These Bones Live?*; and Harmon, *Towards Baptist Catholicity*.

4

Recovering Sacramentalism in the Baptist Tradition

By the early twenty-first century sacramentalists had produced numerous biblical defenses and even some theological defenses of their view of baptism, but a lingering concern was the ordinance-only Baptist objection that sacramentalism is not and never was a genuine part of the Baptist tradition. In response, sacramentalists addressed the objection directly, demonstrating how their view is not an intrusion onto Baptist theology that is motivated by ecumenism. Rather, sacramentalism is a recovery of a much older Baptist view. Likewise, Baptists have historically been concerned with their relations to other Christian traditions, so neither sacramentalism itself nor ecumenical concerns go against one's Baptist heritage.

PHILIP E. THOMPSON

Thompson's works address not only baptism itself but also historical Baptist views and Baptist historiography on ecumenism and sacramentalism in general.[1] In his article, "A New Question in Baptist History," he appeals to seventeenth-century General Baptist positions for evidence that ecumenical concerns are rightly part of the Baptist tradition. Thompson is not interested in repeating anti-ecumenical Baptist tendencies here. Rather, he wants to analyze the underlying mindset that fuels them. He

---

1. Thompson's works on seventeenth-century Baptist thought include "People of the Free God," "Practicing the Freedom of God," "Seventeenth-century Baptist Confessions," and "Baptists and 'Calvinism.'"

argues that Baptists once operated with a catholic mind and spirit, but contemporary Baptists deviated from this attitude and "the atrophy of a catholic spirit . . . has rendered them unable to see themselves as responsible to the church's tradition."[2]

Thompson supports his argument with two major sections. The first section traces the nineteenth-century rise of Landmarkism among Southern Baptists, which is the belief that certain churches alone stand in continuity with New Testament churches through a historical succession of the proper theology of the church and its ordinances. Thompson then argues that E. Y. Mullins's emphasis on soul competency, which is the belief that people, as created in God's image, are fully competent and capable of directly responding to God, successfully supplanted Landmarkism in the twentieth century as the dominant Southern Baptist ecclesiology.[3] Both Landmarkism and soul competency were popular among Baptists during their respective periods because they utilize the same themes and principles, namely the primacy of the individual and/or individual local churches. Thompson rightly links both Landmarkism and soul competency to ordinance-only Baptist opposition to sacramentalism, because all three rely on individualism. As a result, Baptists during these periods distanced themselves from the tradition of the catholic church as if Baptists have always operated with such an individualistic impulse. Thompson argues that in contrast Baptists should ask whether "early Baptists understood the catholicity of the church better than their descendents have. Their voice is effectively silenced along with the rest of the catholic tradition. What are Baptists' options? They could continue to accept a self-understanding that has proved time and again to quench the catholic spirit. Or, by listening anew to the forebears, they may receive a Baptist witness to catholicity of mind and spirit.[4]" Thompson opts for the latter and briefly presents what such historic Baptist catholicity looked like in the second section of his article.

Thompson's historical treatment focuses on the General Baptist theologian Thomas Grantham (1634–92) and the *Orthodox Creed* of the General Baptists of the Midlands. He finds that neither Grantham nor the authors of the *Orthodox Creed* base their opposition to infant baptism

---

2. Thompson, "New Question," 52.

3. Mullins explains his understanding of soul competency in *Axioms of Religion*, 53–57.

4. Thompson, "New Question," 58.

on historical successionism as Landmarkists did or soul competency as Mullins and subsequent Southern Baptists did. Rather, these General Baptists largely followed the Reformed tradition in granting God's sovereign freedom to add to the church as he sees fit, and these Baptists argued that infant baptism, especially when performed by a state church, undermines such divine freedom. However, they never transferred their emphasis on divine freedom to human religious freedom or an individual believer's soul competency. Grantham criticizes the Quakers in particular for rejecting all religious externals, even baptism, because Quakers thereby violate God's freedom to use religious externals in salvation and sanctification. In response, Grantham affirms the possibility of such religious externals because he thinks God normatively leads his people into Christ's image through the church and its ordinances, which are religious externals. And likewise, the *Orthodox Creed* urges Christians to join themselves to the church and to look nowhere else for eternal life, which leads to an article in the creed on the marks of a true church. In this article, the creed clearly states there is one holy catholic church and that it includes more than just Baptist churches.

Thompson argues that such teaching provided early Baptists "a context within which they could affirm the importance of the church's tradition."[5] While this context in itself does not prove that early Baptists had a catholic spirit, Thompson demonstrates this greater point by focusing on three things that contemporary Baptists typically reject: creeds, the episcopacy, and the sacraments, because "the way early Baptists regarded these will reveal to us their catholic spirit as well."[6] To be sure, early Baptists did not think the state should impose creedal forms for churches, but they nonetheless thought true religion required creeds—so they wrote their own. The *Orthodox Creed* includes an article that calls for Baptists to receive and believe the ancient ecumenical creeds of the faith. Grantham even thought such creeds could bring unity to an otherwise fractured state of Christianity. Regarding the episcopacy, Thompson points readers to the General Baptist office of the bishop, who ordained local pastors and guarded the doctrinal purity of the churches under him. Lastly, Thompson argues that these early Baptists employed not only

---

5. Ibid., 63.
6. Ibid., 64.

sacramental concepts but also sacramental terminology. Grantham even believed that sacraments serve as seals of the covenant.

Thompson builds his case for the catholic spirit among early Baptists by also showing the humility these Baptists had regarding their own unique beliefs and practices as prone to correction by Scripture *and* church tradition. He contrasts their attitude toward church tradition with the arrogance that Landmarkism and soul competency instilled in Southern Baptists during the last two centuries when they distanced themselves from church tradition in general. Such humility, Thompson argues, gave early Baptists a sense of oneness with other communions that many contemporary Southern Baptists lack but ecumenically minded Baptists continue today. Thompson concludes that these early Baptist views disclose a self-understanding that differs from what is often presented today as Baptist traits, whether it be historic succession or the theological principle of soul competency. Thompson believes that this difference should lead contemporary Baptists to reconsider whether their anti-ecumenical and anti-sacramental posture carries on the best part of the Baptist tradition.

In another article, "Re-envisioning Baptist Identity," Thompson provides more support for his claim that the Baptist heritage legitimately includes sacramentalism. He argues that early Baptist theocentrism emphasized God's freedom in salvation, including his communal design for bringing people into his covenant and church, symbolized through its sacraments. In this way, Thompson covers similar ground to that of Ellis, Fiddes, and Haymes, but he researches and uses Baptist history to support his own baptismal theology more than they do. He also goes further in analyzing the shift in Baptist thought during the nineteenth century in which various factors led to an almost completely different Baptist identity when it comes to that period's Baptist theology of the church and its sacraments or ordinances.

In this article, Thompson highlights the rise of individualism and the scorning of physical creation as symptoms of a theological shift to anthropocentrism in Baptist theology during the nineteenth century from the theocentrism of earlier Baptist thought.[7] This shift directly affected Baptist theology of the church and sacraments. Thompson concludes: "By replacing theocentrism with anthropocentrism, Baptists shifted

---

7. Thompson develops these arguments in "Sacraments and Religious Liberty."

affirmations concerning God's freedom to human freedom, discarding those aspects such as sacraments and the church which make sense in light of the former but not the latter. God may freely use physical creation in salvation, but physical creation can be only an encroachment upon the freedom of the spiritual human individual."[8]

While Thompson is right in asserting that sacramentalism is part of the Baptist tradition, he overstates the differences between seventeenth-century Baptists and their successors. For example, he argues that the nineteenth-century shift in Baptist thought from theocentrism to anthropocentrism ultimately "became almost total. Apart from affirmation that humanity must honor God's freedom, God, bereft of those means by which God freely works for salvation, must now honor human freedom."[9] Such a statement ignores contemporary Baptist use of the preaching of the Word and theology of the Spirit, who graciously prompts people to faith—elements that have much continuity with historical Baptist thought—as means by which God freely works for salvation. There is much common ground between ordinance-only Baptists and sacramentalists, and a preferable strategy of defending sacramentalism would be to maximize this common ground instead of accusing Baptists today of replacing God with human beings in their theology.

In another article, "Memorial Dimensions of Baptism," Thompson extends his historical research on Baptist theology beyond seventeenth-century Britain to late colonial America. He cites baptismal prayers and hymns from this period that stress the communal aspects of baptism as evidence that historical Baptist notions about the church and its sacraments came across the Atlantic in the eighteenth century. In the prayers of these Baptists, "it is not simply the one seeking baptism, but the gathered community that remembers the saving acts of God in Christ. The Lamb of God is bidden to meet not the individuals awaiting baptism, but the community of disciples gathered on the riverbank. Indeed, there is even a certain priority given to the community, for the common life provides the context within which the rite is performed."[10] Such prayers also admonish "the newly baptized . . . to consider the day of their baptism

---

8. Thompson, "Re-envisioning Baptist Identity," 302.
9. Ibid.
10. Thompson, "Memorial Dimensions of Baptism," 310.

as the day of their new birth into the Christian community."[11] Baptists of this period were also comfortable in their hymnody to ascribe great significance to baptism as a symbol of initiation into Christ's name and salvation. Some hymns even mention the Spirit's role in bringing together Christ, the community, and the individual through baptism. For example,

> Eternal Spirit, heavenly Dove,
> On these baptismal waters move;
> That we through energy divine,
> May have the substance with the sign.[12]

In contrast to the prayers and hymns of late Colonial American Baptists, Thompson argues that most contemporary North American Baptists practice baptism as an individual monologue rather than a communal prayer. They also do not sing any hymns or songs that celebrate baptism, either in a baptismal service or in any other service. Thompson links this contrast in baptismal practice between the periods to underlying differences in baptismal theology. Contemporary North American Baptists emphasize the individual and his or her faith to the point that baptism has meaning only for the person being baptized. Thompson finds this emphasis wrongheaded because, "baptism for Southern Baptists seems either to remember not the gospel rooted as it is in flesh and matter, but individual, spiritual appropriation of it; or to reduce the gospel to individual saving knowledge or experience. . . . The individual believer and her belief have come to displace the one in whom she believes in baptismal memory."[13]

To be sure, there are important differences between the theology of baptism among Baptists today and their late Colonial predecessors, but Thompson once again overstates the differences between historical and contemporary Baptists. Thompson conflates emphasizing one's belief *in* the gospel of Jesus Christ in baptism with letting that belief *displace* the gospel itself in baptism. Nonetheless, Thompson's method of contrasting the worship and practice of historical and contemporary Baptists and analyzing their differing underlying theologies remains well grounded. His gleaning of baptismal theology from prayers and hymns is also

11. Ibid., 311.
12. Clay, *Hymns and Spiritual Songs*, hymn 260. Quoted in Thompson, "Memorial Dimensions of Baptism," 317.
13. Ibid., 322.

helpful in assessing historical Baptist thought and only supports his case that sacramentalism is truly part of the Baptist tradition. Two other authors who have also made such arguments are Fowler and Cross.

STANLEY K. FOWLER

Fowler's monograph, *More Than a Symbol*, presents historical and contemporary sacramentalist baptismal theology from the seventeenth century to 1966. He analyzes and defends sacramentalism in light of both the biblical witness and the baptismal views of other Christian traditions. But the most significant contribution Fowler makes to sacramentalism is how he traces historical Baptist baptismal theology from 1600 to 1900 by looking at communal confessions and creeds as well as individual tracts and treatises from the periods. His research leads him to conclude that the dominant seventeenth-century Baptist view "was very much like the Puritan-Calvinist understanding of baptism as both sign and seal of entrance into salvific union with Christ. . . . Although this Reformed sacramentalism was still evident in major Baptist writers at the end of the 17th century, it was either ignored or rejected by most Baptists in the following two centuries."[14] Fowler's historical research ends with the dawn of the twentieth century, by which time Baptists thought baptism was merely a symbolic ritual undergone by a confirmed believer. It was in this milieu that twentieth-century sacramentalists did their work, and Fowler concludes that they often faced misunderstandings and charges of incoherence because they varied in the language they used regarding whether baptism itself bestows Christ's benefits or symbolically ratifies them to the believer. Fowler argues that, despite the varied language of sacramentalists on this point, the two positions are "in the end functionally equivalent. To say that these benefits of Christ are actually bestowed in baptism is to say that as far as our perception of them is concerned, they are bestowed in this context."[15]

One method Fowler uses to demonstrate the coherence of sacramentalism is to compare it to the sacramental theology of other Christian traditions. Among his comparisons, the differences he cites between

---

14. Fowler, *More Than a Symbol*, 248–49. Fowler's understanding of Reformed sacramentalism centers on an understanding of the sacraments as signs and seals of God's grace that mediate consciousness of salvific union with Christ (as applied to confessing believers).

15. Ibid., 211.

sacramentalism and the baptismal theology of the Stone-Campbell movement (Churches of Christ) is most helpful since both groups oppose infant baptism. Critics of sacramentalism often claim that it is nothing more than the Stone-Campbell view by another name, and Fowler addresses this issue in more detail with a subsequent article, "Baptists and Churches of Christ in Search of a Common Theology of Baptism."[16]

In this article, Fowler provides a helpful survey of recent North American Baptist sympathies toward sacramental concepts, even if few North American Baptist theologians embrace sacramental terminology. Whereas former North American Baptists typically avoided claiming that baptism is an instrument of grace in salvation in any sense, not a few contemporary North American Baptist theologians now argue that the straightforward reading of many baptismal texts is that baptism is an instrumental cause in the application of salvation—God is always the efficient cause. That is, using Aristotelian terms, God is the reason baptism has any effect on believers and the instrument God uses to apply that effect is baptism. It is similar to saying that Charlie Parker is the reason one can hear beautiful saxophone music in his recordings and the instrument he uses to make that music is a saxophone. The key in either case is the efficient cause, not the instrumental cause.

Fowler argues that the recovery of sacramentalism among Baptists opens up the possibility of rapprochement between Baptists and the Churches of Christ because the latter insist that baptism is an instrumental but not efficient cause of salvation. Rapprochement cannot be one-sided, so Fowler also traces recent trends in the Churches of Christ that recognize genuine remission of sins among those who are neither baptized within the Churches of Christ nor baptized at all.[17] Fowler argues that this recent trend is closer to Alexander Campbell's own view than the dominant Churches of Christ position after his death. The latter view held that those baptized outside the Church of Christ or not baptized at all are probably unsaved because they never received the instrumental means of salvation. In contrast to this claim, Fowler argues that Campbell believed baptism is the instrumental cause of a believer's *assurance* of forgiveness of sins, which is similar to Baptist sacramentalist accounts and different

---

16. Caneday also argues for some rapprochement between Baptists and Stone-Campbell Restorationists regarding a shared view of baptism, ("Baptism").

17. Fowler points readers to the following Churches of Christ writings, which demonstrate these trends: Hicks and Taylor, *Down in the River*; and Baker (ed.), *Evangelicalism*.

from subsequent Churches of Christ accounts, which proclaim baptism to be the instrumental cause of forgiveness of sins. Given these changing trends among both North American Baptists and Churches of Christ theologians, Fowler concludes,

> It does not take a huge paradigm shift on either side to effect a convergence of Baptists and the Churches of Christ in the area of baptismal theology. For Baptists it means being prepared to admit that baptism is the climax of conversion and the act of a penitent sinner, not of a confirmed saint, so that the baptizand is turning to Christ for the conscious experience of salvation. For the Churches of Christ, it means admitting that while the grace of entrance into union with Christ is normatively mediated through baptism, it is not the exclusive means, so that the negative inference, "No valid baptism implies no salvation," is invalid.[18]

Fowler's conclusion shows that sacramentalism and Churches of Christ baptismal theology share many things in common, including the rejection of baptismal regeneration. Both positions hold baptism to be the normative instrumental means through which one deepens his or her *experience* of salvation. For them, God prescribed baptism as the normative outward act that confirms one's inward faith. This conclusion should disarm the ordinance-only Baptist objection to sacramentalism that it sounds too much like Churches of Christ theology, or, in other words, a position that entails baptismal regeneration.

Fowler's works also provide a firm foundation on which to build a theological defense of sacramentalism. His analysis and defense of the first generation of sacramentalists is crucial for making the case that sacramentalism is a genuinely Baptist position. However, one weakness in Fowler's works is that he defines and explains his sacramental theology in ways that are prone to misunderstanding. For example, in a few places he speaks of the baptizand coming to the waters as a penitent sinner rather than a confirmed saint. But in other places, he insists that baptism is a seal of one's experience of salvation, implying that salvation itself begins before baptism, at the point of faith. This raises the question, what does he mean by "penitent sinner" and "confirmed saint"? Does Fowler want to emphasize that the baptizand is a sinner, prompted by faith to come penitently to the grace promised in baptism? Or does he want to emphasize baptism's instrumental role in confirming the baptizand's faith? In other

---

18. Fowler, "Baptists and Churches of Christ," 269.

words, does Fowler consider the baptizand to be an unconfirmed saint, but a saint nonetheless, prior to baptism? Fowler's works overall tend to affirm the previous question, but the way he defines and explains sacramentalism reasonably leads Schreiner and Wright to claim that "Fowler's book suffers from lack of clarity in using the word 'sacramental,' and the vagueness of his language makes it difficult to determine precisely what he means."[19] This problem is not unique to Fowler and is one that sacramentalists should resolve with clearer claims.

If sacramentalists do not address these misunderstandings with clearer defenses, they can continue to expect a cold reception to their views. As Baptists misunderstood or misapplied Beasley-Murray's explanation of conversion-baptism decades ago, they can also do the same to Fowler's talk of baptism being for the penitent sinner rather than the confirmed saint. Sacramentalists need to tighten their description of the meaning of baptism, and placing it within a greater theological framework such as covenant theology could help them in this task. Despite some vagueness in his definitions and brief explanations of his views, the substance of Fowler's works is clearer than that of many works from the twentieth-century sacramentalists that he covers. This is a trait that Fowler shares with other members of the resurgence of sacramentalism, such as Anthony R. Cross. Whereas Fowler's language on the relation between faith and baptism tends toward the latter mediating one's experience of salvation, Cross's baptismal theology tends the other way, in which baptism is part of conversion, or even justification, itself. As a result, Cross's works demonstrate the current state of sacramentalist literature by building on historical arguments with a biblical approach.

ANTHONY R. CROSS

Cross's monograph, *Baptism and the Baptists*, traces both the baptismal theology and the baptismal practice of British Baptists in the twentieth century. After examining events of the century closely, he concludes that "there is no single Baptist theology or practice of baptism, only theologies and practices, and this diversity accords with Baptist ecclesiology

---

19. Schreiner and Wright, introduction to *Believer's Baptism*, 2n4. Moody also stumbles over Fowler's claims, saying that Fowler's view of sacramentalism is more Lutheran than it is Reformed, ("American Baptist Sacramentalism?" 174). Fowler's writings themselves clearly negate Moody's charge, since Fowler delineates Baptist sacramentalism from both Lutheran and Reformed sacramental theology, (*More Than a Symbol*, 237–40).

which continues to tend towards independency, each local church and individual minister exercising their liberty in the administration and interpretation of Christ's laws."[20] Cross does not think this is a healthy state of affairs for Baptists:

> As far as Baptists are concerned, a century of baptismal debate and controversy, both internal and external, discussion and developments, seems to have created a schizophrenic denomination in which the ones apparently interested in the theology and practice of baptism appear to be those involved within the ecumenical movement. Further, Baptists are themselves no nearer consensus in answering the most important theological question than they were at the beginning of the century—is baptism a mere symbol however important a one, or an effective rite? This second position now commands more respect than in earlier years, but no one side has convinced the other and Baptists are left with competing theologies and practices of baptism/initiation.[21]

While it would be too much to expect Baptists to present a monolithic theology and practice of baptism, the debates among British Baptists that Cross presents and analyzes did sharpen the self-understanding and baptismal theology of these Baptists. The baptismal debates among North American Baptists that started much later in the twentieth century will most likely lead to the same results—both positive and negative. Despite Cross's somewhat grim overall conclusion, his research and analysis of twentieth-century British Baptist theology has some implications for the present study as it relates to North American Baptists today.

Cross argues that British Baptists "view baptism pragmatically, a point supported by the fact that discussion of baptism is now often found within discussions of related subjects which are apparently regarded as more important."[22] This point holds for North American Baptists as well, considering the most in-depth work on baptismal theology in recent years, *Believer's Baptism*, a North American Baptist book that contains many sacramental concepts of baptism even though its editors purposely avoid sacramental terminology, is aimed in part at the related subject of "correcting" Reformed paedobaptist theology. This subject is considered important because North American Baptists who are attracted to Reformed

---

20. Cross, *Baptism and the Baptists*, 455.
21. Ibid., 463.
22. Ibid., 454.

soteriology are prone to be attracted to Reformed paedobaptist theology as well.[23] While there is much merit to addressing practical concerns with negative theological arguments, this tendency can limit positive theological explorations on the topic itself. More theological reflection on the meaning of baptism that is severed from the pragmatic goal of pursuing other subjects is needed among North American Baptists today because it is important enough to study in its own right.

Cross also argues that between 1966 and 1997 "the overwhelming majority of Baptists writing on baptism have done so within the ecumenical context, which suggests that Baptists hold an ambivalent attitude towards baptism."[24] This trend has not changed in the last fifteen years. What Cross means by "ambivalent attitude" is that Baptists often vehemently defend believer baptism as opposed to infant baptism, but outside of such debates they make little of the meaning of believer baptism. The turn to receptive ecumenism lowers the stakes of these debates between Baptists and others over baptism and should also spur Baptists to plunge the depths of the meaning of believer baptism. As a result, Baptists can continue to engage other Christians with their unique baptismal theology as well as give needed depth to the rite itself that is often lacking in their baptismal theology and practice, without desiring to win the debate over which baptismal theology is correct. As will be seen in the next chapter, Cross's evaluation of ambivalence applies to Baptist attitudes on covenant theology, because Baptists often oppose covenant theology due to its link to paedobaptist theology, but they often do not develop a positive theology of the covenants for themselves.[25]

In another article, "The Myth of English Baptist Anti-sacramentalism," Cross surveys four centuries of Baptist sacramentalism. He builds on Fowler's and Thompson's works, agreeing with them that "by the close of the nineteenth century . . . baptism was, with a few exceptions, described as an ordinance, the subjective, personal testimony of a believer's faith in Christ and not an objective means of conveying the grace of God and

---

23. Schreiner and Wright, introduction to *Believer's Baptism*, 6–7. Akin's article on the meaning of baptism appears in a volume aimed at correcting the eroding integrity of Southern Baptist churches, including its distinction of holding to believer's baptism by immersion, ("Meaning of Baptism").

24. Cross, *Baptism and the Baptists*, 454.

25. Two welcome exceptions in recent literature are Nichols, *Covenant Theology*; and Gentry and Wellum, *Kingdom through Covenant*.

the benefits of redemption through Christ to those who believe."[26] But Cross also claims that there has always been a strand of sacramentalists throughout Baptist history. This strand continued into the twentieth century and flourished during this time because the ecumenical movement helped fuel it. As a result, twentieth-century Baptists reflected more on baptismal theology than in previous centuries, but in Cross's opinion their works fell short of offering a "truly Baptist sacramental theology of baptism. . . . Further, these developments have had little effect on the practice of baptism. . . . Two challenges for Baptists to take up, then, are to explore further baptismal sacramentalism and to translate it into baptismal practice."[27] One way of tying these two challenges together is to explore sacramentalism in a theological manner that directly addresses practical issues, which is one goal of this book.

Like Fowler, Cross has contributed to the development of Baptist sacramental theology not only as a historian but also as a theologian.[28] In the following articles he continues much of the biblical theology of the first generation of sacramentalists by taking their positions to a new generation.

In "'One Baptism' (Ephesians 4:5): A Challenge to the Church," Cross argues that the "one baptism" in Ephesians 4:5 is "conversion-baptism" and that neither paedobaptist nor credobaptist churches currently practice it; the verse thus presents a challenge to both church traditions.[29] Cross builds on the writings of Beasley-Murray and others to argue that the NT, especially the baptismal accounts in Acts, teaches conversion-baptism. Conversion-baptism holds that baptism is but one element in the complex but unified experience of Christian initiation that includes other elements such as faith, forgiveness, justification, and the gift of the Spirit. Such a complex experience is a process in which differing orders and timelines of people's experiences of these elements do not affect the overall effectiveness of the process.

---

26. Cross, "Myth," 152.

27. Ibid., 162.

28. His theological works include "'One Baptism,'" "Spirit- and Water-Baptism," "Meaning of 'Baptisms,'" "Being Open," "Faith-Baptism," "Evangelical Sacrament," "Baptismal Regeneration," and *Recovering*.

29. Cross, "'One Baptism,'" 207–9.

Cross argues that this understanding of Christian initiation explains the variety in Luke's accounts in Acts in which there is no normative ordering of the elements of conversion:

> Which is the normative order of conversion: repentance, water-baptism, forgiveness and reception of the Spirit (Acts 2:28, 41); believing, water-baptism, laying on of hands and reception of the Spirit (Acts 8:12–17); reception of the Spirit, speaking in tongues and water-baptism (Acts 10:44–48); believing and water-baptism (Acts 16:31–33); or believing, water-baptism, laying on of hands, reception of the Spirit and speaking in tongues (Acts 19:1–6; see also 9:17–18; 22:16)? But when we recognize conversion as a process, that is conversion-initiation, such questions lose their relevance, as the sovereign activity of the Spirit of God is recognized along with the probable explanation that Luke was not concerned with providing a pattern of conversion-initiation.
>
> Further, when the use of metonymy is acknowledged, the absence of reference to one or more of these "aspects" of conversion-initiation, or the mention of only one of them, ceases to be problematic.[30]

What Cross means by the NT authors' use of metonymy is the practice of using one element of Christian initiation, such as faith or baptism, to refer to the whole process. In NT texts that specifically refer to baptism (e.g., 1 Cor 12:13), Cross argues that it is best to understand "baptism" as a synecdoche that refers to "both Spirit- and water-baptism and the rest of the conversion-initiation process."[31]

Instead of defending conversion-baptism against the critiques of fellow Baptists, Cross addresses developments in biblical theology after Beasley-Murray in which NT scholars such as James D. G. Dunn explain the data in Acts above and in other NT baptismal texts by concluding that the primitive church had various theologies and practices of baptism rather than a unified baptismal theology.[32] Cross rightly defends the notion of a unified baptismal theology in the early church against such authors. But he does not take the same measures to clarify and defend his

---

30. Ibid., 176–77.

31. Cross, "Spirit- and Water-Baptism," 148. Cross goes into more detail in this article about his understanding of baptism as a metonymy and synecdoche in which the latter term is more precise than the former one.

32. Cross, "'One Baptism,'" 178–81. Cross refers primarily to Dunn's *Unity and Diversity*; and Hartman's *"Into the Name."*

own understanding of conversion-baptism against objections from ordinance-only Baptists. Instead, Cross merely acknowledges that objections exist, saying, "While many will reject this position on baptism, it is nevertheless a plausible interpretation."[33] It would be helpful and would make the position more plausible if he presented the reasons why many Baptists reject conversion-baptism, along with his responses to their objections.

Nonetheless, Cross argues in the rest of the essay that conversion-baptism is the "one baptism" of Ephesians 4:5 and that churches should alter their theology and practice accordingly in order to testify to this one baptism. He proceeds to give some suggestions as to what this modified practice may resemble. However, if one is unconvinced of conversion-baptism in general, he or she will not agree with Cross that it is the key to understanding the "one baptism" of Ephesians 4:5 and will not take his practical suggestions seriously.

In this way, Cross's theological articles continue both the strengths and weaknesses of the first generation of sacramentalists by focusing on biblical theology at the expense of systematic theology. While it is plausible to argue that the NT presents conversion as a process, Cross does not explain the relationship between the elements within this process. Are all elements equal, or are some elements more important than the others? For ordinance-only Baptists, faith is the key to conversion and other elements are subordinate to it. Moreover, ordinance-only Baptists may understand Christian initiation as a process that includes faith and baptism among other things, but they would not consider "conversion" to be synonymous with the greater process of Christian initiation. For them, conversion refers to justification by grace through faith alone. Likewise, they consider baptism to be only believer baptism, so faith must precede it and must be more important than it.[34] Cross seems to ignore their concerns.

Cross's treatment here is reminiscent of some of Beasley-Murray's arguments in which faith and baptism are so connected that "baptism is the moment of faith in which the adoption is realized—in the dual sense of effected by God and grasped by man—which is the same as saying that in baptism faith receives Christ in whom the adoption is effected."[35] Beasley-Murray calls this faith-baptism, which holds together objective

---

33. Cross, "'One Baptism,'" 181.
34. Moody, "American Baptist Sacramentalism?" 199–202.
35. Beasley-Murray, *Baptism in the New Testament*, 151.

and subjective aspects of the gospel, but this concept still falls short of answering ordinance-only Baptist questions regarding the precise relationship between faith and salvation. Elsewhere, Beasley-Murray also claims that faith precedes baptism and one should not reverse Paul's emphasis of faith over baptism.[36] But it seems that Cross wants to do exactly that in this and other articles, exposing sacramentalism all over again to objections that Beasley-Murray had to address long ago. Despite these similarities between Cross's and Beasley-Murray's baptismal theologies, Cross's sacramentalism appears to be more like Gilmore's than Beasley-Murray's in that faith and baptism are inherently tied to one another, yet they each have distinct but equally important roles within the process of conversion. For Gilmore, genuine faith necessarily leads to baptism, but faith acts almost as a prerequisite for baptism, which itself is the means through which a believer is united to Christ. Cross considers baptism to be an objective means of conveying the grace of God and the benefits of redemption through Christ to those who believe, and he clarifies his baptismal theology by going further in the direction of Gilmore in another article, "Baptismal Regeneration: Rehabilitating a Lost Dimension of New Testament Baptism," where he explores how baptism objectively conveys the benefits of redemption through Christ.

In this article Cross addresses the Southern Baptist Convention position that Baptists do not and have not viewed baptism as either sacramental or regenerative, given that Scripture teaches otherwise.[37] While many works have addressed sacramentalism, Cross makes the unique argument here that evangelicals and Baptists should embrace baptismal regeneration because it is a biblical doctrine. This is a surprising claim and one that marks a change in his own understanding of Baptist theology, because he previously claimed that Baptists have always "staunchly opposed" baptismal regeneration.[38] This change may be somewhat overstated, because in his earlier work he lumped all views of baptismal regeneration together in such a way that there was no distinction between what he now calls a "biblical" view and an *ex opere operato* view. In this article, he wants to delineate the biblical view of baptismal regeneration from other versions of it, but the concept he refers to with the phrase

---

36. Ibid., 304.
37. International Mission Board, "Position Paper."
38. Cross, *Baptism and the Baptists*, 28.

baptismal regeneration appears to be none other than sacramentalism by another name.

According to Cross, the biblical view of baptismal regeneration recognizes "that it is possible to be regenerated and saved without baptism, but equally that not everyone baptized will be regenerated and saved—the key in both scenarios is clearly the presence or absence of saving faith."[39] As such, this version of baptismal regeneration claims that baptism is a sacrament of regeneration, but only so as it depends on faith. This view requires more qualification regarding what Cross means by regeneration since he could mean either the confirmation of one's cleansing from sin or the means through which one's sins are cleansed. Unfortunately, Cross does not qualify his position. Instead, he argues that one can find this form of baptismal regeneration in the writings of the seventeenth-century Particular Baptist William Mitchell, who adopts a Reformed sacramental theology that understands baptism and the Lord's Supper as signs of the covenant of grace that represent Christ and his benefits in such a way that they are means of grace though the action of the Spirit working with the Word. Cross reaffirms Fowler's claim that Particular Baptists of this period patterned much of their theology on the Westminster Confession of Faith, so it should be no surprise that Reformed theology influenced their sacramental theology.

Cross further defends his historical claim by presenting a few Baptist theologians from the last few centuries who espouse some form of baptismal regeneration because they think baptism confesses and consummates one's faith, thereby making it the focal point of one's remission of sins and reception of the gift of the Spirit. Cross argues that this formulation of biblical baptismal regeneration was not a new innovation by these Baptists or their Reformed counterparts. Rather, they continue a strand of teaching that was very popular in the early church. Up until Augustine, even after the rise of infant baptism, the early church used the pattern of seeing "the work of the Spirit and the faith of the believer expressed in water-baptism."[40]

Cross ties Baptist accounts of baptismal regeneration to historical precedents, including baptismal regeneration in the Reformed tradition,

---

39. Cross, "Baptismal Regeneration," 155.

40. Ibid., 162. Cross refers to a few church fathers to build his case, and this section will not assess his claims, because they fall outside the scope of this study. Ferguson gives a more complete treatment of this topic in *Baptism in the Early Church*.

Recovering Sacramentalism in the Baptist Tradition

but he does so without first demonstrating that the Reformed tradition in the seventeenth or any other century held to baptismal regeneration. While Fowler rightly demonstrates the similarities between Baptist sacramentalism and Reformed sacramentalism, Cross has a more difficult time using the primary sources to demonstrate his claim that both traditions share similar accounts of baptismal regeneration. Cross considers only Calvin's view of baptismal regeneration, as representative of other Reformers, to be important for the discussion, but a closer look at Calvin's writings reveals that Cross cannot rightly use them as evidence of baptismal regeneration in the Reformed tradition.

Cross presents some of Calvin's theological reflections on certain baptismal passages in which Calvin ties the work of the Spirit to faith expressed in baptism in such a way that baptism is also tied to newness of life or regeneration itself.[41] Cross thinks such claims demonstrate that Calvin held to a doctrine of baptismal regeneration, but a closer look at Calvin's writings reveals otherwise. Calvin's commentary on Titus 3:5 connects faith to God's saving grace and baptism to confirmation of one's faith: "I have no doubt that he [Paul] alludes, at least, to baptism, and even I will not object to have this passage expounded as relating to baptism; not that salvation is contained in the outward symbol of water, but because baptism seals to us the salvation obtained by Christ. Paul treats of the exhibition of the grace of God, which, we have said, has been made by faith. Since therefore a part of revelation consists in baptism, that is, so far as it is intended to confirm our faith, he properly makes mention of it."[42] Calvin does go on to say here that baptism is "fitly and truly said to be 'the washing of regeneration,'" but the efficacy lies in the Spirit's residing in one who has what the sign of baptism signifies, namely faith.[43]

Cross points to Calvin's discussion of "baptism as token of mortification and renewal in Christ" in the *Institutes* as further evidence for his theology of baptismal regeneration. But here again, Calvin says the efficacy of baptism's role in tying the believer to Christ's death lies in the Spirit, and so the benefits of baptism are what it demonstrates to believers who already have new life.[44] In this section, Calvin points the reader to

---

41. Cross, "Baptismal Regeneration," 163–65. Cf. Cross, "Baptism in Calvin and Barth."

42. Calvin, *Commentaries*, 332–33.

43. Ibid., 333.

44. Calvin, *Institutes*, 4.15.5.

his previous treatment of baptism in which he claims its virtue is not in water without the Word: "For Paul did not mean to signify [in Titus 3:5] that our cleansing and salvation are accomplished by water, or that water contains in itself the power to cleanse, regenerate, and renew; nor that here is the cause of salvation, but only that in this sacrament are received the knowledge and certainty of such gifts."[45]

According to these writings, Calvin does not hold to baptismal regeneration if by that phrase one refers to the view that baptism is a symbol that also bestows what it signifies, the cleansing of sin. The same holds true for Particular Baptist William Mitchell because he conceives of baptism as the sign of the covenant of grace and as such a means through which the Spirit and Word work to the benefit of the believer by confirming his or her faith. Calvin and Mitchell held to a sacramental view of baptism, but most would not say that they also held to baptismal regeneration.

Baptismal regeneration typically means that baptism itself washes sins away and as such is a necessary part of salvation; this is not the same as saying that baptism is a means of grace. The authors of *Christian Baptism*, including Beasley-Murray, distanced their sacramental theology from baptismal regeneration because of how most people understand the phrase. Can such a view rightly be called "baptismal regeneration" when it allows for God to regenerate people apart from baptism? Most Christians probably would not consider such a view to be baptismal regeneration at all, but rather sacramentalism by another name. Unlike the use of sacramental terminology, Cross's use of the term *baptismal regeneration* causes more problems than it solves. Moreover, what Cross calls baptismal regeneration here is what he calls sacramentalism elsewhere. For example, he gives the biblical case for baptismal regeneration in his article, "Baptismal Regeneration," by repeating arguments that he and others have presented elsewhere as the biblical case for sacramentalism with no distinction. By including baptismal regeneration in the discussion of sacramentalism, Cross only clutters the discussion and provides no tangible benefits for sacramentalists. If anything, he invites the aforementioned objection from ordinance-only Baptists that sacramentalism entails baptismal regeneration.

Cross's arguments reveal a distinction between his version of sacramentalism and that of Fowler, because Cross holds to faith-baptism

---

45. Ibid., 4.15.2

in which baptism is itself part of the gospel presentation, the conversion process, and the doctrine of salvation.[46] Cross distinguishes this understanding of believer baptism from another form of believer baptism in which those who have already come to faith and been regenerated come to baptism. It appears that Fowler's insistence that baptism is the means of one's experience of salvation technically falls into this other category, and this book will later argue that Fowler's view is closer to seventeenth-century Baptist sacramental theology than that of Cross.

While Cross clearly distinguishes his view from other Baptist sacramental theologies, he never addresses his equivocal use of regeneration. When Calvin, Mitchell, and others refer to regeneration within the context of baptism, they are referring to baptism's benefit as a sign of the washing away of sin that occurs by grace through faith. Cross seems to make regeneration (within the context of baptism) refer to conversion itself in which baptism is the instrumental means through which the Spirit bestows the cleansing itself that baptism signifies. In other words, Cross does away with the distinction between the sign and that which it signifies—a distinction that most other theologians want to keep in order to ensure that salvation is by grace through faith in Christ alone. Cross's view is clearer than twentieth-century sacramentalists who, when pressed, may also have espoused this understanding of baptism, but Cross's clarity comes at the price of more objections—this time from fellow sacramentalists as well as ordinance-only Baptists.

While Cross's historical arguments in this article fall short of supporting his overall thesis, they certainly encourage further exploration of the relationship between seventeenth-century Baptist and Reformed theologies, especially covenant theology. Given the centuries-old connection between sacraments and covenants, if the two groups shared a similar sacramental theology, then they most likely also shared a similar covenant theology. Moreover, if historians such as Thompson, Fowler, and Cross are right that sacramentalism is part of the Baptist tradition, then demonstrating how Baptists employed sacramental theology in other realms of theology, such as covenant theology, would help strengthen their case.

In his most recent article, "The Evangelical Sacrament," Cross shifts from historical Baptist theology to the global evangelical tradition, calling for the reform of how evangelicals in general and Baptists in particu-

---

46. Cross, "Baptismal Regeneration," 174.

lar understand baptism. He wants both groups to turn to what he calls faith-baptism, in which God saves people through spiritual and material means—faith and baptism respectively. While others may want to understand fully how God does this, Cross argues that such a desire is wrongheaded: "We cannot explain and understand everything (the felt need to do so is driven by an Enlightenment impulse, I believe) and sometimes we simply need to accept in faith that God works in his ways, and that we are not always privy to his reasons (cf. Isa. 55:8)."[47] But there is a difference between the desire to understand fully what God does not reveal about baptism and to understand clearly what God has revealed about it in Scripture. Cross is aware of this distinction and delves once again into a biblical theology of baptism to support his claim.

Cross presents here, as he has before in other writings, his conception of conversion-initiation and how faith-baptism fits within it, in order to suggest how evangelicals should reform their baptismal theology. He argues that Scripture clearly teaches conversion as a process with many elements. The NT authors often use synecdoche to let one element refer to the process as a whole and thus attribute the whole process to faith or baptism. Within this conception of conversion, Scripture claims that baptism itself is an instrumental means of the Spirit, effecting certain aspects of salvation. Cross does not explain in great detail what these aspects are, and both versions of sacramentalism (as expressed above) fit Cross's definition here. If churches are to honor and value this understanding of baptism, they should include baptism in their presentations of the gospel, regularly preach and teach on baptism, and urge people to refer to baptism as the commencement of their lives of discipleship.

Cross traces familiar ground here when he again presents the biblical case for sacramentalism, but he applies his findings from biblical theology to systematic concerns as if they are sufficient to the task. For instance, he claims people should be less concerned with the ordering of the elements in conversion (e.g. repentance, faith, baptism, etc.) because the process as a whole is key. But he only defends this claim with the variety of conversion accounts in the NT, especially Acts, and the NT usage of synecdoche when referring to conversion. These data do not support only Cross's understanding of conversion-baptism. If baptism is faith-baptism, or an act of faith in which baptism expresses—maybe even consum-

---

47. Cross, "Evangelical Sacrament," 205.

mates—one's prior faith, then one may use the same data as Cross does to defend another understanding of conversion. One could understand it to mean that it is punctiliar at the moment of one's faith, so the ordering of the elements of Christian initiation does matter, especially when some of them are inherently tied to a prior faith. Moreover, these other elements are tied to faith in such an asymmetrical way that true faith is still possible without baptism, but true baptism is impossible without faith. It is not clear in Cross's writings whether baptism is more than the moment of the assurance of one's faith or is in fact the true moment of faith itself. The criticism above of Cross's version of baptismal regeneration also applies here to his understanding of faith and baptism in general. He appeals to evidence that supports sacramentalism in general, but this evidence does not prove only Cross's understanding of conversion-baptism as opposed to other Baptist sacramental theologies.

Instead of restating the biblical witness on baptism in ways reminiscent of Beasley-Murray, sacramentalists need to build on this exegesis by developing a more systematic account of baptism. This is because systematic questions and concerns, such as the meaning of baptism in relation to faith and conversion, require systematic answers. Cross does not provide such answers here, once again exposing his work to the same objections that twentieth-century sacramentalists faced. Nonetheless, he has greatly contributed to the discussion of Baptist sacramental theology with his treatment of twentieth-century British Baptist baptismal theology and practice, and his theological works have uncovered some problems within the literature on sacramentalism that were unclear in earlier years.

CONCLUSION

Thompson, Fowler, and Cross added a historical dimension to sacramentalism, so that the doctrine is no longer considered an alien disruption of Baptist theology; rather, it is a recovery of an older Baptist view. The literature has also expanded beyond a discussion that was once exclusively among an earlier generation of British Baptists to now include North American Baptist voices that speak within their own contexts to North American Baptist concerns and objections. This can only help increase the reception of sacramentalism among North American Baptists. It also calls for more research on specifically North American Baptist issues, such as the practice of baptizing young children.

Contemporary Baptist sacramentalism has built on the strengths of the first generation's works and carried on some of the pervasive weaknesses in the literature. Despite the increase in theological and historical discussions of sacramentalism, authors still misapply biblical theology to concerns and objections that are systematic in nature. This reliance on biblical theology has also continued to mark sacramentalism with unclear explanations and descriptions of the doctrine, exposing the contemporary movement to old objections and misunderstandings. More systematic defenses of sacramentalism are needed to address this ongoing weakness in the literature so that authors can take sides on these systematic issues rather than claiming that what appear to be different accounts of the meaning of baptism are in reality nothing more than functionally equivalent doctrines.

Taking sides on this issue requires that one formulate a systematic understanding of baptism, and the covenantal view aims to do exactly that. But first, the next few chapters will provide some historical depth to the covenantal view, demonstrating that it too should be considered a recovery of an older Baptist view rather than an alien intrusion of Reformed theology into Baptist doctrine.

5

Covenant Theology in the Baptist Tradition

MANY BAPTISTS THINK COVENANT theology is incompatible with believer baptism, which is why they do not consider placing believer baptism within a covenantal framework. To be sure, covenant theology provides a solid theological framework for infant baptism, but seventeenth-century Baptists modified covenant theology to make it compatible with believer baptism and apply its many benefits to their own theology and practice. These Baptists used covenant theology to strengthen their own Free Church ecclesiology in general and their baptismal theology in particular. They also used covenant theology to show Christians from other traditions that they were less sectarian than some other Free Church groups, because covenant theology was a mainstream position at the time. While these reasons, along with its biblical support, made covenant theology a popular position among seventeenth-century Baptists, its popularity waned during the next two centuries as Baptists gradually abandoned it for various reasons—reasons this book will not address. What this chapter will address is how seventeenth-century Baptists contributed to the development of covenant theology by offering their own versions of it that made room for believer baptism. The covenantal view of baptism will carry their contribution even further.

BAPTISTS AND THE "TWO TRADITIONS"

Before giving the basic elements of seventeenth-century Baptist covenant theology, a fair question, especially from Reformed Christians, is How can Baptists be a genuine part of the development of covenant theology? After all, most of the literature on covenant theology comes from the

Reformed tradition, and historians of covenant theology typically do not discuss Baptists in their writings. In fact, most historical literature on covenant theology focuses exclusively on Reformed writings, constructing two Reformed traditions—neither of which includes Baptists.

While there is much literature that defends two Reformed traditions of covenant theology during the sixteenth and seventeenth centuries, reassessments of the primary sources reveal a single tradition in which there is much variety on the number of, conception of, relationships between, and terminology for covenants throughout the seventeenth century. In light of these reassessments the variety within this tradition should also extend to Baptist accounts that show believers as the only proper subjects of baptism. These Baptist versions of covenant theology still honor that which unites all versions of covenant theology—the belief in one people of God under the headship of Christ with distinctions between the old and new covenants, among which is the belief that baptism is a sign of the new covenant rather than the old covenant. Baptist versions of covenant theology simply add to the diversity of the greater tradition by focusing on how covenant theology can support believer baptism.

Most historical accounts of the origins and development of covenant theology during the Post-Reformation period lack the English Baptists' adoption of and contribution to it, making their versions of covenant theology largely unknown today. This is one reason why today's Baptists and even Reformed Christians have a more narrow understanding of what constitutes a covenantal view of baptism than historical evidence allows. While there are other factors for this lacuna in the secondary literature on covenant theology, a major one is the dominance of the "two-traditions" thesis, which divides sixteenth- and seventeenth-century covenant theology into a Rhenish and a Genevan tradition.[1] This thesis has acted as a grid through which scholars have approached and defined the origins and developments of covenant theology. This grid has also encouraged extensive discussion of Calvin's own covenant theology and the place of legalism in the so-called Rhenish tradition while ignoring other historical developments such as Baptist modifications of covenant theology. Despite its enduring popularity among some historians, reassessments of the primary sources have shown the two-traditions thesis to be untenable, which in turn encourages other areas of research on the

---

1. Discussion of this thesis below relies primarily on the analysis of Beach in *Christ and the Covenant*, 23–47.

variety of covenant theology in this period—including Baptist contributions to it. The rest of this section of the chapter will give the details of the rise and fall of the two-traditions thesis for those who are interested. For those who are not, the following sections of the chapter will present the Baptist contributions.

A few nineteenth-century figures, such as Alexander Schweizer, were important in shaping subsequent historical treatments of Post-Reformation covenant theology,[2] but Heinrich Heppe's work was most influential in the rise and dominance of the two-traditions thesis.[3] He saw in the primary sources a German Reformed covenant theology that softened the more rigid predestinarian theology of Geneva. Heppe claimed this separate German tradition sprang from the desire of German Reformed theologians such as Boquinus (d. 1582), Ursinus (1534–1583), Hyperius (1511–1564), and Olevianus (1536–1587) to offer an alternative to predestination, as if covenant theology and predestination were opposed to one another. Heppe himself focused on the origins and development of covenant theology on the continent because of his desire to unite nineteenth-century German Protestant churches. Subsequent historians applied Heppe's thesis to Puritan covenant theology in Great Britain and in New England.

Perry Miller's works were the most influential in extending the two-traditions thesis to the Puritans. Miller claims that Calvin's theology of a transcendent God that elects people almost capriciously led to a crisis among his followers over their assurance of salvation, which was tied to a greater crisis over the place of human involvement in salvation or the lack thereof. According to Miller, the Puritans responded to this crisis by embracing and developing the Rhenish tradition of covenant theology because it stresses human faith and obedience. This theology assured people of their salvation as long as they were fulfilling their end of the covenant (understood by Miller as a contract) that God made with them.[4]

Other historians, such as Leonard J. Trinterud, Jens Møller, and Richard L. Greaves modify Miller's view.[5] Trinterud thinks the main dif-

---

2. Schweizer, *Die Glaubenslehre*. Another key work from this period is Gass, *Geschichte*.

3. Heppe, *Dogmatik*, 1:139.

4. Miller, *New England Mind*, 395–97; and *Errand*, 54.

5. Trinterud, "Origins of Puritanism"; Møller, "Beginnings"; and Greaves, "Origins." Other historians who embrace the two-traditions thesis, but write on matters other

ference between the two traditions is how they understand the nature of covenants. According to Trinterud, Calvin's Genevan tradition stressed divine election because it understood covenants to be monopleuric, or divine promises that only God himself faithfully fulfills. This tradition affirmed only the covenant of grace. In contrast, Zwingli's Rhenish tradition used a nearly synergistic understanding of salvation because it understood covenants to be dipleuric, or conditional agreements in which people are responsible for meeting God's conditions. This tradition developed multiple covenants including the covenant of works. Trinterud thinks the Puritan Westminster standards of faith favor the Rhenish tradition over Calvin.[6] Møller claims William Tyndale (1494–1536) compared covenants to ethical vows by focusing on the conditions in covenants. For this reason, Møller includes Tyndale in the Rhenish tradition, claiming it holds to a fundamentally different way of understanding covenants than the Genevan tradition. Møller concludes that inasmuch as the Puritans followed Tyndale's cruder covenant theology they deviated from Calvinism and came closer to views that were common in medieval Catholicism.[7] Greaves offers a slightly different account than Trinterud and Møller because he recognizes elements of God's grace and human responsibility in both the Zwingli-Tyndale and the Calvinist traditions. Greaves finds Calvinist strands within Puritan covenant theology and argues that the development of Puritan covenant theology reached the point at which certain theologians such as Dudley Fenner (1558–87), Thomas Cartwright (1535–1603), and William Perkins (1558–1602) merged the two traditions before subsequent theologians separated them again.[8] Baptist historians such as B. R. White have also extended Miller's

---

than British Covenant theology include Baker's works on Heinrich Bullinger, *Heinrich Bullinger and the Covenant*; and "Heinrich Bullinger"; as well as Weir's argument that covenant theology developed as a legalistic response to the dominance of Bezan predestinarian theology in *Origins*. Venema has countered Baker's work by offering a more accurate analysis of Bullinger's covenant theology in *Heinrich Bullinger*. Muller offers a better treatment of Beza's doctrine of predestination than Weir does, ("Use and Abuse of a Document").

6. Trinterud, "Origins of Puritanism," 45.

7. Møller, "Puritan Covenant Theology," 66–67. McGiffert offers a more accurate analysis of Tyndale's covenant theology in which it is not contractual, "William Tyndale's Conception of Covenant." However, McGiffert for the most part affirms the two-traditions thesis in "Grace and Works"; and "From Moses to Adam."

8. Greaves, "English Covenant Thought," 32.

two-traditions thesis by arguing that Separatists (and later, the Baptists) departed from their Puritan Calvinistic roots by adopting a more conditional view of covenant theology.[9]

Not long after historians embraced the two-traditions thesis, theologians used it to critique many aspects of seventeenth-century theology. Theologians such as Karl Barth, James B. Torrance, Holmes Rolston III, David N. J. Poole, R. T. Kendall, Stephen Strehle, and Mark W. Karlberg critique the Rhenish tradition in particular with its multiple covenants for being too legalistic, for yielding to voluntarism and/or nominalism, for being grounded in speculation rather than Scripture, and for departing from true Reformed theology—which for most of these theologians is tantamount to the Genevan tradition alone.[10] These theological critiques often stress the discontinuity between the Reformers, often synonymous with these theologians' interpretations of Calvin, and the Post-Reformation orthodox. As a result, they ignore the variety of the Reformers' theology and its continuity with that of the Post-Reformation orthodox, thereby misconstruing the theology from both eras.

Historians such as Richard A. Muller have demonstrated that this historical and theological focus on the discontinuity between the Reformers and the Post-Reformation orthodox is the product of an improper methodological approach to the primary sources.[11] For example, he argues that one should not make too much of Calvin's contribution to the Reformed identity as if he were the chief codifier of a monolithic tradition. Even so, one should approach Calvin's theology by looking at all of his writings (instead of using the *Institutes* alone as Baker does) and by comparing his theology to that of his contemporaries. The overemphasis on Calvin is just one example of historians misapplying modern categories and theories to historical documents. Another example is Muller's argument that historians should focus on the concepts expressed by historical figures rather than the terms they use, because the development of a concept will always precede the development of its terminology in the literature.

9. White, *English Separatist Tradition*.

10. Barth, *Church Dogmatics*, IV.1, 54–66; Torrance, "Covenant or Contract?"; Rolston III, "Responsible Man in Reformed Theology"; Poole, *History of the Covenant Concept*; Kendall, *Calvin and English Calvinism*; Kendall, "Puritan Modification"; Strehle, *Calvinism, Federalism, and Scholasticism*; and Karlberg, "Reformed Interpretation."

11. Muller demonstrates this in *After Calvin*, especially 63–102. Cf. Muller, "Problem of Protestant Scholasticism"; and Trueman, "Calvin and Calvinism."

Diverse and fluid covenantal terminology in the primary sources has fueled the two-traditions thesis, but most of the above historians use this diverse terminology to support traditions that they have manufactured. They have failed to demonstrate the development of two conceptual traditions in the literature and instead wrongly place historical figures into one so-called tradition or another based on terminology alone.

As the two-traditions thesis developed and gained momentum during the twentieth century, its opposition also increased. In the early twentieth century, Geerhardus Vos dismissed Heppe's two-traditions thesis on the grounds that Heppe presents covenant theology as some sort of alien synergistic development within the Reformed tradition.[12] In the middle of the twentieth century, Everett H. Emerson, Elton M. Eenigenburg, Anthony Hoekema, and George Marsden rightly showed that proponents of the two-traditions thesis such as Miller often use a faulty historical method by focusing solely on Calvin only to end up getting his theology wrong.[13] During the last thirty years, Lyle D. Bierma, Muller, Peter A. Lillback, and others have continued reassessing the validity of the two-traditions thesis by looking at primary sources from Calvin and other figures in the Reformation and Post-Reformation era.[14] Their reassessments of the origins and development of covenant theology challenge the heart of the two-traditions thesis by demonstrating that the covenant theology of Calvin and other members of the so-called Genevan tradition had much in common with that of members of the so-called Rhenish tradition. The two so-called traditions have much in common because covenant theology was never fundamentally legalistic and predestination was never a central dogma that sixteenth- and seventeenth-century theologians felt needed further support or softening from covenant theology. These reassessments propose that historians abandon the two-traditions thesis and replace it with a single, variegated tradition in which

---

12. Vos, "Doctrine of the Covenant," 235.

13. Emerson, "Calvin and Covenant Theology"; Eenigenburg, "Place of the Covenant"; Hoekema, "Calvin's Doctrine"; Hoekema, "Covenant of Grace"; and Marsden, "Perry Miller's Rehabilitation." A later reassessment of Calvin's theology along these lines is Helm's "Calvin and the Covenant." Muller provides many general rules for properly assessing Calvin's theology in *Unaccommodated Calvin*.

14. Bierma, "Federal Theology"; Bierma, "Covenant or Covenants"; Bierma, "Role of Covenant Theology"; Muller, "Covenant and Conscience"; Muller, "Covenant of Works"; Lillback, "Ursinus' Development"; Lillback, "Continuing Conundrum"; and Lillback, *Binding of God*.

theologians used fluid covenantal conceptions and terms throughout the sixteenth and seventeenth centuries. Likewise, reassessments of the Separatist and Baptist traditions have shown how they have contributed to this single, variegated tradition of covenant theology by having both unconditional and conditional aspects to their covenants—much like everyone else in the period.[15]

Muller's article on the seventeenth-century development of the covenant of works in the writings of Herman Witsius (1636–1708) and Wilhelmus à Brakel (1635–1711) is a helpful example of these reassessments.[16] In the article he argues that covenant theologians in this period considered divine initiative alone to be the reason for the establishment of covenants, making the covenants monopleuric. These same theologians, however, also recognized that all covenants had genuine mutuality, or dipleuric dimensions.[17] Thus, one should not conclude, especially appealing to terminology alone, that one tradition of covenant theologians considered covenants to be monopleuric while another tradition considered them to be dipleuric. Muller also argues that theologians developed the covenant of works out of their exegesis of texts that concern soteriology, especially original sin, rather than out of applying legalistic standards onto divine-human relationships. Covenant theologians desired to uphold the role of grace in salvation, and they did not think the covenant of works undermined it. Rather, they thought the law predated sin and was thus joined to love because both flow from God's own nature. Law and grace, like God's graciousness and righteousness, are not opposed to one another, so there is no grace without law and no law without grace. If God never repeals the law, and he should not since it is a natural law, then it must also apply to Christ's atonement in which he fulfills the law with his perfect obedience—making the covenant of grace a fulfillment rather than a repudiation of the covenant of works. According to Muller, those who developed the covenant of works did not intend to offer a legalistic theology of salvation because they thought their view upheld God's grace in the person and work of Jesus Christ.

Muller's presentation of the covenant theology of Witsius and à Brakel comes to more accurate conclusions than those of his two-

15. Brachlow, *Communion of Saints*, 4–13.

16. Muller, "Covenant of Works." Cf. Beach's summary of Muller's arguments in *Christ and the Covenant*, 44–46.

17. Muller, "Covenant of Works," 86–87.

traditions counterparts because he lets the primary sources speak for themselves, especially when it comes to explaining the motivations behind the development of a covenant of works and a covenant of redemption.[18] A desire to uphold God's grace motivated these covenants rather than a desire to inject legalism into Reformed theology. However, Muller's historical argument does not extend to defending the theological results of those who developed the covenant of works. One might argue that the end result of their theology gives the law a foundational role that may indeed undermine grace, but such an argument would be theological in nature rather than historical. One is free to critique historical versions of covenant theology, and more accurate historical assessments of such theology will lead to more accurate critiques of it. The two-traditions thesis is an inaccurate assessment of the origins and development of covenant theology, so the theological critiques that use it need revision.

Reassessments from Muller and others should lead historians and theologians alike to abandon the two-traditions thesis and aim their efforts toward more contextual research on the seventeenth-century development of a single, variegated tradition of covenant theology. Further contextual research is needed in the literature from regions outside Germany and England, such as Switzerland and France, and in the literature from other Protestant traditions, such as the Baptists.[19] Further research on Baptist covenant theology in particular would provide more examples of how members of this single tradition used fluid concepts and terminology throughout the sixteenth and seventeenth centuries to reflect their various understandings of the nature of, number of, and relationships between covenants. Further research on how historical figures understood these relationships would also uncover more variety in the tradition regarding its use of sacramental theology and eschatology, which have been largely ignored by historians.

Just as there were not two distinct traditions on the nature of the covenants, there were also not two distinct traditions, a Reformed one and a Baptist one, on how to understand the relationship between and the continuity of the signs of the old and new covenants. Seventeenth-

---

18. Muller has another article on the development of the covenant of redemption or *pactum salutis*, "Toward the *Pactum Salutis*." Cf. Beach, "Doctrine of the *Pactum Salutis*"; and VanDrunen and Clark, "Covenant before the Covenants."

19. This conclusion follows that of Beach, save the part about the Baptists, *Christ and the Covenant*, 61–62.

century Reformed covenant theologians espoused varying degrees of continuity and discontinuity between the old and new covenants.[20] Thus, seventeenth-century Baptist covenant theology, with its emphasis on the discontinuity between the old and new covenants, differs from its Reformed counterparts only in degree—not in kind. In other words, it is a genuine version of covenant theology that has a rightful place in the greater development of seventeenth-century covenant theology. Seventeenth-century Baptists contributed to covenant theology's development with their modifications of it that allow for believer baptism.

GENERAL AND PARTICULAR CONTRIBUTIONS

Both branches of seventeenth-century British Baptists, General and Particular Baptists, included theologians who modified covenant theology so that it would support believer baptism.[21] Particular Baptists affirmed most of the basic elements of Reformed covenant theology, arguing that such elements need not entail infant baptism. For example, the Particular Baptist Second London Confession of 1677 follows the Westminster Confession by including basic elements of Reformed covenant theology such as the covenant of works, the covenant of grace, and the covenant of redemption.[22] In contrast, prominent General Baptists such as Thomas Grantham used a form of covenant theology that supported both Arminian soteriology and believer baptism. Baptist covenant

20. For example, seventeenth-century Puritan John Ball lists four different views among Reformed divines in his day on the relationship between the old and new covenants in *Treatise of the Covenant of Grace*, 92–102.

21. Baptist historians are still debating the issue of Baptist origins and the influence of different groups on the movement. For example, Brackney thinks that "the extent to which Anabaptist ideas directly influenced English dissenters may never be known with certainty," (*Genetic History*, 12). That being said, most historians agree that two separate Baptist groups emerged in the seventeenth century with different antecedents and influences that will not be dealt with in detail in this chapter beyond describing the contribution of both groups to the development of covenant theology. The first group was the General Baptists, which was more in line with Arminian soteriology, and the second group was the Particular Baptists, which was more in line with Reformed soteriology. Their respective labels came from their different positions on the extent of the atonement. White gives more details on the origins of these two groups in *English Baptists of the Seventeenth Century*. Wright has recently modified White's account, successfully arguing that the two groups were quite interrelated until the middle of the seventeenth century, (*Early English Baptists*).

22. *Confession of Faith*, 26–27, 28, and 67 respectively.

theology was not just the product of one or two theologians because the list of influential seventeenth-century Baptists who espoused versions of covenant theology includes John Bunyan (1628–1688), John Tombes (d. 1676), Benjamin Keach (1640–1704), Philip Cary (Active 1685–1695), Edward Hutchinson (Active 1670–1690), Thomas Patient (d. 1666), and John Spilsbury (b. 1593).[23] Their writings influenced the theology of prominent eighteenth-century Baptists such as John Skepp (1675–1721), John Gill (1697–1771), and Abraham Booth (1734–1806).[24] Space does not permit covering all these Baptist contributions to covenant theology, so this chapter will use Thomas Grantham and Nehemiah Coxe as representatives of seventeenth century General and Particular Baptist covenant theologies respectively.[25]

THOMAS GRANTHAM (1634–1692)

Grantham's works provide a representative account of typical General Baptist views in his day.[26] He pastored and planted Baptist churches before being imprisoned for his religious views. Official toleration of the Baptists allowed for his release from prison, after which he preached, wrote, and published for over twenty years. Like many other Baptists in

---

23. The list below is by no means exhaustive, because many of these authors published several treatises and sermons on covenant theology: Bunyan, *Doctrine of the Law and Grace Unfolded*; Tombes, *Short Catechism*, which gives the essence of the arguments of the third part of his treatise, *Anti-paedobaptism*; Keach, *Ax laid to the Root*; David B. Riker covers Keach's covenant theology as a whole in *Catholic Reformed Theologian*; Cary, *Solemn Call*; Hutchinson, *Treatise*; Patient, *Doctrine of Baptism*; Spilsbery [Spilsbury?], *Treatise*; and Spilsberie [Spilsbury?], *Gods Ordinance*.

24. Skepp, *Divine Energy*; Gill, *Cause of God*; and Booth, *Essay on the Kingdom*.

25. A few Baptist historians have covered Grantham to some extent. Brackney has an article on Grantham's life and contribution to the development of Baptist theology, "Thomas Grantham." Nettles also presents an overview of his life and theology, *Baptists*, 1:71–93. Walker includes him in his article on the place of infants in seventeenth-century Baptist theology, "Relation." Garrett also summarizes Grantham's life and work in *Baptist Theology*, 42–43. Thompson discusses Grantham's view of catholicity in "New Question," 58–71. Cross and Fowler both briefly present his sacramentalism, but they do not discuss his covenant theology, Cross, "Myth," 137–39; and Fowler, *More Than a Symbol*, 27–28. As for Coxe, the only notable source is Renihan's short biography, "Excellent and Judicious Divine."

26. Grantham's works include *Christianismus Primitivus*, which is an edited compilation of many of his other individual works. These other works include: *Paedo-Baptists Apology, Religious Contest, Quaeries Examined, Presumption no Proof, Infants-Advocate*, and *Truth and Peace*.

his day, he received no formal theological training, but his writings reveal much self-study as he often draws from the Church Fathers as well as Reformed figures Calvin, Musculus (1497–1563), Diodati (1576–1649), and Wollebius (1586–1629).

Grantham has no major treatises on covenant theology, but he often employs it in his writings. In his major work, *Christianismus Primitivus*, Grantham uses covenant theology in his theologies of the church, salvation, and especially baptism. Covenant theology also comes up in his numerous tract wars with paedobaptists because one of the major issues in these debates was the relationship between God's covenant with Abraham with its sign of circumcision and the new covenant with its sign of baptism. Accounting for his fluid terminology, Grantham's covenant theology includes the covenant of works, or covenant of nature, with Adam; the covenant of grace, or covenant of mercy and justice for all generations, with Adam, Noah, and Abraham; the covenant of circumcision, or the old covenant, with Abraham and Israel; and the new covenant, or the covenant of gospel, with those who believe the gospel of Christ. Grantham may not always clearly explain the relationships between these covenants in his writings, but he unequivocally thinks covenant theology can support believer baptism instead of infant baptism. A look at his conception of the covenant of works, the covenant of grace, the covenant of circumcision, the old covenant, and the new covenant in his writings will demonstrate how he modifies covenant theology to support believer baptism.

Grantham does not mention the covenant of works very often in his writings because it is little more than a backdrop to the covenant of grace in his theology. He mentions it in his reply to Samuel Petto's (d. 1711) arguments for infant baptism in which Grantham argues that all infants are a part of the covenant of grace and the universal church of God until they depart from that covenant by voluntarily choosing sinful ways.[27] He goes on to contrast the covenant of grace with the "covenant of intire Nature made before the Fall. And that Covenant of Nature being broken by *Adam*, and in him by all his Posterity, it being not a Covenant of Grace, could not afford means to justify the Offenders in the Sight of God."[28] The covenant of works differs from the covenant of grace because the former has no means of salvation for its offenders while the latter does. When

---

27. Grantham, *Presumption no Proof*, 19. Grantham is responding to Petto's *Infant Baptism*. Petto later responded to Grantham in *Infant-Baptism Vindicated*.

28. Grantham, *Presumption no Proof*, 20, emphasis his.

Adam sinned, he broke the covenant of works for himself and for his posterity, but, unlike Adam, his posterity did not break the covenant of grace in his sin. Thus, original sin applies to all people in Adam, but it does not exclude infants from being under the covenant of grace in Christ: "And therefore Infants are not guilty of any Sin committed against the Covenant of Grace, and consequently are not deprived of the Benefit of it. Otherwise if the Sin of subsequent Parents should make void the Grace of the second Covenant, as the sin of *Adam* made his Posterity guilty of the Breach of the first Covenant, we may then cry out, *who can be saved?*"[29] Grantham affirms original sin because he thinks all people in Adam are unclean from birth and will invariably choose to sin themselves because of their uncleanness. For this reason, death reigns over all of Adam's children, even infants,[30] and yet physical death and moral uncleanness is the extent of the consequences of original sin.[31]

Grantham thinks the covenant of grace is between God and fallen Adam, including all those in Adam. God first revealed this covenant to Adam and Eve in Genesis 3:15, and no one, not even God himself, will ever repeal it.[32] Grantham appeals to the writings of Richard Baxter and reasons that since God made the covenant with all people fallen in Adam, then Christ likewise brings those same people under his covenant of grace.[33] Infants are born into this covenant of grace until they themselves

---

29. Grantham, *Presumption no Proof*, 23, emphasis his. See also p. 26.

30. Grantham, *Christianismus Primitivus*, II.1:77–79 (Book II has two parts with separate pagination). Firmin charged Grantham of denying original sin because of his views on infants, *Scripture-Warrant*, 44. Grantham responds to Firmin by repeating his section on original sin from *Christianismus Primitivus* written a decade earlier than *The Infants Advocate*, 28.

31. Grantham, *Christianismus Primitivus*, II.2:4. Cf. Grantham, *Presumption no Proof*, 23. Grantham is presenting confessional General Baptist doctrine on this point, according to Article X of *Brief Confession*, 6.

32. Grantham thinks God renewed the covenant of grace with Noah after the flood rather than repealing the covenant of grace altogether through the flood, *Christianismus Primitivus*, II.2:52.

33. Grantham, *Christianismus Primitivus*, IV:129. Grantham appeals to Baxter a few times on this point, *Christianismus Primitivus*, II.2: 4; *Quaeries Examined*, 7; *Presumption no Proof*, 20; and *Infants Advocate*, 19. Baxter and Tombes, a Baptist, had a few exchanges over baptism that Grantham cites repeatedly in *Christianismus Primitivus*. Baxter's view of baptism is complicated, and Boersma has a helpful guide to it: *Richard Baxter's Understanding of Infant Baptism*. Tombes has a brief statement of his baptismal beliefs in *Short Catechism about Baptism*. Half of the catechism deals with covenantal issues.

consciously sin,[34] after which they themselves must consciously believe in the gospel of Christ in order to be in the covenant of grace again. While faith is the means through which sinners come back to the covenant of grace, Grantham thinks the Holy Spirit applies Christ's saving work to infants who have not yet sinned, but he does not speculate as to the exact means God uses to save them.[35] Grantham's covenant theology placed the infants of both believers and unbelievers in the covenant of grace, which exposed his view to the charge that it offers no advantages to the children of believers.

Grantham addresses this charge by claiming that Baptists have always maintained that infants of Christian parents enjoy benefits such as having parents who consciously bring them up in the Christian faith. These children will have a constant relationship with a visible church, including a state of blessing through their infant dedications.[36] Grantham lists several advantages the church provides to children of Christian parents, but he does not think they should be subject to church duties such as baptism and the Lord's Supper until they can better understand what these duties entail. Besides, infants do not need baptism because they are already in the covenant of grace without the sacrament.[37] The mistake for paedobaptists, according to Grantham, is that they make circumcision a sign of the covenant of grace instead of linking it to a separate covenant that was instituted with Abraham and expired once Christ came.[38] This is seen in the fact that Abraham was part of the covenant of grace on account of his faith in God some twenty-four years before God made a covenant of circumcision with him.[39]

In *Truth and Peace*, Grantham presents his most detailed account of the covenant of circumcision. He first argues that the lengthy gap in time itself between God's promise to Abraham in Genesis 12 and his covenant

---

34. Grantham, *Presumption no Proof*, 21.

35. Grantham, *Infants Advocate*, 29.

36. Grantham, *Christianismus Primitivus*, II.2:5–6. Baptists had to address the issue of infants, children, and the church given their baptismal views, so dedication was and still is a common practice among Baptist churches. West discusses this practice in great detail, "Child and the Church," 75–80.

37. Grantham, *Christianismus Primitivus*, IV:106.

38. Grantham, *Presumption no Proof*, 8; *Infants Advocate*, 17, 20; and *Truth and Peace*, 2–4.

39. Grantham, *Presumption no Proof*, ii–iii. Cf. Acts 7:8.

of circumcision in Genesis 17 shows that circumcision cannot be linked to the much earlier covenant of promise, or covenant of grace. Grantham supports his argument by noting that figures such as Melchizedek were also part of the covenant of grace without being circumcised.[40] He also appeals to Paul's treatment of these two covenants in Romans 4. In this chapter, Paul says that the promise was not given to Abraham or his seed through the Law, so Grantham asks, "what Law was *Abraham* under, but the Law or Covenant of Circumcision?"[41] Grantham supports this claim by looking at Galatians 4:9; 5:2; and Romans 2:25 in which Paul ties circumcision to the law, not the gospel. Grantham thinks the widespread practice of linking baptism to circumcision mistakenly holds onto the "weak and beggarly" ceremonial Law that has ceased after Christ.[42] For the covenant of circumcision was folded into the Law to point to Christ.[43] This connection between the law and circumcision leads to Grantham's explanation of the relationship between the old and new covenants.

Regarding the old covenant, Grantham believes Christ's work abrogated it and its ceremonial Law, so Christians are free to worship on Sundays instead of Saturdays. However, the moral requirement of the Sabbath, like the rest of the moral law, is still in place after Christ.[44] Grantham considers the moral law to be a natural law that includes the Decalogue, but the ceremonial signs of the natural law given in the OT were only temporary. Thus, the Sabbath, animal sacrifices, and circumcision were all merely signs that have passed away because all have been fulfilled in Christ.[45]

Regarding the new covenant, its community includes only regenerate people, calling every member to perform such duties as repentance, faith, believer baptism, and perseverance—duties that were never required for

---

40. Grantham, *Truth and Peace*, 2. Cf. Grantham, *Presumption no Proof*, 9 and 11–12. Grantham published *Truth and Peace* in response to Hickes's *Case of Infant-Baptism*.

41. Grantham, *Truth and Peace*, 4, emphasis his.

42. Ibid., 5.

43. Ibid., 10.

44. Grantham, *Christianismus Primitivus*, II.2:156. Grantham spends an entire chapter giving numerous reasons why the Sabbath was a temporary ceremonial sign, (pp. 156–174).

45. Grantham spends an entire chapter on this issue giving six reasons why Christ fulfilled the old covenant and its signs are no longer in effect, (*Christianismus Primitivus*, III:73–78).

every member of the old covenant community.⁴⁶ Despite the differences between the old and new covenants and their communities, Grantham still calls Abraham the father of the faithful when talking about baptism, stressing the differences between circumcision and baptism:

> This great Prophet [Jesus] gave clear notice, that God was now purposed to raise up Children another way then by natural extraction, even by Heavenly birth or being born from above John 3.3, and therefore this holy rite was adapted or fited only for such Children (professedly at least) as the very title thereof (the Baptism of repentance) doth plainly shew. And here we find a clear difference between Circumcision and Baptism, in the first Institution of each, the first taking in all the natural seed of Abraham, though not concern'd in the Covenant made with Abraham (as in the case of Ismael) the other leaving out the natural seed of Abraham, though in possession of the Covenant made with Abraham, Act. 3.25, unless they did the works of Abraham. Matt 3.8, 9. John 8.39.⁴⁷

Members of the new covenant are the spiritual seed of Abraham because they also have faith. For Grantham, another difference between the old and new covenants is that the former was for Abraham's natural seed alone, but the latter requires that everyone, Jews and Gentiles alike, hear and obey the gospel of Jesus Christ.⁴⁸

In summary, Grantham applied covenant theology to many other doctrines and considered it a central part of his greater theology. His covenantal framework was common among General Baptists of the period, and he modified covenant theology, especially the covenant of works and the covenant of grace, to allow for a rather Arminian soteriology in which Christ's atonement covers, at least initially, all people without distinction. This is one way that Grantham's covenant theology differs from Particular Baptist accounts that more closely follow Reformed theology. However, both General and Particular Baptist accounts of covenant theology distinguish God's promise to Abraham from God's subsequent covenant of circumcision with him. This distinction is the heart of Baptist covenant theology, because it separates baptism from circumcision. A look at the details of Nehemiah Coxe's covenant theology will reveal more similarities and differences between General and Particular Baptist views.

---

46. Grantham, *Christianismus Primitivus*, IV:33, 102.
47. Ibid., II.2:18.
48. Grantham, *Truth and Peace*, 8. Cf. Grantham, *Infants Advocate*, 18.

NEHEMIAH COXE (D. 1689)

For most of his adult life, Nehemiah Coxe pastored a large church in London. Despite his death in 1689, Baptist historians think he served as either the editor or co-editor of the version of the Second London Confession that Particular Baptists adopted later that year.[49] His 1681 work, *A Discourse of the Covenants*, is in part a response to Joseph Whiston's (d. 1690) paedobaptist arguments, but Coxe intended it to be a primarily positive account of Baptist covenant theology that addresses the "main hinge" of the controversy, namely the nature of the covenant in Genesis 17.[50] Coxe begins the work with an introductory chapter on covenant relationships in general followed by three chapters on God's transactions with Adam, his covenant with Noah, and the covenant of grace he revealed to Abraham. Coxe then spends the next three chapters on the covenant of circumcision with Abraham in which he presents his main arguments against infant baptism. He concludes the work with a chapter on the promises made to Abraham. He does not include chapters on the old and new covenants because he refers the reader to the third volume of John Owen's (1616–1683) commentary on Hebrews that was published a year earlier.[51] As a Particular Baptist, Coxe was more interested than Grantham was in presenting a mainstream account of covenant theology. Besides Owen, Coxe also favorably quotes Reformed writers such as Cocceius (1603–1669), Junius (1545–1602), and Pareus (1548–1622) in his *Discourse*.

In the first chapter, Coxe argues that covenant theology is necessary for affirming and explaining the mutual respect the Old and New Testaments have for one another. He then explains the nature and elements of covenants in general. For Coxe, divine-human covenants do not carry any mutual benefits, because God initiates them and his creatures receive everything from him. Coxe defines *covenant* by endorsing Cocceius's definition: "A declaration of his Sovereign Pleasure concerning the Benefits he will bestow on them [his covenant people], the Communion they will have with him, and the way and means whereby this shallbe injoyed

---

49. Renihan, "Excellent and Judicious Divine," 20.

50. Coxe, *Discourse*, A4. Whiston wrote at least seven tracts on infant baptism, and in the preface to *Discourse*, Coxe mentions Whiston's *Infant-Baptism Plainly Proved*. Whiston responds to Coxe in *Energiea Planes*.

51. Coxe, *Discourse*, A6–A7. Cf. Owen, *Continuation*.

by them."⁵² Coxe notes that all biblical covenants share this definition, but they do not all share the same conditions. Some covenants are better than others. All covenants have a representative head, whether the covenant is for all people or only a select few. Divine revelation is the only source from which one can discern divine covenants because they "flow only from his [God's] *good pleasure,* and *the counsel of his Will.*"⁵³ Coxe considers covenant theology to be biblically grounded because it is the product of a humble person's careful exegesis of Scripture rather than careless speculation.

In the second chapter, Coxe covers God's transactions with Adam, which include both law and covenant. Coxe believes God created Adam upright, so his soul was in perfect harmony with God's eternal law. Adam knew this law perfectly by intuition, needing no outside source of revelation. God did reveal to Adam his "*positive precept*" not to eat of the tree of the knowledge of good and evil, because this precept was not in and of itself a part of the eternal law.⁵⁴ However, the foundation of the precept was God's will, or the eternal law, so disobedience to this precept was also disobedience to the eternal law. God's grace was the foundation of this precept, because he intended to encourage Adam's obedience and manifest his riches and glory to Adam through it. In order to be the means of such grace, this precept was conditional, promising Adam eternal life for his obedience and death for his disobedience. This conditional precept was the covenant of works in which God promised to bless Adam on the condition that Adam obey his precept—representing his obedience to the eternal law.

Coxe is aware that Genesis has no explicit covenantal language between God and Adam, so Coxe defends the biblical grounding of the covenant of works by reflecting on the curse of death in Genesis chapter 3. Coxe gives three reasons why the curse in the text implies God's promise to reward Adam: first, God put Adam in a trial state; second, people are naturally inclined to expect a reward for obeying God; and third, there was a sacramental use of the tree of life as "a Sign and Pledg of *that eternal life,* which *Adam* should have obtained by his own personal, and perfect obedience to the Law of God, had he continued therein."⁵⁵ These argu-

52. Coxe, *Discourse*, 6.
53. Ibid., 12-13, emphasis his.
54. Ibid., 19, emphasis his.
55. Ibid., 22, emphasis his.

ments also show that God created Adam upright and set him in his way toward eternal rest by making him capable of obeying the eternal law.

Having established the promises of the conditional covenant of works, Coxe supports this covenant further by arguing that Adam was both a natural and federal root for all people. He reasons from Scripture's claim that in Adam's fall all people fell (Rom 5:19) that likewise "in his standing all Mankind stood."[56] Thus, God's covenant with Adam was a covenant with all people in him as their head. Adam broke the covenant by sinning, leaving humankind "altogether *helpless and without Strength*, being utterly disabled to stand before God upon Terms of a Covenant of Works, and as uncapable to bring himself upon other Terms with God."[57] While it would be impossible for God to renew the covenant of works with people in their fallen state, there is nonetheless hope for them because God wisely foresaw Adam's fall and graciously decided to redeem a remnant of fallen people through Christ.

For Coxe, God's decision to redeem this remnant is itself another covenant. It is the covenant of redemption, or *pactum salutis*, made between God the Father and God the Son in which God pledges to save some sinful people through their mediator, Christ. On the basis of this covenant, Coxe argues that God approached fallen Adam in Genesis 3 and "held a Treaty with him, which issued in a Discovery of Grace."[58] Without this covenant, God would have had to execute "the Rigor of the Law upon" Adam, which would have resulted in his eternal death.[59] God's treaty with Adam in Genesis 3 lessened some of the consequences of the fall for all people, but it did not lift all the effects of God's curse such as misery on earth, temporal death, and natural evil.

On account of the covenant of redemption, Coxe also thinks God revealed to Adam that a Redeemer would come from Eve's seed, and God even gave Adam faith in this promise. For this reason, Coxe comfortably refers to Adam as a member of the church. However, God did not reveal more of the covenant of grace with Adam, "much less was the Covenant of Grace established with him as a *publick Person* or Representative in any kind; but as he obtained Interest for himself alone, in the Grace of

---

56. Ibid., 26.
57. Ibid., 35, emphasis his.
58. Ibid., 38.
59. Ibid.

God thus revealed, *by his own Faith*, so must those of his Posterity that are saved thereby."[60] Thus, Adam's fall affected all people in him, but his subsequent faith was for himself alone. Adam's children are born under original sin as covenant breakers that remain obligated to obey God's eternal law. As such, they are in need of salvation by grace through their own faith in Christ. Thankfully, the full execution of the law's curse is delayed, so there is still time for those fallen in Adam to accept the gospel of Christ.

In the third chapter, Coxe covers the covenant God established with Noah. This covenant required faith on Noah's part to build an ark. God promised to reward Noah's faithful obedience with three benefits and blessings for Noah and all of humanity after him: "1. Fruitfulness for the replenishing of the Earth. 2. Dominion over the Creatures, and the free use of them for Food. 3. Assurance that the Judgment which they had now escaped should not be *repeated*."[61] Coxe recognizes that these are all temporal blessings, but he also thinks this covenant assured the promise of eternal salvation for Noah and others because it allowed the human race to continue and eventually produce the promised seed (Gen 3:15). Like the trees in the Garden of Eden, God also used a created thing, the rainbow, as a sacrament of this covenant.

In the fourth chapter, Coxe discusses the covenant of grace that God made with Abraham. In this covenant God brought Abraham "into such a *Relation* to God, and the whole Church, as was in some respects peculiar to himself, and never was the Lot of any other of the Children of Men either before or since his time, in respect of which *Abraham* may be considered as a Type of Christ, who is eminently *the Head and Prince* of the new Covenant."[62] Coxe holds Abraham in high esteem, and he further supports his position by referring to another transaction between God and Abraham in which the NT claims he served a double capacity as both "the *Father* of all true *Believers*, and as the *Father* and Root of the *Israelitish Nation*."[63] Coxe argues that Abraham's double capacity implies his participation in two covenants, so one must be careful not to conflate these capacities by positing only one covenant with Abraham

60. Ibid., 43, emphasis his.
61. Ibid., 59, emphasis his.
62. Ibid., 68, emphasis his.
63. Ibid., 71, emphasis his.

when there are really two. Coxe spends the next three chapters on the second covenant with Abraham, so he focuses only on the first covenant, the covenant of grace, here.

Coxe's key passage for the covenant of grace with Abraham is Galatians 3:6–9, 16, and 17 in which Paul speaks of God accounting Abraham's faith in him as righteousness. Coxe makes five observations from this passage: first, God revealed the gospel and covenant of grace to Abraham in Genesis 12, not Genesis 17. Second, all the spiritual and eternal blessings of the covenant of grace stem from Abraham's own blessing in which he became the father of all the faithful, even faithful Gentiles. Third, "This Covenant was made with *Abraham* in and thro' *Jesus-Christ*; It is not *Abraham* but *Christ* that is *the first Head* thereof; in and by him all the Promises of it are ratified, as he was the *Surety of the Covenant*."[64] Coxe briefly supports his third point by looking at Genesis. He argues that God makes the covenant of grace with Abraham in Genesis 12 and repeats this same covenant in Genesis 22, but God's covenant with Abraham in Genesis 17 is only a *type* of the covenant of grace. Thus, the natural blessings given to the natural seed of Abraham through the covenant in Genesis 17 only point to Christ and the blessings he bestows on Abraham's faithful, spiritual seed through the covenant of grace in chapters 12 and 22.

After making these points about the covenants in Genesis, Coxe returns to Galatians 3, and his fourth point is that the covenant of grace was made with Abraham "as *a Root* of Covenant-Blessings, and *common Parent* unto all true believers."[65] God blessed Abraham himself directly through Christ, who is Abraham's seed and the Prince of the covenant, "but with respect unto us, The Covenant was first given unto *Abraham*, and we are brought into it in the Interest of Relation to him as Children, which also is by Faith in *Jesus Christ*."[66] Fifth, this covenant shows that the way to salvation is not "by a *natural Descent* from *Abraham*, [or] any *external Priviledg* appendent thereunto, but *by a walking in the Footsteps of* Abraham's *Faith*, Rom. 4:13. who is made the Exemplar of Justification unto all in future Ages."[67]

---

64. Ibid., 77, emphasis his.
65. Ibid., 81, emphasis his.
66. Ibid., emphasis his.
67. Ibid., 82–83, emphasis his.

Covenant Theology in the Baptist Tradition

These points constitute a nuanced and intricate doctrine of the covenant of grace that calls for further clarification. Coxe has Christ as the prince and first head of the covenant of grace in virtue of his role in the covenant of redemption. Christ alone ratifies the covenant of grace through his person and work. Abraham is the second head of the covenant of grace as the one to whom God first revealed the fullness of this covenant's blessings. As a result, God brings other people into this covenant through Abraham, their spiritual father, because they have the same kind of faith in Christ that Abraham had. The spiritual blessings of the covenant of grace are not the same as the special blessings God promises to Abraham's natural seed, signified by circumcision. Those special blessings merely point to the blessings of the covenant of grace that are available to anyone, not just Abraham's natural seed, through faith. God did not reveal any outward seal of this covenant to Abraham. But God did reveal an outward seal for another covenant with Abraham in Genesis 17, and that covenant has temporal blessings for Abraham's natural seed.

Coxe calls this second covenant the covenant of circumcision, and it is the key to Coxe's Baptist covenant theology. It explains how circumcision is indirectly related to the covenant of grace as a sign of another covenant that merely points to the covenant of grace, thus proving circumcision was never a sign of the covenant of grace itself. The covenant of circumcision is the major difference between Baptist and Reformed versions of covenant theology, so Coxe spends three chapters defending it.

Coxe's first chapter on the covenant of circumcision makes a few general observations about it before discussing its promises. He bases his terminology for this covenant on Stephen's phrase, "a covenant of circumcision," in Acts 7:8. Coxe thinks this covenant was another covenant of works full of conditions and terms for Abraham's natural seed to fulfill in order to receive its typical blessings and avoid its curses. The Mosaic Law, which was also signified by circumcision, perfected this covenant, because the Law's promises also merely typified the blessings of the great promise to Abraham. Through the Mosaic Law, God included every member of the church-State Israel under the covenant of circumcision.

After making these general observations, Coxe examines God's promise in Genesis 17:7-8 in which God makes an everlasting covenant with Abraham's seed, promising them the Land of Canaan as their everlasting possession. He discusses this promise first because covenant theologians often point to its use of the word *everlasting* as evidence that this covenant's blessings are spiritual rather than typical, or temporal. Coxe responds to their claim by arguing that this promise uses the word *everlasting* in a precisely temporal sense in which the promise lasts for a long time until the coming of Christ. For support he refers to other OT texts that speak of Levi's "everlasting priesthood" (Num 25:13) and the temple's "everlasting doors" (Ps 24:5) to show that all the word *everlasting* means in Genesis 17:7–8 is "the Continuance of these for a long time, *viz.* throughout the Old Testament Oeconomy, until the days of the *Messiah* commonly spoken of by the Jews under the Notion of *the World to come*; wherein a new State of things was to be expected, and when their old Covenant Right and Priviledge was to expire, as having its proper End and Design now fully accomplished."[68] When the Messiah came, this covenant ceased along with its conditions, blessings, curses, and signs—even circumcision.

Coxe builds a credobaptist argument from Genesis 17 on two propositions: "1. The *mediate and remote Seed* of that Line to which the Promises of the Covenant of Circumcision did belong, were as fully included, and interested in them, as the *immediate Seed*. 2. From the first establishing of this Covenant, some of the *immediate Seed of Abraham* were *excluded* from Interest in it."[69] While these two propositions may seem unrelated to baptismal theology, Coxe derives from them what he considers to be an important argument against paedobaptism. He defends the first proposition by examining the relationship between the nation of Israel, the Mosaic Law, and the covenant of circumcision in which the benefits of the covenant "can rise no higher than the Advantage, and Priviledg of a Jew, by virtue of the Covenant in the Wilderness [the Mosaic Covenant]."[70] In other words, whatever the blessings of this covenant are, they can be no greater than the blessings God promised Israel through the Mosaic Law. While some covenant theologians do not think the covenant of circumcision's conditions, blessings, and curses are directly related to the Mosaic Law, Coxe argues that the NT links them together because they share one sign, circumcision, which signifies the same thing for both the Law and the covenant of circumcision. The NT contrasts the old way of circumcision and law with the new way of the gospel, further splitting the relation-

---

68. Ibid., 98, emphasis his.
69. Ibid., 117, emphasis his.
70. Ibid., 121.

ship between circumcision and the covenant of grace. Coxe defends the second proposition above by looking at the cases of Ishmael and Esau, who had no interest in and received no promise from the covenant of circumcision, despite being Abraham's immediate natural seeds.

Now that he has defended these two propositions, Coxe explains how together they undermine Reformed paedobaptist theology. Given these two propositions, a private believing parent today cannot claim the blessings of the covenant in Genesis 17 for his or her immediate natural seed without also claiming such blessings for his or her mediate and remote seed in future generations. Coxe argues that Reformed theologians apply the covenant's blessings to their immediate seed *only* rather than their mediate and remote seed, which goes against Genesis 17. Thus, Christians who want to use Genesis 17 to support their practice of infant baptism should teach that the mediate and remote seed, or future generations, of every believing parent constitutes a peculiar people to God who have been promised the land of Canaan as their everlasting possession. Coxe points out how absurd this is in a new covenant context, and he notes that no paedobaptist he knows of believes this to be true of his or her mediate and remote seed. Thus, given the absurdity of this notion, Coxe concludes that "*Abraham* was considered in this Covenant, not in the Capacity or Respect, of a *private believing Parent*, but of one chosen of God, to be *the Father of, and a Federal Root unto a Nation*, that for special Ends should be separated unto God by a *peculiar Covenant*: And when those Ends are accomplished, the Covenant it self by which they obtained that Right, and Relation, must cease; And the like cannot be pleaded for by any other, without a reviving of the whole Oeconomy built thereupon."[71] In other words, Abraham was no mere believing parent in this covenant, considering some of his immediate natural seed had no interest in it, but his mediate and remote seed through Jacob did. Rather, God made this covenant with Abraham as the head of a chosen nation for special purposes that included producing the Messiah, Christ. When Christ came, he brought those purposes to an end, rendering the covenant, including its sign of circumcision, to be old and obsolete. Coxe argues that if paedobaptists want to appeal to this old and obsolete covenant for their baptismal theology and practice, they should at least do it

---

71. Ibid., 106, emphasis his.

consistently and take hold of all its promises—including the promises to one's mediate and remote seed.

Coxe's third chapter on the covenant of circumcision discusses the meaning of what he calls the "great promise" in this covenant, which is God's statement to Abraham, "*I will establish my Covenant—to be a God unto thee, and to thy seed after thee. Gen 17:7*."[72] Reformed theologians argue that this great promise is none other than the blessing of the new covenant itself because Romans 9:4 says the covenants and promises brought salvation to Israel. Coxe spends this chapter refuting their claim. He first notes that God considered Israel, under the Mosaic economy, to contain both a carnal and a spiritual seed in which the former overlapped the latter. Individual Israelites were part of the carnal seed by birth, but they needed to have faith in God to become part of the spiritual seed and be saved. On account of their faith and repentance, God gave these individual Israelites the covenant of grace's spiritual blessings. But he gave them and their carnal brothers and sisters only temporal blessings for their keeping of the Law—signified by circumcision. The conditions, blessings, promises, and signs of the old covenant had an indirect spiritual benefit for Israel because they typically pointed to faith in Christ. This is the only sense in which one may properly say the covenants and promises brought salvation to Israel. Such things were only indirectly related to the salvation of Israel's spiritual seed, so they did not bring salvation to Israel's carnal seed, although both seeds benefited from them in a temporal sense. For these reasons, Coxe does not want to attach any spiritual benefits whatsoever directly to the old covenant, despite the language Genesis 17:7 uses to describe its promise.

After Coxe is clear about what this promise does not include he then turns to what it does include. As a temporal promise, it entails that God will extend his grace and mercy through many excellent privileges to Israel. Such privileges may point members of the nation of Israel to the faith in Christ that will save them, but God does not promise to save them through their keeping of this covenant. Therefore, the sign of this covenant, circumcision, may also help point individual Israelites to faith in Christ and remind them of such faith afterwards, but it does not signify their entry into the covenant of grace.

---

72. Ibid., 136, emphasis his.

Coxe concludes this chapter by discussing the church membership of infants, because Acts 7:38 mentions *"the Church in the Wilderness."*[73] Coxe mentions this verse, because Reformed theologians sometimes use it to defend linking Israel to the church in such a way that infant baptism signifies one's entry into church membership today as circumcision marked it for Israel in the past. Coxe first responds by challenging the notion that circumcision was ever tied to church membership in the past. He finds this unlikely, considering God first instituted it with Abraham and it does not even include women or non-Israelite believers. Coxe next mentions that purchased slaves were to be circumcised, though they were not church members, but their children were not to be circumcised. For Coxe, these points show that God's revealed commands governed the practice of circumcision rather than any inherent connection it may have had with church membership or with entry into the covenant of grace. Coxe also rejects the Reformed claim of continuity between the church-state Israel and the NT church as a reason to include infants within the church today. Coxe argues that the gospel dissolved the typical church-state of Israel in which infants were born as members of that church, so the gospel also dissolved the rights and privileges of that former state, including circumcision. He thinks it is preferable to let "the positive Law, and express Will of the Lord" govern both the meaning of circumcision in the past and the meaning of baptism today, so paedobaptists should point to a divine law to baptize infants in order to defend their practice.[74]

Coxe's final chapter discusses God's individual promises to Abraham and to his seed. He focuses on the proper references of Abraham's seed in these promises, reaffirming his distinctions between Abraham's spiritual and natural seed. What is new in this section is his exegesis of Colossians 2:11 and Romans 4:11, which are two NT texts that discuss the meaning of circumcision. Colossians 2:11 states, *"In whom also ye are circumcised with the Circumcision made without hands, in putting off the Body of the Sins of the Flesh, by the Circumcision of Christ."*[75] Coxe thinks "the circumcision of Christ" in this passage relates to believers' justification rather than their sanctification, because it speaks of Christ's own circumcision, or "the *Sign* being put for the *thing signified*; viz. the Circumcision of

---

73. Ibid., 156.
74. Ibid., 160.
75. Ibid., 172.

Christ, for his perfect Obedience, and fulfilling of the law."[76] According to Coxe, Paul uses Christ's circumcision as a shorthand way of referring to his perfect obedience of the law that is imputed to believers for their righteousness. Unlike the sign of the covenant in Genesis 17, this passage speaks of a circumcision that is made without hands. Romans 4:11 states, "*And he* [Abraham] *received the Sign of Circumcision, a Seal of the Righteousness of Faith which he had being yet uncircumcised; that he might be the Father of all them that believe, tho' they be not circumcised, that Righteousness may be imputed unto them also.*"[77] Coxe argues that this passage shows that circumcision sealed the righteousness Abraham already had as a faithful uncircumcised man. Abraham was righteous without being circumcised, which assures uncircumcised Gentiles that they also can be justified by their faith in Christ alone and become Abraham's spiritual children—having the same faith he did. Coxe admits that circumcision confirmed to Abraham God's promise that Abraham would be the father of the faithful, but Coxe claims that circumcision served a different purpose for the individual members of Abraham's natural seed than it did for Abraham himself. It signified for these individuals their inclusion in the old covenant and its Law. For example, Paul claims in this very chapter (vv. 12–13) that circumcision is ineffective for obtaining spiritual blessings that can come only through faith. Coxe thinks this claim puts circumcision under the Law and not under "*the Righteousness of Faith, or Covenant of Grace, as an ordinary Seal thereof.*"[78] Coxe supports his interpretation of Romans 4:11 by looking at other passages that relate circumcision to the yoke of the Law such as Acts 5:10 and Galatians 5:3. For these reasons, Coxe does not consider circumcision to be the sign and seal of the covenant of grace under its old administration. He also does not consider baptism to be the seal of the covenant of grace under its new administration. Rather, he thinks Ephesians 1:13 and 4:30 teach that the Holy Spirit himself is the seal of the new covenant.

Coxe concludes his entire work saying, "if Circumcision and Baptism have the same use, and are Seals of the same Covenant, I can hardly imagine how the Application of both to the same Subjects should at any time be proper; and yet we find those that were circumcised in their Infancy,

---

76. Ibid., 175, emphasis his.
77. Ibid., 185, emphasis his.
78. Ibid., 192, emphasis his.

were also baptized upon the Profession of Faith and Repentance."[79] The old covenant is not the new covenant, and that which God has abolished is not the same as that which remains, so baptism does not replace circumcision. Rather, baptism has its own meaning as expressed in the biblical texts that describe it. Coxe does not delve into baptism's meaning in his *Discourse*.

Coxe's covenant theology is closer to its Reformed counterparts than that of Grantham. Coxe has a Reformed soteriology in which God the Father covenants with God the Son to redeem a remnant of those fallen in Adam. Coxe affirms one people of God under one covenant of grace in which Christ is the covenant's primary head, but Abraham has an important role as its secondary head through which his spiritual seed come to Christ through having the same kind of faith he had. Coxe, like Grantham and other Baptists, differs from Reformed theology by holding to a second covenant between God and Abraham in Genesis 17. This covenant of circumcision is the old covenant intended only for Abraham's natural seed for temporal ends that Christ has fulfilled, bringing this covenant—including its terms, promises, and signs—to an end. For these reasons, Coxe thinks circumcision was never linked to the covenant of grace, and he thinks there is no reason to base new covenant baptismal theology on the terms of an old and obsolete covenant.

CONCLUSION

Grantham's and Coxe's views reveal both the uniformity and the variety among seventeenth-century Baptist modifications of covenant theology. They both argue for a covenant of circumcision in Genesis 17 that allows them to defend believer baptism, but they have different soteriologies influencing their respective understandings of the scope of the covenant of grace. General Baptists, such as Grantham, include all infants under the covenant of grace to magnify God's goodness and grace to all people. Such a view implies for Grantham that infants have no need of baptism. Particular Baptists, such as Coxe, follow Reformed soteriology more closely by holding to a covenant of redemption between God the Father and God the Son that saves a remnant of fallen humanity. Coxe's covenant of redemption stands in the place of Grantham's covenant of grace revealed to Adam and all fallen in him, and this difference between the two

79. Ibid., 194.

positions likely explains Coxe's silence regarding the plight of deceased infants.[80] Rather than saying Christ covers all infants, Coxe's covenant of grace with Abraham is more restrictive. He never claims it is for all people fallen in Adam, because the covenant of redemption extends salvation only to those who were granted the same faith as Abraham. God's mysterious purposes alone are responsible for granting voluntary faith to the remnant. Coxe's restriction of the covenant of grace could also explain why he thinks the covenant with Noah is merely a typical covenant full of temporal blessings while Grantham considers it to be a reissuing of the covenant of grace to all people.

Despite these soteriological differences, both Grantham and Coxe claim God made two covenants with Abraham, which is the key Baptist modification of covenant theology. Coxe and Grantham respectively argue that God made or reissued the covenant of grace with Abraham in Genesis 12, and they both claim God later made a covenant of circumcision with Abraham in Genesis 17. They both defend their distinction between these two covenants with Abraham from the OT versions of the covenants in Genesis and the NT expositions of it, especially in Galatians. Their belief in two covenants with Abraham reveals an intertwined view of the relationship between the two covenants. Grantham and Coxe both argue that God extends eternal promises to Abraham's spiritual seed, believing Jews and Gentiles, on account of this seed's inclusion in the covenant of grace, but God extends only temporal promises that typify spiritual blessings for Abraham's natural seed on account of that seed's inclusion in the covenant of circumcision, or old covenant. The covenant of circumcision is coextensive with the old covenant because it was inherently tied to the Mosaic Law. As such, the coming of the Messiah brought it to its proper end, fulfilling that to which it typically pointed, thereby abolishing it and its signs once Christ came. Thus, circumcision was never directly tied to the covenant of grace as its sign. Likewise, baptism was never directly tied to circumcision as a rite for infants.

Grantham's and Coxe's views show that Baptists and Reformed Christians share much in common in their covenant theology. Both groups include the covenant of works and also the covenant of grace under the headship of Christ in whom there is one people of God. The

---

80. Walker lists four lines of Particular Baptist thought on the relationship of original sin and an unbaptized infant, and one position is agnostic on whether deceased infants of believers and/or unbelievers are elect ("Relation," 258–60).

Particular Baptist version of Baptist covenant theology shares even more in common with Reformed covenant theology because both groups share the same soteriology, including the covenant of redemption. In light of the reassessments of the origins and development of covenant theology, Baptist covenant theology clearly contributes to the variegated tradition of covenant theology in this period. Thus, Baptist covenant theology was and still is a genuine version of covenant theology.

Seventeenth-century Baptists embraced covenant theology for not only its biblical grounding and systematic coherence, but also its practical benefits for Baptist theology and practice. The next two chapters will build on Grantham's and Coxe's accounts by exploring how other seventeenth-century Baptists used the basic tenets of covenant theology expressed here to enhance their ecclesiology and baptismal theology.

6

Covenant Ecclesiology in the Baptist Tradition

DESPITE THE FIRM ESTABLISHMENT of covenant theology in both the General and Particular Baptist traditions, contemporary literature on Baptist covenant theology has followed a strikingly similar path to that of contemporary Baptist sacramental theology by aiming exegetical arguments against paedobaptism.[1] These works rarely acknowledge that their exegetical arguments are a recovery of an older Baptist view, and none of them positively applies the benefits of covenant theology to other aspects of Baptist theology and practice today. As a result, these works either knowingly or unknowingly do little more than repeat the same kinds of arguments that seventeenth-century Baptists used in the past. While such works may carry value in debates with other Christian traditions, they alone do not give a clear meaning to believer baptism for their fellow Baptists. Thankfully, there are other contemporary treatments of Baptist covenant theology that apply historic understandings of Baptist covenant theology found in the writings of John Smyth (1570–1612), Benjamin Keach, John Gill, and others for the purpose of enhancing Baptist theology and practice today rather than converting paedobaptists

---

1. These works include Kingdon, *Children of Abraham*; Jewett, *Infant Baptism*; Malone, *Baptism*; Waldron, *Biblical Baptism*; and Wellum, "Baptism and the Covenants." One exception is Meyer's positive theological study of the mosaic covenant as it compares to the new covenant in Paul's writings, but he does not pursue the baptismal aspects of the new covenant (*End of the Law*).

to the Baptist cause.² Among these contemporary works, Fiddes's essay, "'Walking Together,'" and Lee's essay, "Covenant and Baptism," stand out because they demonstrate the practical benefits of covenant theology for Baptist faith and practice in the past.³

Although discussions of covenant theology, as expressed in the previous chapter, can be complex, Baptists defended it vigorously because of its role in shoring up their understanding of the nature of the church. As will be seen in this chapter and the next one, Baptists used covenant theology to shape their understanding of the church's identity, mission, membership, rites, and purpose. In essence, covenant theology was not an academic enterprise. Rather, it was the backbone of their understanding of how God relates with his people and also how his people ought to relate to one another.

FIDDES'S "'WALKING TOGETHER'" (1999)

In "'Walking Together,'" Fiddes presents covenant theology as a historic Baptist position with many benefits for Baptist faith and practice today, especially as it relates to ecclesiology. Fiddes draws from the works of seventeenth-century Baptists such as John Smyth, Benjamin Keach, and others to identify "four threads of significance of the term 'covenant' within the cloth of English Puritan and Separatist theology. Failure to identify these will undoubtedly lead to confusion in any discussion, as will failure to notice where they are woven together in a harmonious pattern or even into a single multiple-stranded thread."⁴ Fiddes believes

---

2. These works include Fiddes, "'Walking Together'"; Fiddes, "Church and Trinity," which is a slightly revised version of an earlier essay entitled "Church, Trinity and Covenant"; Lee, "Baptism and Covenant"; the essays in Fiddes et al., *Bound to Love*; Killacky, "Covenant Theology"; the essays in Kidd (ed.), *Something to Declare*; several essays in Clarke (ed.), *Bound for Glory?*; Sherman, "Baptized"; Ballard, "Baptists and Covenanting"; Deweese, *Baptist Church Covenants*; Hammett, *Biblical Foundations*; Wright, "Covenant and Covenanting"; Elliott, "Theology of Congregation"; George and George (eds.), *Baptist Confessions*; and Roberts, "Call to Covenant." An older valuable work on historic and early twentieth-century Baptist covenant ecclesiology is Burrage, *Church Covenant*.

3. This group of literature does not include works that discuss what is known as "New Covenant Theology." While some Baptists affirm new covenant theology because of its compatibility with believer baptism, it is not a uniquely Baptist view and does not have its roots in the Baptist tradition. Wells and Zaspel explain its contours in *New Covenant Theology*.

4. Fiddes, "'Walking Together,'" 25.

these four threads are still discernible even though there is much variety within the Baptist tradition on the definition of, relationships between, and terminology for covenants. The four threads are: first, the covenant of grace between God and his one people, which is mediated by Christ under old and new administrations; second, the covenant of redemption between the divine Persons concerning the salvation of people[5]; third, the covenant between God and his church, which Baptists often, but not always extended to each local church; and fourth, the covenant between church members within a local church. According to Fiddes, Smyth, like many other Baptists in his day, linked these last two threads together as two parts of the covenant between God and the Saints.[6] These Baptists considered the fourth thread, the covenanting together of each church's members, to be the instrumental means through which Christ rules each church, giving it the seals of the covenant, "that is, the power to elect its own ministry, to celebrate the sacraments of baptism and the Lord's Supper, and to administer discipline (the authority to 'bind and loose')."[7] Fiddes claims the earliest Baptist churches used the first two threads to include themselves among God's covenant people throughout the ages.

---

5. Chapter 5 highlighted some differences between General and Particular Baptists on covenant theology, and Fiddes presents even more of the diversity among Particular Baptists themselves. For example, Keach argues that the covenant of grace is primarily with Christ and secondarily with believers (*Display*, 285). In contrast, Gill argues that the covenant of redemption is virtually the covenant of grace, so he breaks the connection between the second thread of covenant theology from the last two threads, using Fiddes's terminology (*Body of Divinity*, 1: 306–9 [page citations are to the reprint edition]). Ascol confirms what Fiddes says about Gill's treatment of the covenants of grace and of redemption. Ascol contrasts Gill's covenant theology with that of Andrew Fuller, who provides yet another conception of these covenants ("Doctrine of Grace"). Another difference between Gill's account and that of other Baptists is how he involves the Holy Spirit in this covenant while they typically do not. Cf. Muller, "Spirit and Covenant."

6. Smyth, *Principles*, 1:254. Fiddes follows B. R. White in rightly arguing that Smyth links his covenant ecclesiology (what Fiddes calls the third and fourth threads of covenant theology) to covenant theology, namely the covenant of grace (Fiddes, "'Walking Together,'" 32). Cf. White, *English Separatist Tradition*, 128. In contrast, Coggins argues that Smyth did not link his covenant theology to his covenant ecclesiology, because Smyth would have considered a covenant between God and the elect to be too different from a covenant between church members with one another ("Theological Positions"). Lee rightly finds Coggins's claim unpersuasive for two reasons: "First, the Separatist background from which Smyth drew related the two concepts [or covenants]. Second, the fact that Smyth used the terms in close relationship and in reference to the same groups shows some connection," ("Baptism and Covenant," 125).

7. Fiddes, "'Walking Together,'" 33.

Such identification allowed them to be in continuity with the catholic church despite their separatist stance. They used the last two threads to strengthen their ecclesiology, because it provided a theological framework within which church members could commit themselves to God's promises and to one another.

After demonstrating the multi-stranded use of covenant theology among seventeenth-century Baptists, Fiddes argues that Baptists today should follow the lead of their predecessors by also using covenant theology—with some contemporary modifications—to enhance other areas of Baptist faith and practice, because "a renewed theology of covenant will be fruitful for several concerns that face Baptists in the context of the 'inter-church process' and the secular culture of today, and especially through the tendency of covenant towards openness to others and the whole of creation."[8] First among these concerns is that covenant theology can help Baptists today recognize Christ's universal church as more than a collection of individual churches, the denial of which can limit cooperation with other churches for worship and service to the community. Covenant theology can help address this problem because it holds to God's eternal covenant that constitutes and predates each local church. In other words, "there is a universal reality which *pre-exists* any local manifestation of it, as God's eternal covenant with humankind pre-exists the local covenant bond. Covenant and catholicity belong together."[9] For Fiddes, Baptists can and should apply covenant theology to their understanding of the universal church, so they can conceive of God's eternal covenant as the bond that strongly holds it together.

The second concern Fiddes addresses is the secularization of the term *covenant*. He thinks covenant "has become a dead metaphor" today that often refers to voluntary societies, so he suggests rooting it "in the life and mission of the triune God" in order to give it more theological depth.[10] At first glance, this appears to be a contemporary modification of covenant theology, but Fiddes thinks seventeenth-century Baptist views prompt his suggestion. He notes that seventeenth-century Baptists such as Keach considered the covenant between God and a particular church to be in a line of succession of renewals of the one covenant of grace. Within

---

8. Ibid., 24.
9. Ibid., 32, emphasis his.
10. Ibid.

this succession, the fourth thread of covenant theology, the covenanting between church members with one another, along with baptism and of the Lord's Supper, are all things through which the Spirit "renews and confirms" the taking of someone into the covenant of grace.[11] Smyth and Keach both think people in churches participate in the covenant of grace through their mutual covenanting with one another. Fiddes argues that these historical precedents authorize contemporary Baptists to recover the theological depth of *covenant* by expanding the believer's participation in God's covenants.

Fiddes expands the believer's participation in God's covenants by re-conceiving the second thread above, the covenant of redemption, as God's invitation for others to take part in his own life rather than a mere agreement among divine Persons about the salvation of humans. Historical precedents merely suggest this new conception of the covenant of redemption, so Fiddes turns to more recent theologians such as Barth for his formulation of it. Fiddes draws from Barth to propose "that as God the Father makes covenant of love eternally with the Son in the fellowship of the Spirit, so simultaneously God makes covenant in history with human beings. In one movement of utter self-giving God elects both the divine Son and human children as covenant partners."[12] Fiddes thinks this expansion of the covenant of redemption guards against any reduction of covenant to a mere alliance of people that are formed for certain mundane purposes. Rather, it denotes that covenant has an ontological element in which the being of God and of his people underlies their actions—actions in which God's people participate in his mission.

The third concern Fiddes addresses is an understanding of salvation in which there is little room for spiritual renewal after the moment of one's faith. He argues that Keach and Andrew Fuller (1754–1815) both used covenant theology to "preserve the mystery of grace and freedom."[13]

---

11. Ibid., 34. Cf. Keach, *Display*, 285.

12. Fiddes, "'Walking Together,'" 36. Fiddes summarizes Barth's view of covenant in "'Walking Together,'" 35–36. Cf. Barth, *Church Dogmatics*, II.2, 79–80, 123–25, 161–69, 175–94; and IV.1, 6–7, 36–38, 45–46. McCormack offers a helpful explanation of Barth's doctrine of election in "Grace and Being." Elsewhere, Fiddes argues that another benefit to this version of covenant theology is that it is not elitist or exclusive, because it fosters Christian mission and religious liberty, although he recognizes that the more traditional accounts of covenant theology also foster such things ("Mission and Liberty").

13. Fiddes, "'Walking Together,'" 39. Cf. Keach, *Display of Glorious Grace*, 282; and Fuller, *The Gospel Worthy of All Acceptation*, 112–14.

According to them, one's entrance into the covenant of grace came by way of the Spirit enabling faith in the gospel, but one's assurance of said faith partly comes by way of proper church order, including the making of and assenting to a church covenant that addresses discipline. These historical Baptists thought proper church order was part of the means of one's assurance of salvation, so Fiddes suggests that their practice of church covenants "imprinted on Baptist minds the sense that salvation was not merely a point but a process or a story."[14] In this process, the assurance and renewal of one's salvation comes through such means as entering into church covenants, being baptized, and partaking of the Lord's Supper. Fiddes does not think covenant theology is necessary for the bestowing of rich meaning to these acts, but he does think it confers onto them a helpful theology of renewal of salvation.

The fourth concern Fiddes addresses is the tendency of Baptists to consider their churches to be merely voluntary societies in which even the fourth thread of covenant theology, the covenant between church members with one another, acts as little more than an easily forgotten contract. In response, Fiddes argues that divine initiative is present in all four threads of covenant theology. In the fourth thread, Christ and the Spirit gather together the members of each church, so church members themselves cannot and do not constitute their churches through their resolution alone.[15] Fiddes's claim goes against other accounts that say the Enlightenment concepts of individual freedom and voluntaristic societies influenced historical Baptist church polity more than covenant theology ever did.[16] While there may be some merit to these accounts, Fiddes rejects them because Baptists themselves have insisted otherwise. According to Fiddes, they connected all four threads of covenant theology together in order to tie each Baptist church to God's greater work in the world, including his work in other Baptist and non-Baptist churches. Fiddes argues that this same connection should likewise lead modern Baptists to discern God's leading within not only their local churches, but also their local unions of Baptist churches and, by extension, their ecumenical relations with other Christian traditions.

14. Fiddes, "'Walking Together,'" 39.

15. Ibid., 42.

16. In two works, Brackney argues that voluntarism is the basis of free church life and as God's gift it does not diminish the fact that free churches must depend on God (*Voluntarism*; and *Christian Voluntarism*). Cf. Fiddes, "'Walking Together,'" 41.

The Fifth and final concern Fiddes addresses is the danger of basing covenants between churches on a uniform acceptance of some modern confession of faith. Fiddes admits that seventeenth-century Baptists connected covenants to confessions, but he maintains that it is not altogether clear what these same Baptists thought the proper relationship between covenants and confessions should be. Fiddes argues that uniform adoption of a confession is not necessary for the covenanting together between churches insofar as they share enough beliefs in common to walk together fruitfully with one another in a relationship of mutual openness and trust. Covenants foster these kinds of relationships while confessions often do not, so Baptists should be wary about requiring confessing for covenanting.

Fiddes's analysis of historical and contemporary covenantal positions and concerns are helpful for the covenantal view of baptism. Given the influence that Barth's baptismal theology had on twentieth-century Baptists, some may find it appealing that Fiddes appropriates other aspects of Barth's theology in Fiddes's modification of the covenant of redemption, which gives it more of an ontological element.[17] However, others may prefer to keep the older versions of the covenant of redemption intact, which claim that God calls his people to participate in his continual saving work as his children and witnesses. Such participation, when linked to a theology of union with Christ and his eternal life, can also provide an ontological element to covenant theology in which God's people intimately share in his life and mission. The covenantal view of baptism also extends the instrumental participation of God's people beyond his saving work to his sanctifying work.

Fiddes's "'Walking Together'" also provides helpful suggestions for applying seventeenth-century covenant theology to contemporary

---

17. Barth developed his baptismal theology during his lifetime. In his 1943 lectures on baptism, he separated water baptism from Spirit baptism, conceiving of the former as an act of obedience, but a sacrament nonetheless (*Teaching Regarding Baptism*). Later in his life he repudiated any sacramental understanding of it (*Church Dogmatics*, IV.4, 212). His former view encouraged Baptists who also separated water baptism from Spirit baptism, and his latter view encouraged Baptists who also rejected sacramental theology. Cross argues that it is difficult to "overestimate" the impact Barth's baptismal theology had on twentieth-century Baptists (*Baptism and the Baptists*, 131n21). Elsewhere, Cross discusses Barth's baptismal theology in more detail by comparing it with that of Calvin ("Baptism in Calvin and Barth"). Colwell also discusses Barth's baptismal theology (*Promise and Presence*, 114–19).

Baptist theology and practice. Fiddes's identification of four strands of covenant theology in the Baptist tradition reveals how seventeenth-century Baptists applied covenant theology to other areas of their theology, including baptism. Fiddes does not develop the historic link between covenant theology and baptism very much in this essay, but what he does say about it, namely that it occupies a role as a means of renewal of salvation, fits nicely with sacramentalism in general and the covenantal view of baptism in particular.[18] Moreover, his presentation of a multi-threaded seventeenth-century Baptist covenant theology offers concrete ways the covenantal view of baptism can apply the benefits of covenant theology to multiple aspects of Baptist baptismal theology and practice today, especially its covenantal roles for both the individual baptizand and the covenant community.

As helpful as it is, Fiddes's essay leaves much room for further research on the relationship between covenant theology and baptism in seventeenth-century Baptist theology. Jason Lee's essay, "Covenant and Baptism," is one example of such research that presents how Smyth related his covenant theology to his baptismal theology.

JASON LEE'S "BAPTISM AND COVENANT" (2008)

In his "Baptism and Covenant," Lee explores the benefits Baptist churches would receive by recovering the seventeenth-century Baptist theology and practice of church covenants, or what he calls covenant ecclesiology. Lee begins his presentation of seventeenth-century views with Smyth's covenant ecclesiology and its connections to covenant theology in general.[19] According to Lee, Smyth considered the church covenant to be an instrumental means through which people marked their faithfulness to God's eternal covenant of grace. As Fiddes also claims above, Lee likewise argues that Smyth considers the church covenant to be the grounds on which God grants each church Christ's own authority and power, making that church a true church. This power enables separatist and Baptist churches alike to "baptize, administer the Lord's Supper, elect leaders, and

---

18. Lee claims that Fiddes, "due most likely to the ecumenical aims of Fiddes's call for renewed covenant . . . does not connect the themes of believer's baptism with covenant" in his essay, "Baptism and Covenant," 132. But Lee overlooks the places in which Fiddes speaks of baptism being a means, along with covenant, of one's renewal of salvation.

19. Lee presents other aspects of the life and thought of John Smyth in *Theology of John Smyth*.

even ordain ministers," despite having no chronological succession from the Apostolate.[20] Rather, Christ's authority passes through the church's covenant, because it has a vertical dimension as a covenant between God and his faithful people (of which each church is but one part of this greater group) and a secondary, horizontal dimension between the faithful saints themselves that constitute a local church. Smyth held both dimensions together, because he thought that saints obediently placed "themselves under the discipline and authority of that church specifically and of Christ ultimately" in their one act of covenanting together.[21] In this one act, Smyth derives one covenant from the other, because "the person who accepts the covenant of grace offered by God should respond by agreeing to covenant with other believers to form a church."[22] Thus, Smyth clearly distinguishes God's eternal covenant from church covenants, but he also freely relates the two covenants together with such fluid language that it is difficult to know which covenant he is referring to in some of his writings. Lee analyzes Smyth's covenantal claims and concludes that Smyth's language reveals that he has a two-part church covenant: "The first part is between God and the faithful. Smyth sees this first part of the local church covenant as the acceptance of the eternal covenant of grace. After this is complete, then the Christian can agree to be obedient and demonstrate love to his fellow Christian. So, Smyth saw the church covenant as applying to the faithful who had responded to God's eternal covenant and then bonded together to be obedient to him and faithful to each other.[23]" Smyth's twofold church covenant calls for a church made up of believers alone, complete with a theology and practice of baptism that excludes infant baptism. In Smyth's theology, believer baptism naturally flows from covenant ecclesiology.

Lee argues that Smyth's theology and practice of church covenants was not unique among historical Baptists, because many seventeenth-century Baptists that came after him also embraced covenant ecclesiology. While this was once a popular position among Baptists, it is an uncommon position today. Lee laments that most Baptists today neither use it nor know of its history in the Baptist tradition. Given that most

20. Lee, "Baptism and Covenant," 123–24.
21. Ibid., 123. Cf. Smyth, *Principles and Inferences*, 1: 254.
22. Lee, "Baptism and Covenant," 125.
23. Ibid., 127.

contemporary Baptists would not find historical tradition a decisive enough reason to embrace covenant ecclesiology, Lee briefly presents its biblical grounding in the language of specific covenants in OT Scripture (e.g., Gen 12–17; Exod 19–20; 2 Sam 7; Jer 31; Josh 24; 2 Chr 34; and Neh 9) and reasonable inferences from certain NT passages (e.g., Matt 26:28; 2 Cor 8:5; and Heb 10:19–26) in which churches seem to operate with an underlying communal bond.[24]

Given its historical support and biblical grounding, Lee argues that Southern Baptists in particular need to recover the use of church covenants in order to strive as much as possible at ensuring that their churches are composed of only truly regenerate members.[25] Lee thinks it is obvious that church covenants will add much needed theological support to church membership and discipline, which are two areas of concern for many North American Baptist churches today. Many Baptists avoid both issues because of their negative implications, but Lee encourages churches to consider their benefits, "while anticipation of church discipline does not make it painless, the church covenant puts discipline in the context of mutual accountability and indicates its redemptive purposes."[26] Such a context provides a firm framework within which to renew many areas of Baptist theology and practice, including baptism.

Lee argues that Smyth integrated baptism into his covenant ecclesiology, making baptism more meaningful for Smyth than for many Baptists today. However, Smyth's view was not the only seventeenth-century Baptist understanding of the relationship between baptism and church covenants. According to Lee, Keach also held that churches should baptize people upon their profession of faith, and after their baptism they can then agree to a church covenant and thereby enter into church membership.[27] Lee criticizes Keach's practice because it undermines the meaning of baptism as the means through which one is initiated into the church. Lee thinks that in Keach's view "baptism may be downgraded to a Christian ordinance, by which a person merely professes his or her own faith instead of a church ordinance, by which acceptance of the church's doctrine and practice is displayed along with a profession of personal

24. Ibid., 128–29.

25. Ibid., 132–33. Lee draws from Deweese and Hammett for this point. Cf. Deweese, *Baptist Church Covenants*, 90; and Hammett, *Biblical Foundations*, 117.

26. Lee, "Baptism and Covenant," 134.

27. Keach, *Glory of a True Church*, 5–7. Cf. Lee, "Baptism and Covenant," 134–35.

faith. In order to recover church covenants and still reiterate the corporate nature of baptism, the relationship between church covenant and baptism must be clearly defined.[28]"

This temporal separation between baptism and church membership has led to a downgrade in contemporary Baptist baptismal theology where church covenants are often nonexistent. Lee argues that recovering church covenants today will make a substantive effect on Baptist baptismal theology only if Baptists use Smyth's understanding of the relationship between baptism and church covenants in which baptism is the means through which a new believer visibly shows to fellow believers his or her consent to the twofold church covenant. In other words, baptism itself is a new believer's faithful act through which he or she confirms acceptance of God's covenant.[29] For Smyth, baptism carries this confirming role because it demonstrates one's agreement to God's eternal covenant.[30] Lee concludes that Baptists today should also give baptism this same kind of confirming role by linking it to a church covenant, in order to give both baptism and church membership a solid grounding.

Lee's appropriation of Smyth on church covenants and baptism is helpful for the covenantal view of baptism because it explains how baptism can at the same time confirm one's acceptance of the blessings and responsibilities of both God's eternal covenant and a church covenant. Smyth's view is a solid foundation from which to emphasize the communal aspects of baptism, especially baptism's inherent connection to church membership. Churches need to reconnect what should have never been severed, namely one's visible commitment to both Christ and his church through baptism. Lee's essay provides several arguments that favor a recovery of seventeenth-century Baptist covenant ecclesiology, including its enhancement of the theology and practice of baptism today.

CONCLUSION

Fiddes's and Lee's articles show why some contemporary Baptists argue for a recovery of seventeenth-century Baptist covenant theology: it gives

---

28. Lee, "Baptism and Covenant," 135.

29. Consequently, this is one of Smyth's reasons for rejecting infant baptism, since infants cannot consent to or accept God's covenant without their own faith (*Character of the Beast*, 2:645). Cf. Lee, "Baptism and Covenant, 135.

30. Lee, "Baptism and Covenant," 135–36. Cf. Smyth, *Character of the Beast*, 2: 659.

much needed theological support to neglected aspects of contemporary Baptist faith and practice such as the church and baptism. These two articles demonstrate covenant theology's practical benefits for seventeenth-century Baptists by arguing that these Baptists used their multi-threaded understanding of covenant theology to enhance their ecclesiology and baptismal theology. Despite its biblical grounding, systematic coherence, and practical benefits, as now expressed by Fiddes and Lee, Baptists today do not usually value covenant theology in their tradition. Perhaps their overly narrow view of covenant theology extends beyond their association of it with infant baptism to specific understandings of soteriology and eschatology that they do not accept, such as Reformed soteriology. Despite the presence of Arminian Baptist advocates of covenant theology in the Baptist tradition in the works of theologians such as Grantham, many Baptists today tie covenant theology exclusively to Reformed soteriology. To be sure, covenant theology fits more naturally within a Reformed soteriological scheme than an Arminian one, but Reformed soteriology is not and never was a necessary part of Baptist covenant theology. This raises the question, what elements of Baptist covenant theology are necessary and sufficient for developing Baptist covenant ecclesiology and using its practical benefits?

Neither Fiddes nor Lee discusses which historical and/or contemporary accounts of Baptist covenant theology reap the practical benefits of covenant ecclesiology. Given that seventeenth-century Baptists derived their twofold church covenant from God's eternal covenant with one people—past, present, and future—under Christ's headship, then all that is minimally necessary and sufficient to reap the practical benefits of covenant ecclesiology is to affirm the covenant of grace, understood in a Baptist sense in which circumcision was never its sign of initiation. This is just the minimum, so more elaborate accounts of covenant theology, such as those of Grantham and Coxe, are also compatible with covenant ecclesiology.

The upshot for the covenantal view of baptism is that it need not be inherently connected to any one account of Baptist covenant theology, soteriology, or eschatology. If a Baptist wants to adopt the covenantal view of baptism, then he or she only needs to affirm the covenant of grace between God and his one people under the headship of Christ in which baptism is its confirming sign for believers after the coming of Christ. Thus, the covenantal view of baptism is compatible with a variety of

Baptist views on the number of covenants, the relationships between the covenants, soteriology, eschatology, the nature of God's kingdom, and the Israel-Church relationship. It is even possible for dispensational Baptists to utilize the ecclesiological benefits of the covenantal view of baptism by focusing on its understanding of the meaning of baptism in light of the new covenant.

Moreover, the covenantal view may also keep intact the variety of Baptist views on the meaning of baptism itself, namely the ordinance-only and sacramentalist views. Fiddes and Lee do not explore how seventeenth-century Baptists related covenant ecclesiology to the meaning of baptism, neither do they give their own understanding of the meaning of baptism in these articles. Lee *seems* to operate with an ordinance-only understanding of baptism, and he does not discuss how baptism relates to salvation and sanctification in his article. Rather, he focuses only on how baptism relates to church covenants. Fiddes hints in a few places that historical Baptists considered baptism to be an instrumental means of one's renewal of salvation, but he does not explicitly say if these Baptists considered such a means to be a gracious part of one's conversion and/or sanctification. Moreover, Fiddes, who has researched much on sacramentalism, does not investigate seventeenth-century and/or contemporary Baptist understandings of the relationship between covenant theology and sacramentalism.

Thus, the next chapter will build on Fiddes's and Lee's arguments by taking their historically informed covenantal views of baptism beyond the realm of seventeenth-century Baptist covenant ecclesiology and into the realm of seventeenth-century Baptist views of the meaning of baptism. Covenant theology clearly enhances a sacramental understanding of the meaning of baptism by making it clearer, more coherent, and more practically meaningful for Baptists. But this is not to say that ordinance-only Baptists could not also reap the benefits of covenant ecclesiology for their own view of baptism, and, were they to do so, Baptists should seriously consider it. Nonetheless, the covenantal view of baptism favors a sacramental view of baptism, as the next chapter will show.

7

A Historic Link between Covenant and Sacrament

THE PREVIOUS TWO CHAPTERS demonstrated that seventeenth-century Baptists embraced covenant theology for many reasons, including its strengthening of Baptist ecclesiology. Covenant theology connects each church to the universal church, affirming God's work through and interest in each local church. Covenant theology also binds the members of a local church to one another. Seventeenth-century Baptists used covenant theology to strengthen the genuineness of their churches, the authority of their ministers, the effectiveness of their discipline, and the maintenance of their ministries. On top of these uses for covenant theology, seventeenth-century Baptists also used covenant theology to enhance their sacramental theology of baptism. Recovering this historic link between covenant theology and sacramentalism will inform the covenantal view of baptism, demonstrating its roots in the Baptist tradition as a genuine Baptist view, and helping it address ordinance-only Baptist objections that claim otherwise. This chapter will look at examples of the link between covenant and sacrament in the writings of Benjamin Keach, Robert Garner and Thomas Patient.[1] But first, it is necessary to answer ordinance-only Baptist objections against seventeenth-century Baptist sacramentalism in general, which naturally extends to historic versions.

---

1. In their various works, Thompson, Fowler, and Cross have all presented the sacramentalism of several authors, including Keach, Garner, and Grantham, but they have not focused on how these authors have tied their covenant theology to their sacramentalism.

IS SACRAMENTALISM A GENUINELY BAPTIST DOCTRINE?

Chapter 4 summarized the sacramentalist argument that many seventeenth-century Baptists shared. Although this argument is based on research in the primary sources, ordinance-only Baptists, such as Moody, offer a few reasons to reject it.[2] Moody's first reason is that seventeenth-century Baptist confessions support an ordinance-only view of baptism rather than a sacramental one: "Baptist convictions about Baptism *prior* to the twentieth century are adequately chronicled in the London Confession of 1677 and the Orthodox Creed of 1678. Both confessions simply interpret Baptism as an ordinance ordained by Christ, that is, as a sign of fellowship and forgiveness. Sacramental nuances are completely missing from both of these substantial confessions.[3]" What is odd about Moody's claim here is that even if these two confessions adequately represent the breadth of seventeenth-century Baptist baptismal theology, which they do not, one of the confessions he mentions does not even support his claim. The 1678 Orthodox Creed's article on baptism and the Lord's Supper states, "These two Sacraments, (*viz.*) Baptism, and the Lord's Supper are Ordinances of Positive, Soveraign, and holy Institution, appointed by the Lord Jesus Christ."[4] The next article in this confession, which is specifically on baptism, calls it "an Ordinance of the New Testament . . . a Sign of our entrance into the Covenant of Grace, and ingrafting into Christ, and into the Body of Christ, which is his Church," and it later calls baptism a "holy Sacrament."[5] It is hard to imagine that the authors and signers of this confession had no sacramental nuances in their theology when they call baptism and the Lord's Supper *sacraments* and then conceive of the former as a sign of one's engrafting into Christ and his body.

---

2. Moody, "American Baptist Sacramentalism?" 168–72. Cf. Harsch, "Meaning of Baptism."

3. Moody, "American Baptist Sacramentalism?" 75n8, emphasis his. Moody references Tull in this footnote, but Tull does not share Moody's conclusion that sacramental nuances are completely absent in these documents. Tull merely claims that these Baptists preferred *ordinance* to *sacrament*, because the former emphasizes Christ's commands and the latter is associated with the concept that baptism mediates salvific grace ("Ordinances/Sacraments," 191).

4. *Orthodox Creed*, 37.

5. Ibid., 38–39.

A Historic Link between Covenant and Sacrament

Indeed, the other confession Moody mentions, the 1677 Second London Confession, lacks sacramental terminology and refers to baptism as an ordinance, or a sign, of Christ's death, burial, and resurrection.[6] In light of contemporary Baptist use of the terms *ordinance* and *sacrament*, it may be reasonable to affirm Moody's conclusion that the seventeenth-century Baptists that wrote and signed this confession wished to distance themselves from sacramental theology. But Fowler, Cross, Thompson, and others have demonstrated from the writings of individual Baptists who signed this confession that they affirmed sacramental theology, even if they use *ordinance* in their writings. In light of this research, Moody's conclusion here is inaccurate.

Moody's second reason for rejecting the claim that seventeenth-century Baptists embraced sacramentalism is that contemporary sacramentalists, such as Fowler and Cross, have let their own sacramental biases undermine the objectivity of their research. As a result, they mistakenly project their own theology onto their predecessors. For example, Moody thinks Fowler bases many of his arguments for seventeenth-century sacramentalism "on fallacious arguments from silence."[7] Moody gives two examples: First is Fowler's claim that seventeenth-century Baptists clearly rejected a sacramental understanding of infant baptism, but they never explicitly rejected a sacramental understanding of believer baptism.[8] Moody dismisses this claim as a flawed argument because in his opinion Baptists have always distanced themselves from sacramentalism in general rather than just a sacramental theology of infant baptism in particular. As seen above, Moody never substantiates this supposedly widespread seventeenth-century Baptist aversion to sacramentalism, so his argument is from silence. In contrast, Fowler bases his claim on primary sources, and other historians have corroborated it. This chapter will further corroborate it by analyzing the works of Keach, Garner, and Patient. Moody's first example fails to demonstrate that contemporary historians have let their own bias produce seventeenth-century Baptist sacramentalism.

Moody's second example is his claim that Fowler wrongly legitimizes a sacramentalist reading of seventeenth-century Baptist texts because

---

6. *Confession of Faith*, 96–98.
7. Moody, "American Baptist Sacramentalism?," 169.
8. Ibid. Cf. Fowler, *More Than a Symbol*, 32.

Fowler claims they use *sacrament* and *ordinance* synonymously.⁹ This example has actually misread Fowler more than anything, because he never purports to legitimize his sacramentalist reading of seventeenth-century Baptist texts on their use of terms alone. Fowler only mentions the synonymous usage of *sacrament* and *ordinance* in seventeenth-century Baptist texts to caution against anachronistically superimposing more recent definitions of these terms onto historical documents such as the Second London Confession. Moody's argument above reveals that he has exactly done what Fowler cautioned against.

While it is possible that contemporary sacramentalists have let their biases affect their research, Moody's specific examples fall short of providing any proof. His arguments may even reveal that his own bias has undermined his approach to seventeenth-century Baptist texts. Fowler, Cross, Thompson, and other contemporary sacramentalists conclude that sacramentalism is a recovery of an older Baptist view based on the presence of sacramental concepts in seventeenth-century Baptist works. Unlike Moody, they have not hastily based their conclusion on how these documents use certain terms. Thus, any compelling objection against the veracity of their conclusion should likewise be based on the theological concepts in the texts themselves. Moody's objections lack such substance, making them superficial.

While Moody's objections lack substance, they do reveal the need for contemporary sacramentalists to demonstrate further how seventeenth-century Baptists used ordinance terminology for sacramental concepts. As seen above, the 1678 Orthodox Creed uses ordinance and sacramental terminology interchangeably. Christians from other traditions in the seventeenth century—even traditions that unequivocally embraced sacramental theology—also used ordinance and sacramental terminology interchangeably. For example, paedobaptist minister George Day (d. 1697) published a catechism entitled *The Communicants Instructor: Or, a Sacramental Catechism* that begins by defining a sacrament as "an holy Ordinance of Divine Institution, annexed to the Covenants which God hath made with Men;" its second question asks if Scripture refers to ordinances as sacraments."¹⁰ It replies "no," but argues that *sacraments*

---

9. Moody, "American Baptist Sacramentalism?" 170n172. Cf. Fowler, *More Than a Symbol*, 14.

10. Day, *Communicants Instructor*, 1. He published it anonymously in his lifetime, beginning in 1692.

appropriately refer to the ordinances for good reasons. Clearly, ordinance terminology among seventeenth-century Christians does not alone imply their espousal of what is known as the ordinance-only position today. In order to assess why these authors used and sometimes preferred the term *ordinance* to describe baptism in their writings, one must research what things they label as ordinances and what it is about those things that leads them to prefer ordinance terminology in reference. Likewise, the best way to assess these authors' positions on the meaning of baptism is to assess how they conceive of baptism's purpose, use, and meaning. One way of assessing such matters for seventeenth-century Baptists is by examining the primary sources, so this chapter will look at three works by Keach, Garner, and Patient, who all prefer to use ordinance terminology for their conception of baptism as a covenantal sacrament.

BENJAMIN KEACH (1640-1704)

The articles of faith from Benjamin Keach's church in London espouse sacramental theology without using sacramental terminology.[11] Keach, one of the signers of the 1677 Second London Confession that Moody mentions above, was a prolific Baptist theologian and pastor who often defended Baptist covenant theology against paedobaptists.[12] But this section will look only at his covenantal sacramentalism as expressed by his church's articles of faith.

The sacramental concepts in this document begin in Article XX, "*Of the Means of Grace*," which lists several ordinances: "We believe that the outward and more ordinary means, whereby Christ communicates to us the Benefits of Redemption, are his Holy Ordinances, as Prayer, the Word of God, and Preaching, with Baptism, and the Lord's Supper, *&c.* and yet notwithstanding it is the Spirit of God that maketh Prayer, Reading, *&c.* and specially the Preaching of the Word, effectual to the convincing, converting, building up, and comforting, through Faith, all the Elect of God unto Salvation.[13]" Thus, for Keach, the power in the ordinances

---

11. [Keach?], *Articles of Faith*.

12. There is much literature on the life and works of Keach. As seen above, Fiddes draws from Keach's covenant ecclesiology ("'Walking Together,'" 26–27, and 39–40). Riker presents Keach's covenant theology in much greater detail than Fiddes does (*Catholic Reformed Theologian*). Both Cross and Fowler briefly present Keach's sacramentalism, but neither of them analyze the relation between his covenant theology and sacramentalism (Cross, "Myth," 136–137; and Fowler, *More Than a Symbol*, 29–30).

13. [Keach?], *Articles of Faith*, 19.

comes from the Spirit who graciously works through them—making them means of grace, or sacraments. However, they are still ordinary and outward means, which implies that they are not means of justifying or salvific grace. This article does not mention covenant theology, but Keach uses covenant theology as a framework within which baptism is a confirming means of grace for the believer.

The next several articles discuss in more detail each outward means of grace, or ordinance, beginning with baptism:

> We believe that Baptism is a Holy Ordinance of Christ, or a pure Gospel Institution; and to be unto the Party baptized, a sign of his Fellowship with Christ in his Death, Burial, and Resurrection, and of his being grafted into him, and of Remission of Sins, and of his giving himself up to God, through Jesus Christ, to walk in Newness of Life. . . . And that it is the indispensable Duty of such who are baptized, to give up themselves to some particular orderly Church of Jesus Christ, and to walk in all the Commandments and Ordinances of the Lord blameless: Baptism being an initiating Ordinance.[14]

This language is very similar to that of the 1677 Second London Confession concerning the meaning of baptism, and Keach considers such language to be consistent with his understanding of baptism as a means of grace. For Keach, baptism signifies, in a confirming way, one's entrance into God's eternal covenant. He also links baptism to covenant ecclesiology by stating that baptism initiates one into the church. As a result of baptism, one now has the indispensable duty to submit to a church and agree to walk in Christ's commands and ordinances therein. Fiddes has argued that this language of "walking together," or "walking in commandments and ordinances," is typical among seventeenth-century Baptists who espoused covenant ecclesiology. Fiddes also argues that Keach was a strong advocate for covenant theology in his other writings,[15] so it is reasonable to conclude that Keach uses such language in this article to allude to covenant theology and covenant ecclesiology. Thus, there is a link here between covenant and sacramentalism.

Keach may only allude to covenant theology in his article on baptism, but he explicitly discusses it in the next article, "*Of a true Church*":

---

14. Ibid., 20–21.
15. Fiddes, "'Walking Together,'" 24–34.

> We believe a true Church of Christ is not *National*, nor *Parochial*, but doth consist of a number of godly Persons, who upon the Profession of their Faith and Repentance have been baptized, and in a solemn manner have in Holy Covenant given themselves up to the Lord, and to one another, to live in Love, and to endeavour to *keep the Unity of the Spirit in the Bond of Peace*. Among whom the Word of God is duly and truly preach'd; and Holy Baptism, the Lord's Supper, and all other Ordinances are duly administered, according to the Word of God, and the Institution of Christ in the Primitive Church: watching over one another, and communicating to each other's *Necessities*, as becometh Saints; living Holy Lives, as becomes their sacred Profession; *and not to forsake the assembling themselves, as the manner of some is*; or to take leave to hear where they please in other Places when the Church is assembled, but to worship God, and feed in that Pasture, or with that Church, with whom they have covenanted, and given up themselves as particular Members thereof.[16]

In this article, Keach espouses the twofold church covenant through which believers give themselves up to God and one another. Unlike Smyth, Keach does not think believers take hold of this covenant through baptism itself, but he does think baptism, as a confirming sign of initiation into God's new covenant, is a necessary prerequisite for one's taking hold of the church covenant. Keach gives the church covenant an important role in binding together church members to love one another and to maintain unity in the Spirit. Given what he has previously said about the ordinances being the outward means through which Christ communicates his benefits to believers, Keach is likely tying the maintenance of the unity of the Spirit through such means in this article.

He may not explicitly say as much, but the substance of these articles proclaims that covenant ecclesiology is the framework within which the Spirit works in the church through its ordinances as outward means of grace. For Keach, such ordinances are more regular and effective when church members are committed to one another by their covenanting together. Thus, baptism, in and of itself, may not be the means through which a new believer covenants with a particular church, but its confirming role in Keach's theology allows it to be the fitting prerequisite for one's taking hold of the church covenant.

---

16. [Keach?], *Articles of Faith*, 22–23.

Keach's articles of faith demonstrate how a document that lacks the word *sacrament* can still embrace sacramental nuances. These articles also reveal some of the reasons why seventeenth-century Baptists preferred to use the word *ordinance*. Keach considers ordinances to be holy and sacred outward means of grace, listing several of them: baptism, the Lord's Supper, prayer, the singing of Psalms, the reading and preaching of the Word of God, and the laying on of hands. God's explicit command for his covenant people to do them regularly is what ties all these things together. According to Keach, God has commanded that his church do these ordinances in order to convey his benefits to his people through them. For Keach and others, the word *ordinance* fits this common trait well, emphasizing God's role in commanding the ordinances and the church's role in being bound together to observe them regularly. These are some reasons for Keach's preference of *ordinance*, but they do not fully explain his avoidance of *sacrament* in these articles.

Most seventeenth-century Baptists did not regularly call baptism a *sacrament* because of the commonly used paedobaptist definition of sacraments that claims they are covenantal seals that may also convey salvific grace.[17] Keach's avoidance of *sacrament* likely derived from his numerous debates with paedobaptists in his lifetime. In those debates, he and other Baptists often refused to agree with their paedobaptist brothers and sisters that baptism is a seal of the new covenant. Rather, these Baptists appealed to Ephesians 1:13 and 4:30 to argue that the Spirit himself is the seal of the new covenant.[18] They still affirmed that the Spirit graciously works through baptism's confirming role as a sign of initiation into the new covenant, but some of these Baptists, such as Spilsbury, would even explicitly link baptism to the Spirit's confirming or sealing work: "the sealing and confirming ordinances of Christ, ever presuppose faith in the subject, to seal unto, and to be confirmed."[19] For these Baptists, the Spirit only works through baptism and other outward means of grace in a person who has his or her own faith, so baptism cannot act as a seal of the new covenant for infants who lack their own faith. As seen in chapter 5, Coxe, representing most seventeenth-century accounts of Baptist covenant theology, did not even want to say that circumcision was a seal of the old covenant. Rather,

17. Tull, "Ordinances/Sacraments," 191.
18. *Confession of Faith*, 117. Cf. Cary, *Solemn Call*, 57.
19. Spilsbery [Spilsbury?], *Treatise*, 46.

he grounded the meaning and use of circumcision in God's express commands, or ordinances. Thus, many seventeenth-century Baptists avoided sacramental terminology so as not to undermine key parts of their defense of Baptist covenant theology and baptismal theology. They did not avoid it because they rejected sacramental theology altogether. The works of Garner and Patient will support this point further, because they both use ordinance terminology for their covenantal view of sacramentalism.

ROBERT GARNER (ACTIVE 1640–1650)

Garner's *Treatise of Baptisme* is one of the documents that Fowler uses for his presentation of seventeenth-century Baptist sacramentalism, so this section will complement Fowler's research by analyzing how Garner's covenantal themes affect his baptismal theology.[20] In this treatise, Garner explores how Ephesians 4:5, especially its phrase "one Lord, one faith, one baptism," shapes Baptist baptismal theology. This treatise contains six major arguments: first, the "one baptism" in this text is water baptism; second, water baptism is an ordinance of the Lord Jesus; third, God commands that only believers be baptized; fourth, baptism has many privileges for believers; fifth, baptism also has many duties for believers; and sixth, Christ appointed only certain people to administer baptism. Garner weaves covenantal themes throughout these arguments, especially when they lead him to discuss the many ends and uses of baptism. This section will present a few of these discussions, focusing on how he understands the relationship between covenant theology and sacramentalism.

Garner considers baptism to be a mutual pledge and promise between God and believers in which God puts "his Name, that is, his Authority and his Grace, upon them," and believers take on his threefold name.[21] Garner believes that this mutual pledge between God and his people in baptism is no less covenantal than God's pledge and promise with Israel in Numbers 6:22–27. In this passage, God blesses Israel as his people, and they take on his name to be his people, including taking on the duties and obligations thereof. Likewise, Garner thinks baptism is a mutual pledge in which a believer subjects him- or herself to God and to his people, and God, speaking through his community, confirms his acceptance of the believer. Such a mutual pledge makes baptism a covenantal act that

---

20. Fowler, *More Than a Symbol*, 20–24.
21. Garner, *Treatise of Baptisme*, 10.

is between not only God and his people as a whole, but also individual members of his people with one another. This mutual pledge is the key to Garner's covenantal view of baptism.

Like Smyth, Garner argues that baptism, rather than the signing of a church covenant, is the normative means through which believers join a church, because believers take hold of God's covenant, including its blessings and responsibilities, through baptism. Garner is not against the use of church covenants altogether. Rather, he is against disassociating baptism from the means of initiation into a church, because God appointed

> but one way, for the joyning or adding of believers unto his Body. Which sometimes is called an adding to his Church, and some times an adding to the Lord; both which commeth to one and the same thing: for to be added to the Church of the Lord, or the body of the Lord, is to be added to the Lord himself, in a mysticall externall union. And the same Scripture [Acts 2:47; 5:34; 13:24] likewise declareth, that as they entred by baptisme into the union and fellowship of the body: so likewise unto the enjoyment of all the priviledges of the body.[22]

Like Smyth, Garner also advocates a two-part church covenant here. As the means of entry into the church and as a profession of union with Christ, Garner argues that baptism inherently lays on believers the tasks "to walk like such as are dead to sinne, to the world. . . . [and] to seeke after, and set their affections upon things which are above."[23]

Baptism brings much responsibility, but Garner is also quick to emphasize its connection to the lasting power of Christ's resurrection, which enables believers to walk well in their new lives and the new duties therein:

> The Lord puts forth a glorious power to Believers in baptisme, giving in unto their hearts (in what proportion he pleaseth) the power of the death and resurrection of Jesus Christ, acting faith in them to receive the same, whereby they are in some measure enabled to perform that which their baptisme doth engage them unto: Rom. 6:4. . . . Neither doe believers enjoy this fruit and benefit in the present administration of baptisme onely: but this grace

---

22. Ibid., 15.
23. Ibid., 18–19.

and power of Christ in baptism, hath an influence into after times also, even so long as they continue in the state of mortality.[24]

Garner links covenantal stipulations, including the spiritual power for fulfilling them, to baptism, which he prefers to call "a holy and pretious Ordinance of Iesus Christ."[25] Garner uses ordinance terminology for a sacramental understanding of baptism, while arguing that baptism is the means through which believers get the initial and lasting power to live holy lives—such power is a manifestation of God's grace in the life of the believer. Garner's treatise is clearly one example of covenantal sacramentalism, and he is not even afraid to call baptism a seal.

Garner calls baptism a seal because he applies covenant theology to his theology of baptism. As a result, Garner's sacramental theology is much clearer than that of many contemporary Baptists. Garner considers it to be a privilege of baptism that "in this Ordinance, the Lord Jesus by his Spirit acting in a believers heart, doth more richly seal up or confirm to him the free and full remission of all his sinnes, through the blood of Christ."[26] For Garner, sealing and confirming is the same thing, and he directly ties this sealing privilege of baptism to the work of the Spirit:

> [For it is the Spirit's proper grace or work] to witness or confirm to us (by acting faith in us, more assuredly to believe) the remission of all our sinnes by Jesus Christ. In baptisme, as well as in the Lord's Supper (although in another manner) the pretious death and resurrection of Christ, is mystically, yet clearly set forth before believers. And the Spirit of God acting faith in them, in this Ordinance, doth not onely clear up to them more sweetly, the pretiousnesse of the death of Christ, but also confirms to them more rightly their interest in the same: to wit, the remission of all their sinnes, and their peace with the Father, through Jesus Christ.[27]

Garner keeps the Spirit as the agent of baptism's sealing work, so his view does not contradict biblical passages such as Ephesians 1:13 and 4:30 that refer to the Spirit himself as the believer's seal. Garner thinks the Spirit uses baptism as an instrumental means of his sealing work, which confirms a believer's remission of sins through faith in Christ.

---

24. Ibid., 19–21.
25. Ibid., 20.
26. Ibid., 24.
27. Ibid.

Garner distances himself from the view that baptism itself remits sins, because he considers that to be a paedobaptist Roman Catholic position. Rather, he thinks one reason Jesus commands baptism is so he can confirm to believers, through his Spirit acting faith in them, the remission of their sins. For Garner, baptism is the instrumental means through which the Spirit acts faith on the part of the believer to confirm their pledge to God, thereby also confirming God's pledge to them to forgive all their sins on account of Christ. In Garner's formulation, Baptism itself does not justify, but God uses it to confirm one's prior faith that alone justified. Baptism's sealing is a confirming work, not a saving one. For Garner, baptism is not necessary for salvation like faith in the blood of Christ, but, given baptism's privileges, he thinks it is "not a uselesse, but a gainfull Ordinance" that has immediate and lasting benefits.[28]

Garner ties his covenant theology to his doctrine of baptism in many fruitful ways. He considers baptism to be the means through which God and the believer mutually pledge, or take covenant, with one another. God pledges to put his name on the believer, confirming his acceptance of him or her into his covenant as part of his covenant community. The believer takes hold of the covenant, thereby taking on its obligations and receiving its blessings, or privileges. Its blessings include the Spirit's confirming, or sealing, work that assures believers of their faith and gives a lasting bestowal of consciousness of Christ's indwelling resurrection power. Its privileges include the proper duties of taking on God's name, which prompts his people to live holy lives and covenant with one another.

Garner's treatise is another example of a seventeenth-century Baptist using ordinance terminology for sacramental theology. Moreover, this treatise supports Fowler's claim that these Baptists rejected a sacramental theology of infant baptism in part because of their own sacramental theology. Garner argues in several places that each of the privileges, ends, and uses of baptism demonstrate that infants are not capable of pledging themselves to God, undertaking the duties of walking righteously, receiving blessings to resist sin, and needing assurance that God has forgiven their sins—since they do not even know of their sin. Garner does not reject infant baptism because he rejects all sacramental theology, because his treatise argues exactly the opposite. While Keach and Garner both emphasize the role of covenant ecclesiology for their sacramen-

---

28. Ibid., 26.

talism, Patient emphasizes the role of covenant theology in general for his sacramentalism.

THOMAS PATIENT (D. 1666)

Patient was one of the London Particular Baptist pastors who signed the First London Confession, and his arguments in *The Doctrine of Baptism* overlap the above works.[29] Like Garner, Patient also focuses on the theological implications of being baptized into God's threefold name. Like most other Baptist authors from the period, Patient also spends much time discussing the proper mode of baptism, immersion, because it symbolizes Christ's death, burial, and resurrection by offering a visible portrayal. His definition of baptism also includes familiar terminology: "baptism of Believers, is a Solemn Ordinance of the New Testament, enjoined by divers special commands, and incouraged with promises of remission of sins and salvation on the right performance of the same."[30] Patient spends the first half of this work presenting his own understanding of covenant theology, which agrees with most of the points Coxe makes, so there is no need to repeat them here. In the second half of this work, Patient defends his understanding of covenant theology by responding to several objections. In the course of some of these responses, he explains how covenant theology relates to sacramentalism, so this section will look at three of them.

First, Garner argues that one distinction between the old and new covenants is that the latter's signs are vehicles of the Spirit's work that confirm one's prior faith. Garner makes this point in response to a paedobaptist objection that is based on 1 Corinthians 10:1–5 in which all of Israel was baptized and partook of spiritual food and drink without all of them also pleasing God. Paedobaptists use this text to claim that there is always a distinction between one's outward physical obedience to God's covenant signs and one's inward spiritual obedience to God's laws. Patient accepts such a distinction for the old covenant, but he does not want to extend it to the new covenant and its signs: "These signs, I say, these Sacramentall signs that are instituted since Christ came, for the confirming he is come,

---

29. White, *English Baptists of the Seventeenth Century*, 71. Other than Mickle's exploration of Patient's connections to the Puritans, there are no works on his theology ("'To Do Him Special Service'").

30. Patient, *Doctrine of Baptism*, 25–26.

these belong only to the spirituall seed, in whom Christ is come already dwelling in their hearts by faith. Therefore as Christ is a spiritual and substantial Mediator of a Substantial and spiritual covenant, so these spiritual Administrations of the spiritual covenant, belong only to such as are in Christ, and this new Covenant by faith, and that have Christ dwelling in them. . . .[31]" So that there is no confusion over what administrations Patient has in mind, he immediately says that Christ instituted baptism and his Supper to be only for believers.

Patient thinks that under the old covenant God commanded all his people to partake of the outward covenantal signs, or sacraments, without also requiring all of them to have the spiritual reality to which those signs pointed. However, Patient argues that under the new covenant God commands that only those who have faith and repentance are to partake of its signs, because the new covenant is a spiritual covenant for a spiritual seed under the headship of a spiritual mediator with spiritual signs. Carnal people cannot receive spiritual signs, so God requires that faith and repentance precede the spiritual signs of the new covenant, because "baptism is a confirmation of our Regeneration already wrought in us, and our new birth, and our union with Jesus Christ by faith, and therefore belongs only to them, where this Regeneration is to them that are born again of Water, and of the Spirit. . . ."[32] As a vehicle through which the Spirit performs his confirming work in the life of the believer, baptism is a means of grace. Elsewhere, Patient summarizes his understanding of grace and baptism, saying it "is not to convey grace where it is not, but to confirm Grace, and strengthen it where it is."[33] For Patient, covenantal sacramentalism considers baptism to be a means of confirming or sanctifying grace, rather than justifying grace.

Second, Patient reveals why he uses ordinance terminology for his sacramental theology of baptism. His use of ordinance terminology comes up as he responds to the claim that water baptism is unnecessary for those who have the baptism of the Spirit. He rejects this claim because the Spirit's work is itself a ground and reason for one to be baptized in water. According to Garner, the Spirit works with God's commands rather than against them: "Where you may see, that God is so far from giving his

---

31. Ibid., 127.
32. Ibid., 128.
33. Ibid., 152.

Spirit, to the end that souls should plead thereby freedom from the practice of those commanded Ordinances of Christ, that on the contrary, it is the end why God gives his Spirit to enable, and to cause them to walk in his way, and in his Ordinances, and in particular baptism."[34] For Patient, the freedom the Spirit brings is the freedom to obey God's commands, or ordinances, such as baptism. Patient uses ordinance terminology to describe baptism as one of God's specific commands and to discuss the Spirit's role in baptism, because "it is true that the Spirit, in the saving gifts of faith, repentance, and the like, is held to be essential to the Ordinance of Baptism of water, and must be joined together with it, without which it cannot be said to be an Ordinance of God, there must be the inward grace, as well as the outward sign."[35] In other words, the Spirit's saving work, or what some might call his "baptism," is that which makes water baptism a true ordinance of God for a believer rather than an empty rite for an unbeliever.

Patient also uses ordinance terminology to emphasize baptism's lasting role for the church: "It must needs be a solemn standing Ordinance of God, that every soul upon pain of guilt and rebellion against Christ his head and King ought to be subject to. But this of Baptism, hath as aforesaid, many standing Laws left in holy Record, speaking to all that believe and repent, promising remission of sins, and salvation to the right performance of the same, which proves it to be a standing Ordinance of the new Testament.[36]" His use of *ordinance* here emphasizes God's command of baptism and its solemn importance for Christians, but there is no evidence to conclude that he uses it in order to exclude sacramentalism.[37] Rather, as seen above, Patient considers baptism to be a means of grace; he simply finds ordinance terminology helpful in responding to the claim that water baptism is unnecessary, because God commanded water baptism.

---

34. Ibid., 156.
35. Ibid., 157.
36. Ibid., 158–59.

37. Patient does call baptism a "fundamental ordinance" in this work, but this does not mean he thinks it is absolutely necessary for salvation. He lists several fundamental ordinances, including "Prayer, Hearing [of the Word], Baptism and the Supper of the Lord, Thanksgiving, Contribution to the necessity of the Saints, and maintenance of an official Ministry according to the ability that God gives them," (ibid., 171).

Third, Patient explains baptism's role as a gracious means of confirming a believer's faith. This explanation comes in his treatment of Christ's Great Commission in which he responds to others who, according to Patient, ignore this passage and thereby distort their baptismal theology. The Great Commission texts in the Gospels show Christ's specific instructions for churches first to disciple people, second to baptize them, and third to teach them all of Christ's commands. Garner concludes from this order that Christ brings people into his church through both faith and baptism: "The Ordinance of baptism is to confirm our Regeneration, New birth, and Union with Christ in his death, burial and resurrection, *Rom. 6:3–5* with *Col. 2:12; Tit. 3:5*, and therefore is to be received but once, as a man is to be regenerated but once, and born but once; and changed from death to life but once. . . . [Baptism] is for planting them into Christ, signifying the confirmation or washing of Regeneration, and the new birth and Union with Christ the true stock and root from whence all spiritual growth is to be expected.[38]"

Christ brings people to faith and uses baptism as a means to confirm their faith, and baptism is a one-time confirmation that has lasting effects for the believer's spiritual growth. Like Garner, Patient clearly considers faith and repentance, rather than baptism, to be the means of salvation, while baptism is a means through which God confirms his acceptance of the believer: "For we do profess salvation, justification and the spiritual welfare to be meerly of the grace of God in Christ, and that by faith only; and that our obedience to Christ ought to be performed from a principle of Regeneration and union with Christ by faith; and answerable is our practice in that we dare not put any soul on obedience but from that root. For before we baptize any soul, we prove whether a true work of conversion be wrought in his heart or no; and whether he have union with Christ.[39]" Patient ties union with Christ to faith alone. He ties baptism to an act of obedience that only one's prior regeneration and union with Christ can produce. The Spirit graciously confirms the believer's regeneration by way of the obedient act of baptism, an obedient act full of promises, blessings, and duties.

Patient's major work on baptism begins with covenantal theology and ends with its relation to sacramental theology. This work is another

---

38. Ibid., 168.
39. Ibid., 175.

example of seventeenth-century Baptists using ordinance terminology for sacramental theology. Patient emphasizes the distinction between the old and new covenants in which the Spirit primarily characterizes the latter, so it has spiritual signs that require one's faith and repentance in order for them to have meaning. God ordained baptism as a solemn standing ordinance that confirms one's faith in him, so people enter into his church through both faith and baptism.

CONCLUSION

Keach, Garner, and Patient are three seventeenth-century Baptists that used ordinance terminology to refer to their sacramental theology. Moreover, they tied their covenant theology and/or covenant ecclesiology to their sacramentalism. Their covenant theology influenced their conceptions of how the Spirit works through baptism to confirm, or even seal, one's faith. Covenant theology also provided a framework in which Keach and Garner could speak of baptism as a mutual pledge, or promise, between the believer and God that carried along with it many blessings and obligations, including one's obligations to fellow Christians as one who has covenanted together with them.

These seventeenth-century Baptist models of covenantal sacramentalism favor Fowler's contemporary understanding of sacramentalism in which baptism mediates one's experience of salvation rather than Cross's understanding of sacramentalism in which baptism and faith both mediate salvation itself. These three seventeenth-century authors all clearly advocate that salvation, or justification, comes by grace through faith alone. Nonetheless, they all give baptism a critical role in the process of Christian initiation and sanctification as a spiritual means of grace in the life of the individual believer and in churches as a whole.

Unlike many contemporary sacramentalists, these seventeenth-century Baptists used covenant theology as a systematic framework within which to place their theology of baptism. As a result, these seventeenth-century Baptist sacramentalists presented a clearer and more coherent theology of baptism than most of their twentieth- and twenty-first-century successors. The formulation of the covenantal view of baptism in the next chapter aims to recover these seventeenth-century positions in order to enhance its biblical grounding, systematic coherence, and historical rootedness.

8

A Covenantal View of Baptism

THE COVENANTAL VIEW OF baptism states that the Spirit graciously uses baptism as a confirming sign and seal of a believer's initiation into the new covenant, thereby strengthening his or her consciousness of salvation. In other words, God, through his Spirit and community, confirms that he has covenanted with the believer in baptism. Likewise, in baptism, the believer consciously takes hold of God's covenant by receiving its blessings and by pledging to fulfill its duties—both of which are tied to God's covenant community, the church. This covenantal framework also allows a clear definition and explanation of a sacramental view of baptism that will aid its defense against common objections and give theological support to baptismal practices. Thus, the covenantal view may help end the search for the meaning of believer baptism.

THE COVENANTAL VIEW EXPLAINED

The Covenantal View's Biblical Grounding

Ordinance-only Baptists such as Moody question whether baptism signifies or seals one's initiation into the new covenant because Scripture does not explicitly present baptism in this way.[1] Passages that focus on the new covenant often stress its mediator and his work (Heb 7–10; 12:24), the role of the Lord's Supper in it (e.g., Luke 22:20), and the difference between the Spirit's regenerating and sanctifying work in it as opposed to the letter of the old covenant (e.g., Jer 31:31–34; 2 Cor 3:6). Likewise, NT

---

1. Moody, "American Baptist Sacramentalism?" 192–93. Cf. Lewis and Demarest, *Integrative Theology*, 3:286.

passages that speak of the sealing of believers, attribute it to the Spirit and one's faith (2 Cor 1:21–22; Eph 1:13–14; 4:30), not baptism.

Nevertheless, covenant theologians base their claim that baptism is the divinely ordained normative confirming sign and seal of initiation into the new covenant on other biblical passages. They refer to passages that liken baptism to the sign of initiation into the old covenant, circumcision, in which baptism now marks one as a member of Abraham's spiritual seed (e.g., Col 2:11–12; Rom 4:11–12; Gal 3:26–29). Baptist covenant theologians argue from these passages that one major difference between circumcision and baptism, and by extension the old and the new covenant communities, is that baptism is only for believers who have become Abraham's spiritual children through their own faith. For Baptists, only such believers constitute the new covenant community, although not all of them will confirm their faith through the normative means of believer baptism. Likewise, Baptists recognize that not all those whom they baptize upon profession of faith are in fact true members of the new covenant community with genuine saving faith, but they still strive to ensure that they baptize only professing believers in good faith. Despite the division between Reformed and Baptist covenant theologians over the meaning of circumcision, both use certain baptismal passages in similar ways. For example, both groups point to passages that identify baptism as either an instrumental means of signifying one's union with Christ (e.g., Rom 6:3–5; Gal 3:26–29) or as the divinely commanded practice that marks one's initiation into God's name and his people (e.g., Matt 28:19) for their shared claim that baptism is a sign of initiation into the new covenant. Such a claim has biblical grounding.

While there is uniformity among covenant theologians for calling baptism a sign of initiation into the new covenant, they are divided over whether it is also a seal. Reformed covenant theologians appeal to the same texts above that relate baptism to circumcision to support their claim that circumcision sealed the old covenant as baptism now does the new. Baptist covenant theologians, rejecting this connection between circumcision and baptism, are ambivalent about calling baptism a seal of the new covenant. In their debates with paedobaptists, many seventeenth-century Baptist covenant theologians denied that circumcision was a seal of the old covenant. Consistency in their position, along with NT texts such as Ephesians 1:13 and 4:30 that say the Spirit himself seals believers, prompted these Baptists to deny that baptism is a seal of the new covenant. This ambivalence continues today, because few contemporary Baptists use seal terminology for baptism.

Despite its near exclusive association with Reformed paedobaptist theology today, covenantal sacramentalists should comfortably refer to baptism as a seal of the new covenant, because God freely ordained baptism to be the normative means of professing faith in Christ and of signifying unity with him, his covenant, and his covenant community. Part of the Spirit's work through the sign of baptism is to confirm his seal to believers in order to give them greater consciousness of their initiation into the new covenant. To be sure, Scripture clearly says this seal comes to believers on account of their faith in the gospel, but Scripture also uses baptism as a shorthand way of referring to one's faith because of baptism's role in confirming the genuineness of that faith. Moreover, Scripture also links water baptism to the Spirit's work. Thus, believers can and should point to their baptism as the moment in which the Spirit claimed them in full and in which they claimed Christ in full. Baptism does not begin one's relationship with God, because faith accomplishes that. But Scripture does encourage believers to look back on their baptism for assurance that they have faithfully put on Christ, because the Spirit uses baptism as his confirming instrumental means of signifying and sealing their initiation into the new covenant. The covenantal view's claim that baptism is a confirming sign and seal of a believer's initiation into the new covenant is biblically grounded, and, unlike most other sacramental views, it also achieves a high level of systematic coherence that is able to answer objections.

The Covenantal View's Systematic Coherence

The covenantal view of baptism is a systematically coherent theology of the meaning of baptism, because it clearly explains the theological relationship between faith, baptism, conversion, and salvation. There are two major sacramentalist conceptions of this relationship: first is the view of Cross and others, which conceives of faith-baptism, or conversion-baptism, in such a way that baptism (understood as an expression of one's faith) is on an equal footing with faith as an instrumental means of conveying the benefits of salvation to the believer. Second is the view of Fowler and others, which conceives of baptism as God's normative way of mediating to the believer a confirming consciousness of salvation. In the first view, Cross ties baptism to conversion in such a way that the former (understood as an expression of one's faith) is a means of the Spirit's gracious converting, or regenerating, work. The Spirit conveys some of the salvific, or justifying, benefits of Christ to the believer through baptism. In the second view, the Spirit's gracious confirming or sealing work in and through baptism lies outside the realm of justification and in the realm of sanctification. In this view, faith is an instrumental means of one's justification in a way that baptism is not.

While it is possible that either view of sacramentalism is compatible with the covenantal view, the second view is preferable because it is clearer, it better coheres with Scripture, and it is more compatible with the variety of Baptist theology in general and Baptist covenant theology in particular than the first view. As a result, the second view avoids more objections than the first view does, making it a more appealing sacramental theology for Baptists.

Even though the second view is more appealing, chapter one showed how ordinance-only Baptists have still misunderstood it by claiming it entails baptismal regeneration and thereby undermines the doctrine of salvation by grace through faith in Christ alone. One source of this misunderstanding is that Baptists use the terms *grace*, *conversion*, and *salvation* in various ways. Many ordinance-only Baptists use these terms as synonyms to refer to God's salvific justifying work. For these Baptists, any sacramental conception of baptism that speaks of it as a means of grace makes too much of baptism by wrongly incorporating it into justification. In contrast, many Baptist sacramentalists use these same terms (*grace*, *conversion*, and *salvation*) to refer to overlapping aspects of God's broader past, present, and future work (not just his justifying work) in the lives of believers in which baptism rightly plays an important role in this process. For these Baptists, any conception of baptism that either minimizes or removes baptism's normative confirming role as part of God's gracious work in the lives of believers makes too little of baptism. Thus, it is important for sacramentalists to show their fellow Baptists that sacramentalism is a balanced view that makes neither too much nor too little of baptism, and the covenantal view can clearly show its balance through its systematic coherence and its use of baptism's interrelated covenantal roles.

Other sacramentalist accounts often lack the covenantal view's positive systematic presentation of what *is* baptism's role in the process of Christian initiation, using vague phrases such as "a high point" or "a decisive moment" to describe baptism's role in Christian initiation.[2] This vagueness opened such views to the charge that they made too much of baptism by making it absolutely necessary for salvation. While sacramentalists have successfully denied these charges by insisting that they do not make baptism absolutely necessary for salvation, even their defenses against this charge have continued to lack clear and coherent systematic theological presentations of what baptism positively means. In contrast, the covenantal view, as a product of both biblical and systematic theology, provides a clear and coherent account of the meaning of baptism, expressed chiefly through its systematic account of baptism's covenantal roles.

The Covenantal Roles of Baptism

The first covenantal role of baptism is that God designed baptism as a one-time event, or seal, that confirms initiation into his new covenant, carrying with it lasting effects for the individual believer's life. In light of this role, NT authors often appeal to baptism as a shorthand way of referring to the complete process of Christian initiation for good reason. While baptism does not permanently alter people's appearances like circumcision did, God continually evokes people's baptisms through their everyday use of water. Thus, believers may often recall their baptisms through their everyday life, although it was a one-time event. In this way, baptism is a fitting sign for confirming a believer's initiation into the new covenant, and this one-time confirmation of initiation simultaneously marks one's continual belonging in the covenant. Just as Christ died, was buried, and was raised only once to complete his mediation of the new covenant, so also a believer is baptized only once to confirm his or her initiation into the new covenant. Moreover, just as Christ's mediation of the new covenant permanently changed his life and the lives of others, so also a believer's baptism permanently signifies the presence of Christ's lasting power in his or her life—a power from which a believer draws from in times of trial and need. This covenantal role explains further Scripture's claims that baptism has marked and still marks that believers have clothed themselves with Christ (Gal 3:26–27), that they have been buried and raised with Christ (Rom 6:3–5), and that they have pledged their consciences to Christ (1 Pet 3:21). As a one-time decision that marks

---

2. *Believing and Being Baptized*, sec. 8; and Kidd (ed.), *Something to Declare*, 45.

A Covenantal View of Baptism

a believer's pledge to Christ, the believer plays an active role in his or her baptism. This is not to say that believers have an active role in designing the meaning of baptism or even that they have an active role in initiating baptism, because its second covenantal role is how God works in it through his covenant community.

The second covenantal role of baptism is that God designed it to be performed only by representatives of his covenant community because it also marks initiation of a believer's one-time union with it, carrying lasting effects for the community as a whole. The Great Commission charges God's people to make disciples, baptizing them in the threefold name of God, and then teaching them to obey the Lord's commands (Matt 28:19–20). While the individual believer makes an active decision to be baptized, the covenant community plays the primary human role in this process.[3] Individual believers cannot baptize themselves, because baptism confirms the covenant community's reception, acceptance, and support of its newest member. In baptism, believers profess their renouncement of the Devil and all his ways and their inclusion in God's covenant as a member of his covenant community with its blessings and obligations. The former pronouncement is rooted in the baptismal liturgy of the early church,[4] and the latter pronouncement is rooted in early Baptist baptismal theology.[5] This second covenantal role reveals why God ordained that baptism, rather than praying the sinner's prayer or any other individual act, be the confirming sign of a believer's initiation into God's covenant community. God designed baptism in such a way that his Spirit works through his covenant community to confirm one's initiation into his covenant. Likewise, in baptism the believer professes faith in God in front of many witnesses by pledging to take on God's covenant blessings and obligations. This role demonstrates how baptism is a mutual pledge between God, speaking through his community, and the individual, speaking to God and to his covenant community, that mutually signifies and seals confirmation of the relationship between the two parties that began at the moment of faith. Churches should explain to new believers that they are confirming their acceptance of not only God's new covenant, but also the

---

3. Cf. Haymes, "Baptism: A Question," 125–30.

4. Whitaker's English translations of early church baptismal liturgies is a helpful resource for Baptists who wish to root their baptismal services in the Church's Great Tradition (*Documents of the Baptismal Liturgy*). Cf. Haymes, "Baptism as a Political Act."

5. One example is Garner, *Treatise of Baptisme*, 15

local church's covenant in baptism. Catechesis and baptismal preparation classes are helpful tools churches may use to make this clear to new believers and to current members. Such pre-baptismal preparation should also include a discussion of the church's covenant, which explains the church's pledge to the new believer as well as his or her pledge to the church.

God confirms a believer's initiation into and communion with the past, present, and future members of his one people through the local church that represents this greater community. Thus, the local church's decision to baptize a believer represents God's and his one people's reception, acceptance, and support of the believer. Churches should make their representative role clear to prospective baptizands during pre-baptismal preparation, because it gives more depth to the meaning of baptism by connecting believers to God's one people. Baptism marks confirmation that one is now part of God's universal church, and it assures believers that they are part of the communion of the saints. These are more reasons why Scripture uses baptism to represent the process of Christian initiation, thereby encouraging believers to recall their baptism in times of trial and need.

THE COVENANTAL VIEW COMPARED

Moody's Sacred Baptism

Moody contributes to the search for the meaning of believer baptism by presenting a helpful example of contemporary ordinance-only Baptist theology with his "sacred theology of baptism." A comparison of his view with the covenantal view will reveal both the similarities and differences between ordinance-only Baptists and covenantal sacramentalists today.

Moody begins his presentation of a sacred theology of baptism by discussing terms. He prefers *ordinance* to *sacrament* because he thinks it is easier to add to rather than empty out the meaning of a term. He adds sacredness to the meaning of the term *ordinance* because he wants to emphasize that baptism is a holy rite of worship in which believers pledge themselves to obey God's holy standards. He rejects *sacrament* because he claims North American Baptists think that anything with a "slight sacramental overtone would serve to promote something heretical without fail."[6] The heresy he has in mind is a denial of the doctrine of salvation

---

6. Moody, "American Baptist Sacramentalism?" 191.

by grace through faith in Christ alone. He also dismisses the sacramental claim that baptism is a seal of the new covenant because he thinks this claim stems from the questionable ecumenical motives of sacramentalists. Although he opposes sacramental concepts and terminology, he hopes to identify some middle ground between sacramentalism and the ordinance-only positions by enhancing the latter with his sacred theology of baptism. He explains his view by exploring the roles of time, sign, the Holy Spirit, and humanity in baptism.

Regarding the proper timing of baptism, Moody argues that baptism must come after one's justification, or conversion (ordinance-only Baptists use the two terms synonymously), is complete in order for it to be a confirming sign. Moody considers baptism's confirming work to be largely catechetical because it facilitates the testing of the validity of one's faith and gives the church community an opportunity to accept the baptizand as a new member. Baptism is neither part of one's conversion nor is it a special means of grace in the life of the believer. Rather, "baptism benefits the baptizand in the uniqueness of its opportunity to psychologically, relationally, and existentially elicit a deeper faith through obedience to Christ's command and the worship of the Church. . . . A deeper awareness of God's presence, promises, and purposes comes by way of Baptism's function as a sign."[7] Moody thinks God extends this deeper awareness that comes through baptism to the observing congregation as well, because in baptism they see a dramatic portrayal of the gospel itself. For Moody, baptism acts as a sign in this portrayal.

Regarding the role of sign in baptism, Moody discusses baptism's dramatic depiction of one's identification with Christ's death, burial, and resurrection by way of immersion into water. Ordinance-only Baptists do not deny either baptism's symbolic meaning or its power for believers as a visible drama of the gospel of Christ that impacts both the baptizand and the observing congregation. Baptism's symbolism celebrates the relationship between God and his children, and God uses baptism as a visible demonstration of his word. Baptism is a powerful demonstration because it appeals to everyone's universal experiences of bathing to evoke the truths of the gospel. Moody does not want to make baptism a special means of grace because that would undermine God's "immanent presence" in the believer's life "that turns all activities, religious or not,

---

7. Ibid., 207.

into potentially sacred moments."[8] Thus, baptism has no unique power of its own, for it is powerful "in exactly the same way that any part of the Church's proclamation is powerful."[9] However, it is a unique symbol that portrays what it symbolizes, namely one's identification with Christ and his work. This unique symbol gives an opportunity to all who are involved in it to testify, to confirm, and to deepen their faith.[10] In other words, baptism is a unique opportunity for God to express his power—the same power he expresses elsewhere in the everyday life and worship of his people. For Moody, this is not to say that God has no special purposes in baptism, as he acknowledges the Spirit plays an important role.

Regarding the Holy Spirit's role in baptism, Moody argues that the Spirit is the one who gives baptism its power. Moody thinks both sacramentalists and ordinance-only Baptists consider baptism to be a powerful event through which the Spirit influences people's lives.[11] Moody argues that the Spirit strengthens one's faith through baptism because it is an act of obedience, and "obedience always increases faith."[12] The Spirit specifically strengthens the faith of the baptizand and of the community through baptism and other rites in "psychological terms. . . . The community psychologically, not ontologically, maintains and transmits the constitutive vision of God's kingdom through these religious rites. The baptizand receives a deeper consciousness of his or her kingdom identity."[13] Thus, the Spirit uses baptism as a unique "identity conveying opportunity" for the baptizand and the community.[14] According to Moody, God designed baptism to be a unique means of the Spirit's sanctifying work, because "in Baptism, the Holy Spirit is actively setting apart the human candidate for a progressively sanctified life of obedience and ministry within God's Kingdom of priests."[15] While God has a unique purpose in baptism, Moody also wants to stress the baptizand's own purpose in the rite.

Regarding the role of the baptizand in baptism, Moody claims that sacramentalists overemphasize God's role in baptism by making

8. Ibid., 211.
9. Ibid., 213.
10. Ibid.
11. Ibid., 215.
12. Ibid., 216. Cf. Grenz, "Baptism and the Lord's Supper," 89–90.
13. Moody, "American Baptist Sacramentalism?" 216–17.
14. Ibid., 217.
15. Ibid., 218–19.

the baptizand a mere passive recipient in the rite. In contrast, Moody claims the ordinance-only position emphasizes the baptizand's active agency in baptism, which is his or her surrendering act of worship to God. Ordinance-only Baptists depict baptism as an extension of believers' conscious decisions to profess faith in the gospel, to identify themselves with God and his people, and to re-enact their participation in God's economy of salvation in a dramatic way. According to Moody, Baptists should use only this understanding of baptism when they speak of it as a proof of one's faith, because it does not testify to "the reality of grace's transmission."[16] Moody thinks there are other ways for believers to testify to the validity of their faith, but God has commanded baptism to be one of those ways. His command is enough of a reason for Baptists to continue to respect baptism as a sacred rite. They should not respond to his command by formulating overly sophisticated theologies of baptism such as sacramentalism.

As two contemporary theologies of baptism, both the covenantal view and Moody's sacred theology of baptism address some of the same aspects of baptism: namely, its confirming role to the individual believer, its effects on the community, and the baptizand's active agency in it. Comparing the similarities and differences between Moody's sacred theology of baptism and the covenantal view in these three aspects of baptism will show how the covenantal view better meets some of the goals of ordinance-only Baptist views.

The first aspect of baptism is its confirming role to the individual believer, and both views consider baptism to be a confirming sign that takes place after one's justification is complete. Moody wants to separate baptism from justification because he considers baptism to have a confirming work that strengthens a relationship that already began at faith. Likewise, the covenantal view also separates baptism's confirming work from a believer's justification. The covenantal view argues that God graciously confirms a believer's conscious experience of salvation and union to Christ (extended to his body, the church) through baptism, but baptism does not convey Christ's justifying benefits to the believer. In this way, both Moody's view and the covenantal view clearly affirm the doctrine of salvation by grace through faith in Christ alone and clearly avoid baptismal regeneration.

16. Ibid., 223.

The contrast between Moody's view and the covenantal view here is that Moody further separates baptism from its rightful place as the normative confirming sign and seal of initiation into God's new covenant and his covenant community, while the covenantal view does not. As a result, Moody considers baptism to be a special celebration of an already-completed process of Christian initiation. In contrast, the covenantal view presents baptism as the divinely ordained normative confirming sign and seal of initiation into God's new covenant and his covenant community, without which the normative process of Christian initiation is incomplete. Thus, the covenantal view rightly accounts for biblical language that uses baptism as a shorthand way of referring to the entire process of Christian initiation—a process that has lasting effects on both the individual believer and the covenant community as a whole. Moody's view does not adequately account for this biblical language. Instead, he tries to heighten baptism's significance by calling it a sacred, holy, and special opportunity for the believer, but this language is vague and somewhat hollow when compared to how the NT authors describe baptism's significance. It seems that Moody's desire to avoid making too much of baptism has led him to make too little of it instead. In contrast, the covenantal view gives baptism a normative role in the process of Christian initiation, but not one in justification.

The second aspect of baptism to consider is its effect on the church community. Both views aim to elevate the community's role in baptism. Moody does this in two major ways: first, he encourages churches to take baptism seriously as their verification of the validity of the baptizand's faith. Verification will tell the individual believer that the community accepts and supports him or her. Second, Moody argues that the community is also a recipient of the Spirit's ministry through baptism's symbolism and message. Likewise, the covenantal view also emphasizes the church community's role in baptism in two ways: first, it presents baptism as the normative instrumental means of confirming the baptizand's union with God's covenant community through which both parties mutually agree to covenant with one another. Second, the covenantal view considers baptism to be a gracious means of visibly portraying God's covenant blessings and obligations to the members of the observing community, thereby strengthening their faith. The contrast between Moody's sacred theology and the covenantal view here is that the latter's systematic framework integrates the community itself into its understanding

A Covenantal View of Baptism

of baptism, while Moody's view lists a few communal implications for a theology of baptism that is geared toward the individual being baptized. If ordinance-only Baptists desire to emphasize the community's role in baptism, they should consider adopting the covenantal view because it makes the covenant community itself an agent in baptism, clearly delineating its role therein.

The third aspect of baptism is the baptizand's active role in baptism, which both views emphasize. Moody considers baptism to be an extension of the baptizand's profession of faith in Christ as his or her sacred and faithful act of worship. Through baptism, the baptizand consciously decides to join God's community and portray God's gracious work in his or her life. Moody thinks this is the only way in which one can speak of baptism as a proof of faith. Likewise, the covenantal view also emphasizes the baptizand's active role in baptism, but in a greater way than Moody. In the covenantal view, the baptizand actively takes on God's covenant, confirming his or her faith in the gospel. This taking on of God's covenant includes uniting with God's covenant community by way of covenanting with it. As mentioned in the above explanation, the covenantal view considers baptism to be a mutual pledge between the baptizand and God, who is speaking through his community. In light of the covenantal view's emphasis of the baptizand's own agency in baptism, Moody is wrong to claim that all sacramental theologies emphasize God's role in baptism at the expense of the baptizand. In contrast, the covenantal view gives systematic coherence to the baptizand's active role in baptism, while Moody's view in this area appears to be disjointed. If ordinance-only Baptists want to emphasize the baptizand's active agency in baptism, then the covenantal view provides a clear and coherent framework for that emphasis.

Moody's sacred theology of baptism is one example of a promising trend among ordinance-only Baptists to provide a positive theology of baptism. His view of baptism is closer to some sacramental views than he may think, because he often lumps all sacramental views together. He uses a broad-brush to paint all sacramental theologies as improper Baptist views that are more akin to either Lutheran or Churches of Christ baptismal positions than genuine Baptist traditions. However, this book has so far argued that he failed to make a compelling case that sacramentalism is not a genuine Baptist view and that not all sacramentalist views are the same. Thus, he has overstated the differences between covenantal sacramentalism and his own sacred theology of baptism. Both views share many of the same elements, but there are also important differences between them that allow the covenantal view to be more appealing for Baptists, perhaps even for ordinance-only Baptists. Fellow sacramentalists should already be somewhat disposed to the covenantal view, and the next section will compare it with Cross's sacramental view of faith-baptism to see which view is more appealing for them.

Cross's Faith-Baptism

There are roughly two understandings of baptism's meaning among sacramentalists. One view, shared by Cross and others, holds to faith-baptism, in which baptism (understood as one's expression of faith) is rightly part of the conversion process as a proper response to the gospel. The Spirit normatively conveys some of Christ's benefits, namely remission of sins and the gift of the Spirit, to the believer through baptism. Another view, shared by Fowler and covenantal sacramentalists, holds to a different understanding of baptism's meaning, in which the Spirit normatively confirms one's consciousness of salvation (including remission of sins and the gift of the Spirit) through baptism, but it is not part of God's justifying work.

While other sacramentalists, such as Alec Gilmore, espouse the first broad understanding above, Cross goes further than most of them by arguing that faith-baptism is a sort of baptismal regeneration, because God uses baptism as a means of his regenerating work on those who have already professed faith.[17] Cross goes further than most other sacramentalists by also claiming that God mysteriously uses many elements in the conversion process, including faith and baptism, so theologians should not superimpose some proper ordering of these elements. Nonetheless, Cross does stress the role of faith in conversion and insists that baptism is tied to faith in such a way that baptism is for believers alone.

Previous chapters have critiqued Cross's view in several ways. Chapter 4 critiqued Cross for letting the results of biblical theology constitute his answer to a systematic issue, namely the proper understanding of the relationship between faith, baptism, and conversion. Such results underdetermined Cross's case for faith-baptism as opposed to other sacramentalist views. These results also rendered his view to be quite vague

---

17. Cross, "Baptismal Regeneration," 149–74. Cf. Gilmore, *Baptism and Christian Unity*, 55–56.

in many areas, leaving it vulnerable to objections that it entails baptismal regeneration and makes too much of baptism. Cross also fails to demonstrate that Scripture presents baptism as an important element of conversion, or justification, alongside of faith. Once again the biblical data Cross uses underdetermine his conclusion, and Cross does not deal with the biblical data that support other sacramentalist views in which baptism is a normative part of the process of Christian initiation rather than justification. Moreover, Cross's view does not accurately reflect seventeenth-century Baptist sacramentalism, so his view is more innovative than other sacramental views such as the covenantal view. In light of these critiques, the covenantal view better meets biblical, systematic, and historical objections than Cross's faith-baptism.

On top of these considerations, the covenantal view also emphasizes the communal aspects of baptism more than Cross's view does. Like other sacramentalists, Cross wants to emphasize the communal aspects of baptism, but his view does not incorporate covenant theology in any significant way. Instead, Cross's systematic framework for baptism is murky, consisting of an understanding of an individual's conversion as a process with many elements, but there is little to nothing in his works about how baptism relates to the church community as a whole. Thus, Cross has a rather individualistic sacramental theology of baptism in which baptism does much for God's relationship with an individual believer but little for his or her relationship with the church. In contrast, the covenantal view enhances a sacramental theology of baptism by providing a framework within which one can clearly explain baptism's roles for both the baptizand and the covenant community. If Cross and other sacramentalists wish to stress baptism's communal aspects, then they should consider the benefits of the covenantal view in this area.

The covenantal view has all the strengths of Cross's view with fewer weaknesses. The covenantal view meets objections by being biblically grounded and systematically coherent, while Cross's view often exacerbates objections by toying with the idea of baptismal regeneration and tying faith to baptism in such a way that they are nearly equal parts of an individual's response to the gospel call. While Cross may successfully keep the variety of the biblical witness about the meaning of baptism intact, he pays the price for it by insisting that baptism is a normative part of justification. For these reasons, Baptists who are already disposed to sacramentalism should consider the covenantal view to be more appealing than Cross's faith-baptism. A look at how Baptists can apply the covenantal view to knotty issues in baptismal theology and practice will also help its case among sacramentalists and ordinance-only Baptists alike.

THE COVENANTAL VIEW APPLIED

Baptism and Church Membership

Throughout their history Baptists have differed over the proper understanding of the relationship between baptism and church membership. Accounts vary from those that do not consider baptism to be even a church ordinance, because baptism is an absolutely necessary prerequisite for joining a church, to those that appeal to ecumenical concerns to justify allowing unbaptized believers to join Baptist churches. The major reason for this variety in the Baptist tradition is that there is a logical movement from one's theology of the meaning of baptism to its relation to church membership. In other words, there will be as many different understandings of the relationship between baptism and church membership as there are different meanings of baptism itself. The failure of Baptists to present a positive theology of the meaning of baptism exacerbates this issue as well as the other two practical issues below. While any extended positive reflection on the meaning of baptism would help address this issue in some degree or another, the covenantal view has many benefits that apply to this practical area of concern.

The covenantal view builds on historical Baptist views that do not separate the act of baptism from a new believer's act of covenanting with a church, arguing that baptism itself is the means through which the church covenants with, or adds into membership, new believers. Baptism is a mutual pledge between God, speaking through the covenant community, and the baptizand who is confirming that he or she is taking on God's new covenant and by extension covenanting together with God's covenant community. Thus, a church should not baptize people who do not intend to covenant together with them or any other local church. A church should explain to prospective baptizands that the act of baptism binds them to the one people of God expressed in that particular local body. This binding includes many blessings and obligations as expressed through the terms of church membership. Specifics of these terms will vary from church to church, but they all should include pledges to gather together regularly for prayer and worship, to break bread together, to give some of their money and possessions, and to be subject to church discipline. Linking baptism to church covenants does not mean that churches should abolish the practice of having elders who represent the congregation and new members, whether newly baptized or not, sign a written copy of the church covenant. Rather, the covenantal view gives baptism a confirming role as the baptizand's pledge to unite with God's people, the church. Such a pledge carries its own blessings and obligations, including church membership.

In light of baptism's covenantal roles, churches should encourage people to consider their baptism, a much more powerful pledge than signing a piece of paper, in times of trial and need. God ordained baptism as a fitting normative means of confirming one's salvation for several reasons, including its symbolic portrayal of the gospel, its evocative use of water that prompts believers to recall their baptisms when they bathe, and its use of God's community to assure his reception of a new believer. For these reasons, baptism has more to offer for one's assurance of salvation than more common assurances such as praying the sinner's prayer or church membership without baptism. That is one reason why Scripture repeatedly uses baptism as a shorthand way of referring to the whole process of Christian initiation. Moreover, the covenantal blessings and obligations attached to baptism are the basis of a healthy understanding of what it means to be a member of a church, and baptism is the divinely ordained and fitting means through which a new believer and a church confirm initiation of their covenant with one another. The duties of church membership are an important part of the next practical issue, the proper age at which to baptize youth.

Baptism and Youth

North American Baptists typically baptize youth in their churches at a younger age than their British counterparts, and the average age for North American Baptist baptisms has been declining for the past two centuries.[18] While there are many factors for these geographical and chronological trends, among them is the absence of a positive theology of baptism that would suggest the proper age at which to baptize youth. In the place of such theology, many Baptist church leaders either arbitrarily set minimum ages at which to baptize youth, or, even worse, leave it up to

---

18. Cross, *Baptism and the Baptists*, 392–95.

the sole discretion of the young baptizand's parents. Some churches strive to ensure that these young believers know the gospel by having them take pre-baptism classes before baptizing them, but the murky meaning of baptism that underlies this practice is one in which baptism reflects a young person's knowledge of the gospel rather than his or her capacity and willingness to take on the obligations of being a newly confirmed disciple within God's covenant community. The covenantal view's understanding of the meaning of baptism has natural implications for this issue.

As a sacramental view, the covenantal view considers baptism to be a powerful means of grace through which the Spirit confirms one's faith, but it does not consider baptism to be a necessary or even a normative part of justification itself like some other sacramental views seem to suggest. Such views might encourage parents to rush the baptisms of young children who have just made a profession of faith on account of baptism's vital role in justification. In contrast, the covenantal view emphasizes baptism's covenantal role of confirming one's faith, and the lasting effects of this role increases as the capacities of the person who is baptized also increases. In other words, the more mature a person is at the time of baptism, the better he or she can reflect on, appreciate, and understand the meaning of his or her baptism. The covenantal view also conceives of baptism as one's own pledge to take on God's covenant and unite with his covenant community as a full member who will receive its blessings and share in its duties. Such an understanding of baptism itself nearly precludes young children from participating in it until they are mature enough to grasp such things.

The covenantal view's link between baptism and church membership requires the church to baptize only someone who can clearly understand and pledge to the blessings and obligations of being a member of God's covenant community. Although God may graciously minister to young children in various ways, including baptism, these children cannot properly undergo or appreciate the covenantal view of baptism until they are more mature. Thus, it is preferable to withhold baptism from them until they reach an age of greater maturity. This practice would maximize baptism's covenantal roles and strengthen its benefits as a confirming sign to the believer. It is difficult to apprehend one's baptism as his or her own decision to take hold of God's covenant, to profess renouncement of the devil and all his ways, and to pledge to become a full member of God's covenant community by sharing in its duties, when that baptism was performed at a very young age.

While the covenantal view has many applications for the proper age at which to baptize youth, it cannot pinpoint that age for everyone. A practical rule for churches would be to abstain from baptizing youth until they at least reach the age of thirteen, with possible exceptions for exceptional youth. At this age they are able to make a conscious decision to take hold of God's covenant along with its duties, including service and giving. Thus, it is no coincidence that this age mirrors those of the confirmation rites of other Christian traditions. This age is just a suggestion, so pastoral discretion is key, especially in cases of people whose capacities may never reach full maturity this side of the resurrection. For most people, though, the covenantal view implies that one should not be baptized until he or she is mature enough to understand the obligations of being a full member of the covenant community. To be sure, baptism is the commencement rather than the consummation of a believer's life as a confirmed disciple, so pastors should encourage adolescents, teenagers, and adults to consider baptism as a powerful tool in their ongoing spiritual formation. One benefit the covenantal view offers in this area that also applies to the next section is that it would decrease the number of Baptists who, after being baptized as young believers, later request to be rebaptized under the conviction that they were not true believers at the time of their former baptism.

Baptism and Rebaptism

Baptist churches rebaptize prospective members for various reasons, and some reasons are better than others. Landmarkist factions of North American Baptists stress the "proper" administration of baptism so much so that they rebaptize prospective members who received believer baptism from the "wrong" kind of church. Other Baptists stress the proper mode of baptism, immersion, to the point of denying that there are valid believer baptisms that use other modes such as pouring. As a result, these Baptists reject the validity of many North American Anabaptists who only practice believer baptism by immersion into running water, so they practice believer baptism by pouring during the winter months. Many North American Baptists will rebaptize people who were previously baptized as believers but who now request rebaptism under the conviction that they were not truly believers at the time of their former baptism. Almost all North American Baptists will rebaptize prospective members who were baptized as infants and now want to join a Baptist church, because Baptists by and large have not and do not consider infant baptism to be valid, even though that person is a believer in the gospel. However, there is a growing minority among some British and even North American Baptists that does not rebaptize prospective members who were baptized as infants as long as such people later confirmed their faith through the proper means within their former Christian traditions. Some of these Baptists will even refuse to rebaptize such prospective members who conscientiously request rebaptism. What ties these disparate practices together is that they all stem from some understanding of the meaning of baptism, so this section will discuss how the covenantal view of baptism applies to this issue.

The covenantal view of baptism insists on an asymmetrical relationship between faith and baptism, so the meaning of baptism as a confirming sign and seal of initiation into God's new covenant and into his covenant community requires the baptizand to be a believer. This theology of the meaning of baptism links the validity of baptism to the proper subject alone, believers, rather than the proper mode or administrator. Therefore, Baptists should rebaptize only prospective members who were not baptized as believers. While baptism by immersion is important for naturally portraying baptism's rich symbolism, the covenantal view allows for valid, but irregular modes of believer baptism.

As for those who were previously baptized as believers, but now request rebaptism under the conviction that they were not truly believers at the time of their former baptism, the covenantal view encourages them to consider their former baptism to be God's means of confirming their faith in him. Instead of rebaptizing such people, pastors can suggest that they renew their baptismal vows during the next baptismal service. They can even present a public profession of faith before the church at this time. This is a reasonable pastoral response to their request for rebaptism that still honors the covenantal meaning of baptism along with its initial and lasting effects.

As for prospective members who were baptized as infants, the covenantal view discourages pastors from accepting one's infant baptism and subsequent confirmation in another Christian tradition to be valid for his or her membership in a Baptist church. Baptists who argue for accepting infant baptism for Baptist church membership usually

A Covenantal View of Baptism

reason that baptism can either precede or follow faith in the process of Christian initiation, even though they think God commanded that faith should normatively precede baptism. While they consider a reversal of the normative ordering of faith and baptism to be somewhat innocuous for Baptist ecclesiology, in reality they are emptying believer baptism of its very meaning for Baptists and undermining the chief distinguishing mark of Baptist churches. Baptists could construct a positive theology of baptism that shows how infant and believer baptism share the same meaning, but the covenantal view does no such thing. It is a theology of believer baptism whose definition of baptism precludes the validity of infant baptism for one's membership in a Baptist church. While there are diverse meanings of baptism both inside and outside the Baptist tradition, the basis for accepting a baptism as valid for the covenantal view is if it is believer baptism. Thus, the subject of baptism is what matters (not the meaning, mode, or administrator) regarding the proper grounds on which to rebaptize.

That being said, there is a distinction between making baptism absolutely necessary for the confirmation of anyone's Christian initiation and making it the divinely ordained normative means of confirming one's Christian initiation in the Baptist tradition. The covenantal view uses the latter understanding, so it encourages Baptists to strive to obey this norm in their own churches by insisting that their membership includes only those who have been baptized as believers. However, this insistence on obedience to the norm of believer baptism does not extend to matters outside things directly related to church membership such as baptism.[19] Thus, individual Baptists and Baptist churches alike should continue to worship and to work together with individuals from other Christian traditions and their churches. Baptists must recognize that such individuals are also true believers who have been confirmed by their own respective

---

19. There is variety among Baptists regarding what directly relates to church membership. For example, some Baptists hold to "closed communion," in which one is only allowed to partake of the Lord's Supper in a particular local church if he or she is a member of that church. For these Baptists, this position is a matter of proper church order, so it does not imply that others are not genuine believers. Other Baptists hold to "open communion," in which church membership is not related to who partakes of the Lord's Supper. Rather, anyone who believes in the gospel of Jesus Christ is welcome to join them in partaking of the Lord's Supper. The covenantal view of baptism is compatible with either position.

churches, which are true churches, but ecumenical relations do not have to be grounded in belief in a common water baptism.

Nonetheless, no matter how much Baptist covenantal sacramentalists qualify it, their view has the unsavory implication that infant baptism is not really baptism. To be sure, this stance strains ecumenical dialogue and relations between Baptists and paedobaptist Christian traditions. While Baptists reject the validity of infant baptism for membership in their churches, other Christian traditions have similar stances with similar unsavory implications for their own ecumenical relations. For example, if an unmarried male ordained Baptist minister becomes convicted to convert to Roman Catholicism or Eastern Orthodoxy and then minister as one of their priests, he would be required to be reordained first. According to the theology of the priesthood in these Christian traditions, Baptist ordination is not really ordination. Of course, a major difference between the baptismal issue and the priesthood issue is that Ephesians 4:5 does not mention the priesthood, so there are no calls to base visible church unity on a common priesthood as there are for a common water baptism. Baptists want to affirm a common baptism in a sense that does not require them to accept the validity of infant baptism. They point to a sense of "one baptism" in which every believer's same faith in the same gospel of Christ counts for his or her spiritual baptism, even though Paul was referring to water baptism as the sign that points to one's acceptance of the gospel of Christ in this passage. All who have faith in Christ share this baptism, whether they were ever baptized with water or not. On the one hand this stance strains Baptist relations with paedobaptist Christian traditions, but on the other hand it enhances Baptist relations with other traditions that do not practice water baptism at all, such as the Society of Friends and the Salvation Army.[20] In light of Baptist baptismal theology and the theology of these other traditions that do not baptize with water, all Christian traditions should seek visible unity with one another on grounds that are more inclusive than the affirmation of a common water baptism.

CONCLUSION

Unlike other ordinance-only and sacramental accounts, such as Moody's and Cross's, the covenantal view goes beyond establishing biblical

---

20. Ellis, *Together on the Way*, 22.

grounding and systematic coherence in defense of its position to applying helpful theological support to problem areas in current Baptist baptismal practice. As a result, the covenantal view shares the strengths of other theologies of baptism while answering objections and influencing practical concerns better than these other views. These reasons, along with its rootedness in the Baptist tradition, make the covenantal view more appealing to Baptists than alternatives.

9

Beyond the Waters of Promise

PART OF THE BAPTIST identity is its insistence on baptizing disciples alone, but beyond that insistence Baptists have for centuries searched for what believer baptism means for both the disciple and Baptist churches. The covenantal view builds on that search by transforming the waters of baptism into waters of promise between God, his covenant community, and the baptizand. This book has argued that the covenantal view is biblically grounded, systematically coherent, historically rooted, and practically beneficial. As a result, it meets the most common objections to sacramentalism and bridges the gap between sacramentalists and ordinance-only Baptists while allowing for variety within the Baptist tradition in areas such as soteriology. This book gave a multi-faceted defense of the covenantal view, and further research could help bolster its conclusions.

Needed historical research includes a fuller analysis of the covenant and sacramental (extended to the Lord's Supper) theologies of seventeenth- and eighteenth-century Baptists. While this book drew from a handful of seventeenth-century Baptists as representatives of some of the theological trends of their day, it did not discuss historical theology of the Lord's Supper. Neither did it adequately present the full variety of positions in the primary sources from this period. Rather, this book operated from the lowest common denominator of all Baptist covenant theologies, so it did not go into great detail in researching the various views within the Baptist tradition on areas related to covenant theology such as eschatology and moral theology. Such research would add to the current understanding of the Baptist tradition and provide even more historical depth to the covenantal view.

Another important area of historical research is an analysis of the historical factors for the eclipse of British and North American Baptist covenant and sacramental theology in the late eighteenth and nineteenth centuries. This book addressed the content of historic and contemporary Baptist covenant and sacramental theology without exploring the various factors for the eclipse of this theology that began more than two centuries ago in Great Britain and North America. An analysis of these factors could explain why British Baptists are more prone to accept sacramentalism than are North American Baptists today.

More theological research is also needed that will compare the covenantal view with the baptismal theologies of other Christian traditions, including further implications of the covenantal view for ecumenical dialogue. While the covenantal view and Reformed sacramental theology share certain covenantal elements, there are also important differences to explore. The covenantal view has even less in common with the baptismal theologies of other Christian traditions, so comparing these positions with one another would be valuable in helping Baptists understand the meaning, benefits, and weaknesses of the covenantal view.

Another area of theological research that could expand the case for the covenantal view is the relationship between covenantal sacramentalism and the theologies of other sacraments such as the Lord's Supper, the preaching of the Word, and the laying on of hands both historically in the Baptist tradition and today. There is much Baptist literature on the Lord's Supper that discusses it from both sacramental and ordinance-only points of view, but there is no work that offers a covenantal view of the Lord's Supper. It would be helpful to see if a covenantal framework could also enhance Baptist theology of the Lord's Supper. A defense of a covenantal view of the Lord's Supper could even include the same elements as that of baptism allowing for each view to reinforce the other.

Lastly, this book addressed some common misconceptions about Baptist covenant theology and Baptist sacramental theology. It has defended the covenantal view as the most appealing baptismal theology for Baptists on the basis of its biblical, theological, historical, and practical support. This is a strong claim, but it should not be confused with the even stronger claim that believer baptism is more appealing than infant baptism. This book did not directly address or contribute to the debate between credobaptists and paedobaptists on the proper subjects of baptism. Rather, it offered a Baptist solution to a Baptist problem. As a result, it is intended primarily for Baptists who are already convinced of the merits of believer baptism. It is not intended to be a polemical attack on paedobaptist theology.

Christians from other traditions may find this book helpful in raising and explaining some problems and issues within Baptist theology. They may also find it helpful in comparing their own baptismal theologies with those of the Baptists. Such comparisons can only aid ongoing ecumenical dialogue in which each Christian tradition holds to that which makes it unique with the posture of receiving from other traditions that which makes them unique. More than anything else, a rejection of infant baptism is what makes Baptists unique, and this book is intended to help Baptists understand and appreciate the benefits of their baptismal stance for their own tradition—only then can they have clear reasons to hold onto it and show others how it has enriched their faith, worship, and spiritual formation.

In baptism God bestows a promise to his people who, in turn, promise to God and to each other to strive to be all that he calls his people to be both now and in his future kingdom. Much awaits us beyond the waters of promise.

Bibliography

Akin, Daniel L. "The Meaning of Baptism." In *Restoring Integrity in Baptist Churches*, edited by Thomas White, Jason G. Duesing, and Malcolm B. Yarnell III, 63–80. Grand Rapids: Kregel, 2008.
Ascol, Thomas Kennedy. "The Doctrine of Grace: A Critical Analysis of Federalism in the Theologies of John Gill and Andrew Fuller." PhD diss., Southwestern Baptist Theological Seminary, 1989.
Baker, J. Wayne. *Heinrich Bullinger and the Covenant: The Other Reformed Tradition.* Athens, OH: Ohio University Press, 1980.
———. "Heinrich Bullinger, the Covenant, and the Reformed Tradition in Retrospect." *The Sixteenth Century Journal* 29 (1998) 359–76.
Baker, William R., ed. *Evangelicalism and the Stone-Campbell Movement.* Downers Grove, IL: InterVarsity, 2002.
Ball, John. *A Treatise of the Covenant of Grace: wherein the graduall breakings out of gospel-grace from Adam to Christ are clearly discovered, the differences betwixt the old and new Testament are laid open, divers errours of Arminians and others are confuted; the nature of the uprightnesse, and the way of Christ in bringing the soul into communion with himself.* London: Simeon Ash, 1645.
Ballard, Paul. "Baptists and Covenanting." *The Baptist Quarterly* 24, no. 8 (1972) 372–84.
Barth, Karl. *Church Dogmatics.* Translated by G. W. Bromiley. Edited by G. W. Bromiley and T. F. Torrance. 4 vols. Edinburgh: T. & T. Clark, 1936–69.
———. *The Teaching of the Church Regarding Baptism.* Translated by Ernest A. Payne. London: SCM, 1948.
Beach, J. Mark. *Christ and the Covenant: Francis Turretin's Federal Theology as a Defense of the Doctrine of Grace.* Göttingen: Vandenhoeck & Ruprecht, 2007.
———. "The Doctrine of the *Pactum Salutis* in the Covenant Theology of Herman Witsius." *Mid-America Journal of Theology* 13 (2002) 101–42.
Beasley-Murray, G. R. "The Authority and Justification for Believers' Baptism." *Review and Expositor* 77, no. 1 (1980) 63–70.
———. "Baptism in the Epistles of Paul." In *Christian Baptism: A Fresh Attempt to Understand the Rite in terms of Scripture, History, and Theology*, edited by A. Gilmore, 128–49. London: Lutterworth, 1959.
———. "Baptism in the New Testament." *Foundations* 3, no. 1 (1960) 15–31.
———. *Baptism in the New Testament.* Grand Rapids: Eerdmans, 1962.
———. "Baptism and the Sacramental View." *The Baptist Times*, February 11, 1960.
———. *Baptism Today and Tomorrow.* New York: St. Martin's, 1966.
———. "Church and Child in the New Testament." *The Baptist Quarterly* 21, no. 5 (1966) 206–18.

———. "Faith in the New Testament: A Baptist Perspective." *American Baptist Quarterly* 1, no. 2 (1982) 137–43.

———. "The Holy Spirit, Baptism, and the Body of Christ." *Review and Expositor* 63, no. 2 (1966) 177–85.

———. "I Still Find Infant Baptism Difficult." *The Baptist Quarterly* 22, no. 4 (1967) 225–36.

———. "The Problem of Infant Baptism: An Exercise in Possibilities." In *Festschrift Günter Wagner*, edited by Faculty of Baptist Theological Seminary Rüschlikon/Switzerland, 1–14. Bern: Peter Lang, 1994.

———. "The Sacraments." *The Fraternal* 70 (October 1948) 3–7.

———. "The Second Chapter of Colossians." *Review and Expositor* 70, no. 4 (1973) 469–79.

———. "The Spirit Is There." *The Baptist Times*, December 10, 1959.

———. "The Theology of the Child." *American Baptist Quarterly* 1, no. 2 (1982) 197–202.

Believing and Being Baptized: Baptism, So-called Re-baptism, and Children in the Church, A Discussion Document. Didcot, UK: The Baptist Union of Great Britain, 1996.

Berkhof, Hendrikus. *Christ and the Powers*. Translated by John Howard Yoder. Scottdale, PA: Herald, 1962.

Bierma, Lyle D. "Covenant or Covenants in the Theology of Olevianus?" *Calvin Theological Journal* 22 (1987) 228–50.

———. "Federal Theology in the Sixteenth Century: Two Traditions?" *The Westminster Theological Journal* 45 (1983) 304–21.

———. "The Role of Covenant Theology in Early Reformed Orthodoxy." *Sixteenth Century Journal* 21, no. 3 (1990) 453–62.

Boersma, Hans. *Richard Baxter's Understanding of Infant Baptism*. Princeton, NJ: Princeton Theological Seminary, 2002.

Booth, Abraham. *An Essay on the Kingdom of Christ*. Norwich, CT: John Sterry, 1801.

Brachlow, Stephen. *The Communion of Saints: Radical Puritan and Separatist Ecclesiology 1570–1625*. Oxford: Oxford University Press, 1988.

Brackney, William H. *Christian Voluntarism: Theology and Praxis*. Grand Rapids: Eerdmans, 1997.

———. *A Genetic History of Baptist Thought: With Special Reference to Baptists in Britain and North America*. Macon, GA: Mercer University Press, 2004.

———. "Thomas Grantham, Systematic Theology, and the Baptist Tradition." In *From Biblical Criticism to Biblical Faith: Essays in Honor of Lee Martin McDonald*, edited by William H. Brackney and Craig A. Evans, 199–216. Macon, GA: Mercer University Press, 2007.

———. *Voluntarism: The Dynamic Principle of the Free Church*. Wolfville, NS: Acadia University Press, 1992.

A Brief Confession or Declaration of Faith: Set forth by many of us, who are (falsely) called Ana-Baptists, to inform all men (in these days of scandal and reproach) of our innocent belief and practise, for which we are not only resolved to suffer persecution, to the loss of our goods, but also life it self, rather than to decline the same. London: G. D., 1660.

Bunyan, John. *The Doctrine of the Law and Grace Unfolded: or, a discourse touching the law and grace. The nature of the one, and the nature of the other: shewing what they are, as they are the two covenants, and likewise who they be, and what their conditions are, that be under either of these two covenants*. London: M. Wright, 1659.

Bibliography

Burrage, Champlin. *The Church Covenant Idea: Its Origin and Development*. Philadelphia: American Baptist Publication Society, 1904.

Called to Be One. London: Churches Together in England, n.d.

Calvin, John. *Commentaries on the Epistles to Timothy, Titus, and Philemon*. Translated by William Pringle. Grand Rapids: Baker Book House, 2003.

———. *Institutes of the Christian Religion*. Edited by John T. McNeill. Translated by Ford Lewis Battles. Library of Christian Classics 21. Louisville: Westminster John Knox, 1960.

Caneday, A. B. "Baptism in the Stone-Campbell Restoration Movement." In *Believer's Baptism: Sign of the New Covenant in Christ*, edited by Thomas R. Schreiner and Shawn D. Wright, 285–328. NAC Studies in Bible and Theology. Nashville: B&H Academic, 2006.

Cary, Philip. *A Solemn Call: Unto all that would be owned as Christ's faithful witnesses, speedily, and seriously, to attend unto the primitive purity of the gospel doctrine and worship: Or, a discourse concerning baptism*. London: John Harris, 1690.

Clark, Neville. *An Approach to the Theology of the Sacraments*. Studies in Biblical Theology. London: SCM, 1956.

———. "Initiation and Eschatology." In *Baptism, the New Testament and the Church: Historical and Contemporary Studies in Honour of R. E. O. White*, edited by Stanley E. Porter and Anthony R. Cross, 337–49. Journal for the Study of the New Testament Supplement Series 171. Sheffield, UK: Sheffield Academic, 1999.

———. "The Theology of Baptism." In *Christian Baptism: A Fresh Attempt to Understand the Rite in terms of Scripture, History, and Theology*, edited by A. Gilmore, 306–26. London: Lutterworth, 1959.

Clarke, Anthony, ed. *Bound for Glory? God, Church and World in Covenant*. Oxford: Whitley, 2002.

Clay, E. *Hymns and Spiritual Songs, Selected From Several Approved Authors*. Richmond, VA: John Dixon, 1793.

Coggins, James R. "The Theological Positions of John Smyth." *The Baptist Quarterly* 30, no. 6 (1984) 247–59.

Colwell, John E. *Promise and Presence: An Exploration of Sacramental Theology*. Milton Keynes, UK: Paternoster, 2005.

A Confession of Faith: put forth by the elders and brethren of many congregations of Christians (baptized upon profession of their faith) in London and the country. London: Benjamin Harris, 1677.

Coxe, Nehemiah. *A Discourse of the Covenants that God Made with Men before the Law, wherein the covenant of circumcision is more largely handled, and the invalidity of the plea for paedobaptism taken from thence discovered*. London: J. D., 1681.

Cross, Anthony R. *Baptism and the Baptists: Theology and Practice in Twentieth-Century Britain*. Paternoster Biblical and Theological Monographs. Carlisle, UK: Paternoster, 2000.

———. "Baptism in the Theology of John Calvin and Karl Barth." In *Calvin, Barth, and Reformed Theology*, edited by Neil B. MacDonald and Carl Trueman, 57–87. Paternoster Theological Monographs. Milton Keynes, UK: Paternoster, 2008.

———. "Baptismal Regeneration: Rehabilitating a Lost Dimension of New Testament Baptism." In *Baptist Sacramentalism 2*, edited by Anthony R. Cross and Philip E. Thompson, 149–74. Studies in Baptist History and Thought 25. Milton Keynes, UK: Paternoster, 2008.

Bibliography

———. "Baptists and Baptism—A British Perspective." *Baptist History and Heritage* 35, no. 1 (2000) 104–21.
———. "Being Open to God's Sacramental Work: A Study in Baptism." In *Semper Reformandum: Studies in Honour of Clark H. Pinnock*, edited by Stanley E. Porter and Anthony R. Cross, 355–77. Milton Keynes, UK: Paternoster, 2003.
———. "The Evangelical Sacrament: *Baptisma Semper Reformandum.*" *The Evangelical Quarterly* 80, no. 3 (2008) 195–217.
———. "Faith-Baptism: The Key to an Evangelical Baptismal Sacramentalism." *Journal of European Baptist Studies* 4, no. 3 (2004) 5–21.
———. "The Meaning of 'Baptisms' in Hebrews 6:2." In *Dimensions of Baptism: Biblical and Theological Studies*, edited by Stanley E. Porter and Anthony R. Cross, 163–86. Journal for the Study of the New Testament Supplement Series 234. London: Sheffield Academic, 2002.
———. "The Myth of English Baptist Anti-sacramentalism." In *Recycling the Past or Researching History? Studies in Baptist Historiography and Myths*, edited by Philip E. Thompson and Anthony R. Cross, 128–62. Studies in Baptist History and Thought 11. Milton Keynes, UK: Paternoster, 2005.
———. "'One Baptism' (Ephesians 4:5) A Challenge to the Church." In *Baptism, the New Testament and the Church: Historical and Contemporary Studies in Honour of R. E. O. White*, edited by Stanley E. Porter and Anthony R. Cross, 173–209. Journal for the Study of the New Testament Supplement Series 171. Sheffield, UK: Sheffield Academic, 1999.
———. *Recovering the Evangelical Sacrament: Baptisma Semper Reformandum*. Milton Keynes, UK: Paternoster, forthcoming.
———. "Spirit- and Water-Baptism in 1 Corinthians 12:13." In *Dimensions of Baptism: Biblical and Theological Studies*, edited by Stanley E. Porter and Anthony R. Cross, 120–48. Journal for the Study of the New Testament Supplement Series 234. London: Sheffield Academic, 2002.
Cross, Anthony, and Philip E. Thompson, eds. *Baptist Sacramentalism*. Studies in Baptist History and Thought 5. Carlisle, UK: Paternoster, 2003.
———. *Baptist Sacramentalism 2*. Studies in Baptist History and Thought 25. Milton Keynes, UK: Paternoster, 2008.
Cullmann, Oscar. *Baptism in the New Testament*. Translated by J. K. S. Reid. Studies in Biblical Theology. London: SCM, 1950.
Day, George. *The Communicants Instructor: Or, a Sacramental Catechism*. London: Tho. Parkhurst, 1700.
Dever, Mark E. "Baptism in the Context of the Local Church." In *Believer's Baptism: Sign of the New Covenant in Christ*, edited by Thomas R. Schreiner and Shawn D. Wright, 329–52. NAC Studies in Bible and Theology. Nashville: B&H Academic, 2006.
Deweese, Charles. *Baptist Church Covenants*. Nashville: Broadman, 1990.
Dunn, James D. G. *Unity and Diversity in the New Testament: An Inquiry into the Character of Earliest Christianity*. London: SCM, 1977.
Eenigenburg, Elton M. "The Place of the Covenant in Calvin's Thinking." *The Reformed Review* 10 (1957) 1–22.
Elliott, Ralph. "A Theology of Local Congregation." *Foundations* 22 (1979) 13–27.
Ellis, Christopher J. "The Baptism of Disciples and the Nature of the Church." In *Dimensions of Baptism: Biblical and Theological Studies*, edited by Stanley E. Porter and Anthony

R. Cross, 333–53. Journal for the Study of the New Testament Supplement Series 234. London: Sheffield Academic, 2002.

———. "Baptism and the Sacramental Freedom of God." In *Reflections on the Water: Understanding God and the World through the Baptism of Believers*, edited by Paul S. Fiddes, 23–45. Oxford: Regent's Park College; Macon, GA: Smyth & Helwys, 1996.

———. "Embodied Grace: Exploring the Sacraments and Sacramentality." In *Baptist Sacramentalism 2*, edited by Anthony R. Cross and Philip E. Thompson, 1–16. Studies in Baptist History and Thought 25. Milton Keynes, UK: Paternoster, 2008.

———. *Gathering: A Theology and Spirituality of Worship in Free Church Tradition*. London: SCM, 2004.

———. *Together on the Way: A Theology of Ecumenism*. London: The British Council of Churches, 1990.

Emerson, Everett H. "Calvin and Covenant Theology." *Church History* 25 (1956) 136–44.

Ferguson, Everett. *Baptism in the Early Church: History, Theology, and Liturgy in the First Five Centuries*. Grand Rapids: Eerdmans, 2009.

Fiddes, Paul S. "Baptism and Creation." In *Reflections on the Water: Understanding God and the World through the Baptism of Believers*, edited by Paul S. Fiddes, 47–67. Macon, GA: Smyth & Helwys, 1996.

———. "Baptism and Creation." In *Tracks and Traces: Baptist Identity in Church and Theology*, 107–24. Studies in Baptist History and Thought 13. Eugene, OR: Wipf & Stock, 2003.

———. "Baptism and the Process of Christian Initiation." In *Dimensions of Baptism: Biblical and Theological Studies*, edited by Stanley E. Porter and Anthony R. Cross, 280–303. Journal for the Study of the New Testament Supplement Series 234. London: Sheffield Academic, 2002.

———. "Believers' Baptism: An Act of Inclusion or Exclusion?" In *Tracks and Traces: Baptist Identity in Church and Theology*, 125–56. Studies in Baptist History and Thought 13. Eugene, OR: Wipf & Stock, 2003.

———. "The Church as a Eucharistic Community: A Baptist Contribution." In *Tracks and Traces: Baptist Identity in Church and Theology*, 157–92. Studies in Baptist History and Thought 13. Eugene, OR: Wipf & Stock, 2003.

———. "Church and Trinity: A Baptist Ecclesiology of Participation." In *Tracks and Traces: Baptist Identity in Church and Theology*, 65–82. Studies in Baptist History and Thought 13. Eugene, OR: Wipf & Stock, 2003.

———. "Church, Trinity and Covenant: An Ecclesiology of Participation." In *Gemeinschaft am Evangelium: Festschrift für Wiard Popkes*, edited by E. Brandt, P. S. Fiddes, and J. Molthagen, 37–55. Leipzig: Evangelische Verlag-Anstalt, 1996.

———. "*Ex Opere Operato*: Re-thinking a Historic Baptist Rejection." In *Baptist Sacramentalism 2*, edited by Anthony R. Cross and Philip E. Thompson, 218–38. Studies in Baptist History and Thought 25. Milton Keynes, UK: Paternoster, 2008.

———. "Learning from Others: Baptists and Receptive Ecumenism." *Louvain Studies* 33, no. 1–2 (2008) 54–73.

———. "Mission and Liberty: A Baptist Connection." In *Tracks and Traces: Baptist Identity in Church and Theology*, 242–64. Studies in Baptist History and Thought 13. Eugene, OR: Wipf & Stock, 2003.

———. *Participating in God: A Pastoral Doctrine of the Trinity*. London: Darton, Longman and Todd, 2000.

Bibliography

———. "'Walking Together': The Place of Covenant Theology in Baptist Life Yesterday and Today." In *Tracks and Traces: Baptist Identity in Church and Theology*, 21–47. Studies in Baptist History and Thought 13. Eugene, OR: Wipf & Stock, 2003.

———, ed. *Reflections on the Water: Understanding God and the World through the Baptism of Believers*. Oxford: Regent's Park College; Macon, GA: Smyth & Helwys, 1996.

Fiddes Paul S., Roger Hayden, Richard L. Kidd, Keith W. Clements, and Brian Haymes. *Bound to Love: The Covenant Basis of Baptist Life and Mission*. London: Baptist Union, 1985.

Firmin, Giles. *Scripture-Warrant Sufficient Proof for Infant-Baptism: being a reply to Mr. Grantham's "Presumption no Proof" Wherein his pretended answer to two questions propounded to the Anabaptists by G.F. is examined, and found to be no answer.* London: Tho. Parkhurst, 1688.

Fowler, Stanley K. "Baptists and Churches of Christ in Search of a Common Theology of Baptism." In *Baptist Sacramentalism 2*, edited by Anthony R. Cross and Philip E. Thompson, 254–69. Studies in Baptist History and Thought 25. Milton Keynes, UK: Paternoster, 2008.

———. "Is 'Baptist Sacramentalism' an Oxymoron? Reactions in Britain to *Christian Baptism* (1959)." In *Baptist Sacramentalism*, edited by Anthony R. Cross and Philip E. Thompson, 129–50. Studies in Baptist History and Thought 5. Carlisle, UK: Paternoster, 2003.

———. *More Than a Symbol: The British Baptist Recovery of Baptismal Sacramentalism*. Studies in Baptist History and Thought 2. Carlisle, UK: Paternoster, 2002.

Fuller, Andrew. *The Gospel Worthy of All Acceptation*. 2nd ed. London, n.p., 1801.

Garner, Robert. *A Treatise of Baptisme*. n.p., 1645.

Garrett, James Leo, Jr. *Baptist Theology: A Four-Century Study*. Macon, GA: Mercer University Press, 2009.

Gass, Wilhelm. *Geschichte der protestantischen Dogmatik in ihrem Zusammenhange mit der Theologie*. 4 vols. Berlin: Georg Reimer, 1854–67.

Gentry, Peter J., and Stephen J. Wellum. *Kingdom Through Covenant: A Biblical-Theological Understanding of the Covenants*. Wheaton, IL: Crossway, 2012.

George, Timothy. "The Reformed Doctrine of Believers' Baptism." *Interpretation* 47, no. 3 (1993) 242–55.

George, Timothy, and Denise George, eds. *Baptist Confessions, Covenants, and Catechisms*. Nashville: Broadman & Holman, 1999.

Gill, John. *The Cause of God and Truth: In Four Parts*. 4th ed. London: for G. Keith, 1775.

———. *Complete Body of Doctrinal and Practical Divinity: Or A System of Evangelical Truths, Deduced from the Sacred Scriptures*. New ed. London: Thomas Tegg, 1839. Reprint, Grand Rapids: Baker, 1978.

Gilmore, Alec. *Baptism and Christian Unity*. Valley Forge, PA: Judson, 1966.

———, ed. *Christian Baptism: A Fresh Attempt to Understand the Rite in terms of Scripture, History, and Theology*. London: Lutterworth, 1959.

Grantham, Thomas. *Christianismus Primitivus: or, the ancient Christian religion, in its nature, certainty, excellency, and beauty, (internal and external) particularly considered, asserted, and vindicated, from the many abuses which have invaded that sacred profession, by humane innovation, or pretended revelation comprehending likewise the general duties of mankind, in their respective relations; and particularly, the obedience of all Christians to magistrates, and the necessity of Christian-moderation* about things 'dispensible' in matters of religion. with divers cases of conscience discussed and resolved. 4 books. London: Francis Smith, 1678.

———. *The Infants Advocate: against the cruel doctrine of those Presbyterians who hold, that the greatest part of dying infants shall be damned: in answer to a book of Mr. Giles Firmin's entituled, "Scripture warrant, &c."* London: J. D., 1688.

———. *The Paedo-Baptists Apology for the Baptized Churches, shewing the invalidity of the strongest grounds for infant baptism out of the works of the learned assertors of that tenent, and that the baptism of repentance for the remission of sins is a duty incumbent upon all sinners who come orderly to the profession of Christianity: also the promise of the Spirit [b]eing the substance of a sermon on I Cor. 12, I, to which is added a postscript out of the works of Dr. Jer. Taylor in defence of imposition of hands as a never failing ministery.* London: n.p., 1671.

———. *Presumption no Proof: Or, Mr. Petto's arguments for infant-baptism considered and answered, and infants interest in the covenant of grace without baptism, asserted and maintained. Whereunto is prefixed an answer to two questions propounded by Mr. Firmin, about infants church-membership and baptism.* London: n.p., 1687.

———. *The Quaeries Examined, or, fifty anti-queries seriously propounded to the people called Presbyterians occasioned by the publication of fifty queries, gathered out of the works of Mr. Rich. Baxter. By J. B. Wherein the principal allegations usually brought to support infant-baptism are discovered to be insufficient.* London: n.p., 1676.

———. *A Religious Contest, or A brief account of a disputation holden at Blyton in the county of Lincoln between Mr. William Fort minister of the perochial congregation at Blyton on the one part, and Thomas Grantham, servant to the baptised churches on the other part: whereunto is added Brief animadversions upon Dr. Stilling-fleet his digressions about infant baptism in his book intituled, A rational account of the Protestant religion, &c., in both which are shewed that the generality of the nations now professing Christianity are as yet unbaptised into Christ: 1. Because their sprinkling and crossing the fore-head is not the right way of baptising, 2. Because infants ought not to be baptised.* London: n.p., 1674.

———. *Truth and Peace, or, The last and most friendly debate concerning infant-baptism being a brief answer to a late book intituled, "The Case of Infant-Baptism" (written by a doctor of the Church of England)."* London: for the author, 1689.

Greaves, Richard L. "The Origins and Early Development of English Covenant Thought." *The Historian* 31 (1968) 21–35.

Grenz, Stanley J. "Baptism and the Lord's Supper as Community Acts: Toward a Sacramental Understanding of the Ordinances." In *Baptist Sacramentalism*, edited by Anthony R. Cross and Philip E. Thompson, 76–95. Studies in Baptist History and Thought 5. Carlisle, UK: Paternoster, 2003.

Hammett, John S. *Biblical Foundations for Baptist Churches: A Contemporary Ecclesiology*. Grand Rapids: Kregel, 2005.

Harmon, Steven R. *Ecumenism Means You, Too: Ordinary Christians and the Quest for Christian Unity*. Eugene, OR: Cascade, 2010.

———. *Towards Baptist Catholicity: Essays on Tradition and the Baptist Vision*. Studies in Baptist History and Thought 27. Eugene, OR: Wipf & Stock, 2006.

Harsch, Lloyd A. "The Meaning of Baptism among First Generation Baptists." Paper presented at the annual meeting of the Southwestern Region of the Evangelical Theological Society, Ft. Worth, TX, March 25, 2006.

Bibliography

Hartman, L. *"Into the Name of the Lord Jesus": Baptism in the Early Church, Studies in the New Testament in Its World.* Edinburgh: T. & T. Clark, 1997.

Harvey, Barry. *Can These Bones Live? A Catholic Baptist Engagement with Ecclesiology, Hermeneutics, and Social Theory.* Grand Rapids: Brazos, 2008.

Hauerwas, Stanley. *A Community of Character: Toward a Constructive Christian Social Ethic.* Notre Dame, IN: University of Notre Dame Press, 1981.

Haymes, Brian. "Baptism: A Question of Belief and Age?" *Perspectives in Religious Studies* 27, no. 1 (2000) 125–30.

———. "Baptism as a Political Act." In *Reflections on the Water: Understanding God and the World through the Baptism of Believers,* edited by Paul S. Fiddes, 69–83. Macon, GA: Smyth & Helwys, 1996.

———. "Making Too Little and Too Much of Baptism?" In *Ecumenism and History: Studies in Honour of John H. Y. Briggs,* edited by Anthony R. Cross, 175–89. Carlisle, UK: Paternoster, 2002.

———. "The Moral Miracle of Faith." In *Dimensions of Baptism: Biblical and Theological Studies,* edited by Stanley E. Porter and Anthony R. Cross, 325–32. Journal for the Study of the New Testament Supplement Series 234. London: Sheffield Academic, 2002.

Helm, Paul. "Calvin and the Covenant: Unity and Continuity." *The Evangelical Quarterly* 54, no. 4 (1982) 65–81.

Heppe, Heinrich. *Dogmatik des deutschen Protestantismus im sechzehnten Jahrhundert.* 3 vols. Gotha: Perthes, 1857.

Heron, Alasdair I. C. *Table and Tradition.* Philadelphia: Westminster, 1983.

Hickes, George. *The Case of Infant-Baptism: In Five Questions.* London: T. Hodgkin, 1685.

Hicks, John Mark, and Greg Taylor. *Down in the River to Pray: Revisioning Baptism as God's Transforming Work.* Siloam Springs, AR: Leafwood, 2004.

Hoekema, Anthony. "Calvin's Doctrine of the Covenant of Grace." *The Reformed Review* 15 (1962) 1–12.

———. "The Covenant of Grace in Calvin's Teaching." *Calvin Theological Journal* 2 (1967) 133–61.

Hutchinson, Edward. *A Treatise Concerning the Covenant and Baptism: Dialogue-wise, between a Baptist & Poedo-Baptist, wherein is shewed, that believers only are the spirituall seed of Abraham; fully discovering the fallacy of the argument drawn from the birth priviledge.* London: Francis Smith, 1676.

The International Mission Board of the Southern Baptist Convention Board of Trustees. "Position Paper concerning the IMB Guideline on Baptism." International Mission Board. http://www.imb.org/main/news/details.asp?LanguageID=1709&StoryID=3840 (accessed September 12, 2011).

Jewett, Paul K. *Infant Baptism and the Covenant of Grace: An Appraisal of the Argument that as Infants Were Once Circumcised, so They Should Now Be Baptized.* Grand Rapids: Eerdmans, 1978.

Karlberg, Mark W. "Reformed Interpretation of the Mosaic Covenant." *The Westminster Theological Journal* 43 (1980) 1–57.

Keach, Benjamin. *The Ax laid to the Root: Or, One blow more at the Foundation of Infant Baptism, and Church-Membership. Containing an Exposition of that Metaphorical Text of Holy Scripture, MAT. 3. 10. Being the Substance of Two Sermons lately Preached, with some Additions. Wherein is shewed That God made a Two-fold Covenant with Abraham, and that Circumcision appertained not to the Covenant of Grace, but to the Legal and External Covenant God made with Abraham's Natural Seed, as such. Together With an Answer to Mr. John Flavel's last Grand Arguments in his Vindiciarum Vindex, in his Last Reply to Mr. Philip Cary. Also to Mr. Rothwell's Paedo-Baptisms vindicatur, as to what seems most material.* Part 1. London : Printed for the author, and are to be sold by John Harris, [1693].

———. *The Display of Glorious Grace: or, the covenant of peace opened, in fourteen sermons.* London: n.p., 1698.

———. *The Glory of a True Church, and Its Discipline Display'd.* London: n.p., 1697.

[Keach, Benjamin?]. *The Articles of Faith of the Church of Christ, or Congregation meeting at Horsley-down, Benjamin Keach, pastor.* London: n.p., 1697.

Kendall, R. T. *Calvin and English Calvinism to 1649.* Oxford: Oxford University Press, 1979.

———. "The Puritan Modification of Calvin's Theology." In *John Calvin: His Influence in the Western World*, edited by W. Stanford Reid, 197–214. Grand Rapids: Zondervan, 1982.

Kidd, Richard. "Baptism and the Identity of Christian Communities." In *Reflections on the Water: Understanding God and the World through the Baptism of Believers*, edited by Paul S. Fiddes, 85–99. Macon, GA: Smyth & Helwys, 1996.

———, ed. *Something to Declare: A Study of the Declaration of Principle of the Baptist Union of Great Britain.* Oxford: Whitley, 1996.

Killacky, Christopher. "Covenant Theology: A Renewal of Theology for Baptists." In *From Biblical Criticism to Biblical Faith: Essays in Honor of Lee Martin McDonald*, edited by William H. Brackney and Craig A. Evans, 217–49. Macon, GA: Mercer University Press, 2007.

Kingdon, David. *Children of Abraham.* Sussex, UK: Carey, 1973.

Lee, Jason K. "Baptism and Covenant." In *Restoring Integrity in Baptist Churches*, edited by Thomas White, Jason G. Duesing, and Malcolm B. Yarnell III, 119–36. Grand Rapids: Kregel, 2008.

———. *The Theology of John Smyth: Puritan, Separatist, Baptist, Mennonite.* Macon, GA: Mercer University Press, 2003.

Lewis, Gordon R. and Bruce A. Demarest. *Integrative Theology.* 3 vols. Grand Rapids: Zondervan, 1996.

Lillback, Peter A. *The Binding of God: Calvin's Role in the Development of Covenant Theology.* Texts and Studies in Reformation and Post-Reformation Thought. Grand Rapids: Baker Academic, 2001.

———. "The Continuing Conundrum: Calvin and the Conditionality of the Covenant." *Calvin Theological Journal* 29 (1994) 42–74.

———. "Ursinus' Development of the Covenant of Creation: A Debt to Melanchthon or Calvin?" *The Westminster Theological Journal* 43 (1981) 247–88.

Malone, Fred A. *The Baptism of Disciples Alone: A Covenantal Argument for Credobaptism versus Paedobaptism.* Rev. and exp. ed. Cape Coral, FL: Founders, 2007.

Marcel, Pierre Ch. *The Biblical Doctrine of Infant Baptism: Sacrament of the Covenant of Grace.* Translated by Philip Edgcumbe Hughes. London: James Clark, 1953.

Marsden, George. "Perry Miller's Rehabilitation of the Puritans: A Critique." *Church History* 39 (1970) 91–105.

McCormack, Bruce. "Grace and Being: The Role of God's Gracious Election in Karl Barth's Theological Ontology." In *The Cambridge Companion to Karl Barth*, edited by John Webster, 92–109. Cambridge: Cambridge University Press, 2000.

Bibliography

McGiffert, Michael. "From Moses to Adam: The Making of the Covenant of Works." *The Sixteenth Century Journal* 19 (1988) 131–55.

———. "Grace and Works: The Rise and Division of Covenant Divinity in Elizabethan Puritanism." *Harvard Theological Review* 75, no. 4 (1982) 463–502.

———. "William Tyndale's Conception of Covenant." *Journal of Ecclesiastical History* 32, no. 2 (1981) 167–84.

Meyer, Jason C. *The End of the Law: Mosaic Covenant in Pauline Theology*. NAC Studies in Bible and Theology. Nashville: B&H Academic, 2009.

Mickle, Allen, Jr. "'To Do Him Special Service for Church and Commonwealth': The Life and Labors of Thomas Patient." *Eusebeia: The Bulletin of the Andrew Fuller Center for Baptist Studies*, forthcoming.

Miller, Perry. *Errand into the Wilderness*. New York: Harper & Row, 1956.

———. *The New England Mind: The Seventeenth Century*. 1939. Reprint, Cambridge, MA: Harvard University Press, 1954.

Møller, Jens. "The Beginnings of Puritan Covenant Theology." *Journal of Ecclesiastical History* 14 (1963) 46–67.

Moody, Christopher Bryan. "American Baptist Sacramentalism?" PhD diss., Southwestern Baptist Theological Seminary, 2006.

———. *American Baptist Sacramentalism?: Toward a Sacred Theology of Baptism in the Context of Transatlantic Baptist Disagreement*. VDM Verlag, 2009.

Muller, Richard A. *After Calvin: Studies in the Development of a Theological Tradition*. Studies in Historical Theology. New York: Oxford University Press, 2003.

———. "Covenant and Conscience in English Reformed Theology: Three Variations on a Seventeenth Century Theme." *The Westminster Theological Journal* 42 (1980) 308–34.

———. "The Covenant of Works and the Stability of Divine Law in Seventeenth-century Reformed Orthodoxy: A Study in the Theology of Herman Witsius and Wilhelmus à Brakel." *Calvin Theological Journal* 29 (1994) 75–100.

———. "The Problem of Protestant Scholasticism—A Review and Definition." In *Reformation and Scholasticism: An Ecumenical Enterprise*, edited by Willem J. van Asselt and Eef Dekker, 45–64. Texts and Studies in Reformation and Post-Reformation Thought. Grand Rapids: Baker Academic, 2001.

———. "The Spirit and the Covenant: John Gill's Critique of the Pactum Salutis." *Foundations* 24 (1981) 4–14.

———. "Toward the *Pactum Salutis*: Locating the Origins of a Concept." *Mid-America Journal of Theology* 18 (2007) 11–65.

———. *The Unaccommodated Calvin: Studies in the Foundation of a Theological Tradition*. Oxford Studies in Historical Theology. New York: Oxford Univeristy Press, 2000.

———. "The Use and Abuse of a Document: Beza's *Tabula praedestinationis*, the Bolsec Controversy, and the Origins of Reformed Orthodoxy." In *Protestant Scholasticism: Essays in Reassessment*, edited by Carl R. Trueman and R. S. Clark, 33–61. Carlisle, UK: Paternoster, 1999.

Mullins, E. Y. *The Axioms of Religion: A New Interpretation of the Baptist Faith*. Philadelphia: Judson, 1908.

Murray, Paul D., ed. *Receptive Ecumenism and the Call to Catholic Learning: Exploring a Way for Contemporary Ecumenism*. Oxford: Oxford University Press, 2008.

Nettles, Thomas J. *The Baptists: Key People Involved in Forming a Baptist Identity*. Vol. 1. Beginnings in Britain. Fearn, Ross-shire, UK: Christian Focus/Mentor, 2005.

———. *The Baptists: Key People Involved in Forming a Baptist Identity.* Vol. 3. The Modern Era. Fearn, Ross-shire, UK: Christian Focus/Mentor, 2007.

Nichols, Greg. *Covenant Theology: A Reformed and Baptistic Perspective on God's Covenants.* Pelham, AL: Solid Ground Christian Books, 2011.

An Orthodox Creed: Or, a Protestant confession of faith. London: n.p., 1679.

Owen, John. *A Continuation of the Exposition of the Epistle of Paul the Apostle to the Hebrews. Viz. On the Sixth, Seventh, Eighth, Ninth, and Tenth Chapters.* London: for Nathaniel Ponder, 1680.

Patient, Thomas. *The Doctrine of Baptism, and the Distinction of the Covenants or a Plain Treatise.* London: Henry Hills, 1654.

Payne, Ernest A. "Believers' Baptism in Ecumenical Discussion." *Foundations* 3, no. 1 (1960) 32–39.

Petto, Samuel. *Infant Baptism of Christ's Appointment, or a discovery of infants interest in the covenant with Abraham, shewing who are the spiritual seed and who are the fleshly seed.* London: for Edward Giles, 1687.

———. *Infant-Baptism Vindicated: from the exceptions of Mr. Thomas Grantham.* London: T. S., 1691.

Poole, David N. J. *The History of the Covenant Concept from the Bible to Johannes Cloppenburg: De Foedere Dei.* San Francisco: Mellen Research University Press, 1992.

Porter, Stanley E., and Anthony R. Cross. "Introduction: Baptism in Recent Debate." In *Baptism, the New Testament and the Church: Historical and Contemporary Studies in Honour of R. E. O. White*, edited by Stanley E. Porter and Anthony R. Cross, 33–39. Journal for the Study of the New Testament Supplement Series 171. Sheffield, UK: Sheffield Academic, 1999.

Read, L. A. "The Ordinances." *The Fraternal* 67 (January 1948) 8–10.

Renihan, James M. "An Excellent and Judicious Divine: Nehemiah Coxe." In Nehemiah Coxe and John Owen, *Covenant Theology from Adam to Christ*, edited by Ronald D. Miller, James M. Renihan, and Francisco Orozco, 7–24. Palmdale, CA: Reformed Baptist Academic Press, 2005.

Riker, David B. *A Catholic Reformed Theologian: Federalism and Baptism in the Thought of Benjamin Keach, 1640–1704.* Studies in Baptist History and Thought 35. Milton Keynes, UK: Paternoster, 2009.

Roberts, Samuel K. "A Call to Covenant." *American Baptist Quarterly* 21, no. 2 (2002) 163–72.

Robinson, H. Wheeler. *Baptist Principles.* 4th ed. London: Carey Kingsgate, 1960.

———. "Believers' Baptism and the Holy Spirit." *The Baptist Quarterly* 9 (1938–39) 387–97.

———. *The Christian Doctrine of Man.* Edinburgh: T. & T. Clark, 1911.

———. *The Christian Experience of the Holy Spirit.* New York: Harper & Brothers, 1928.

———. "The Five Points of a Baptist's Faith." *The Baptist Quarterly* 11 (1942–45) 4–14.

———. *The Life and Faith of the Baptists.* London: Carey Kingsgate, 1946.

———. "The Place of Baptism in Churches To-day." *The Baptist Quarterly* 1, no. 5 (1923) 209–18.

———. *Redemption and Revelation: In the Actuality of History.* London: Nisbet, 1942.

Rolston, Holmes III. "Responsible Man in Reformed Theology: Calvin Versus the Westminster Confession." *Scottish Journal of Theology* 23 (1970) 129–56.

Schillebeeckx, Edward. *Christ the Sacrament of the Encounter with God.* New York: Sheed and Ward, 1963.

Bibliography

Schmemann, Alexander. *Introduction to Liturgical Theology*. Crestwood, NY: St. Vladimir's Seminary, 1966.

Schreiner, Thomas R., and Shawn D. Wright. Introduction to *Believer's Baptism: Sign of the New Covenant in Christ*, edited by Thomas R. Schreiner and Shawn D. Wright. NAC Studies in Bible and Theology. Nashville: B&H Academic, 2006.

———, eds. *Believer's Baptism: Sign of the New Covenant in Christ*. NAC Studies in Bible and Theology. Nashville: B&H Academic, 2006.

Schweizer, Alexander. *Die Glaubenslehre der Evangelisch-Reformierten Kirche*. 2 vols. Zürich: Orell, Füssli, und Comp., 1844–47.

Sherman, Hazel. "Baptized in the Name of the Father, Son and the Holy Spirit." In *Reflections on the Water: Understanding God and the World through the Baptism of Believers*, edited by Paul S. Fiddes, 101–16. Oxford: Regent's Park College; Macon, GA: Smyth & Helwys, 1996.

Skepp, John. *Divine Energy: or the efficacious operations of the Spirit of God upon the soul of man, in his effectual calling and conversion, stated, prov'd and vindicated*. London: for Joseph Marshall and Aaron Ward, 1722.

Smyth, John. *The Works of John Smyth*. Edited by W. T. Whitley. 2 vols. Cambridge: Cambridge University Press, 1915.

Spilsberie [Spilsbury?], John. *Gods Ordinance, The Saints Priviledge. Discovered and proved in two treatises*. Edited by Benjamin Coxe. London: M. Simmons for Benjamin Allen, 1646.

Spilsbery [Spilsbury?], John. *A Treatise Concerning the Lawfull subject of Baptisme*. London: Henry Hills, 1652.

Strehle, Stephen. *Calvinism, Federalism, and Scholasticism: A Study of the Reformed Doctrine of Covenant*. Basler und Berner Studien zur historischen und systematischen Theologie. Bern: Peter Lang, 1988.

Thompson, Philip E. "Baptists and 'Calvinism': Discerning the Shape of the Question." *Baptist History and Heritage* 39, no. 2 (2004) 61–76.

———. "Memorial Dimensions of Baptism." In *Dimensions of Baptism: Biblical and Theological Studies*, edited by Stanley E. Porter and Anthony R. Cross, 304–24. Journal for the Study of the New Testament Supplement Series 234. London: Sheffield Academic, 2002.

———. "A New Question in Baptist History: Seeking a Catholic Spirit among Early Baptists." *Pro Ecclesia* 8, no. 1 (1999) 51–72.

———. "People of the Free God: The Passion of Seventeenth-century Baptists." *American Baptist Quarterly* 15 (1996) 223–41.

———. "Practicing the Freedom of God: Formation in Early Baptist Life." In *Theology and Lived Christianity: The Annual Publication of the College Theology Society*, edited by David M. Hammond, vol. 45, 119–38. Mystic, CT: Twenty-third, 2000.

———. "Re-envisioning Baptist Identity: Historical, Theological, and Liturgical Analysis." *Perspectives in Religious Studies* 27, no. 3 (2000) 287–302.

———. "Sacraments and Religious Liberty: From Critical Practice to Rejected Infringement." In *Baptist Sacramentalism*, edited by Anthony R. Cross and Philip E. Thompson, 36–54. Studies in Baptist History and Thought 5. Carlisle, UK: Paternoster, 2003.

———. "Seventeenth-century Baptist Confessions in Context." *Perspectives in Religious Studies* 29, no. 4 (2002) 335–48.

Bibliography

Tombes, John. *Anti-Paedobaptism: Or the Third Part. Being, A Full Review of the Dispute Concerning Infant-Baptism*. London: E. Aisop, 1657.
———. *A Short Catechism about Baptism*. London: Henry Hills, 1659.
Torrance, James B. "Covenant or Contract? A Study of the Theological Background of Worship in Seventeenth-century Scotland." *Scottish Journal of Theology* 23 (1970) 51–76.
Trinterud, Leonard J. "The Origins of Puritanism." *Church History* 20 (1951) 37–57.
Trueman, Carl R. "Calvin and Calvinism." In *The Cambridge Companion to John Calvin*, edited by Donald K. McKim, 225–44. Cambridge Companions to Religion. Cambridge: Cambridge University Press, 2004.
Tull, James E. "The Ordinances/Sacraments in Baptists Thought." *American Baptist Quarterly* 1, no. 2 (1982) 187–96.
Underwood, A. C. "Views of Modern Churches (g) Baptist (2)." In *The Ministry and the Sacraments*, edited by Roderic Dunkerley, 223–29. London: SCM, 1937.
VanDrunen, David, and R. Scott Clark. "The Covenant before the Covenants." In *Covenant, Justification, and Pastoral Ministry: Essays by the Faculty of Westminster Seminary California*, edited by R. Scott Clark, 167–96. Phillipsburg, NJ: Presbyterian & Reformed, 2007.
Venema, Cornelis P. *Heinrich Bullinger and the Doctrine of Predestination: Author of "the other Reformed Tradition"?* Texts and Studies in Reformation and Post-Reformation Thought. Grand Rapids: Baker Academic, 2002.
Vos, Geerhardus. *Redemptive History and Biblical Interpretation: The Shorter Writings of Geerhardus Vos*. Edited by Richard B. Gaffin, Jr. Translated by S. Voorwinde/W. Van Gemeren. Revised translation by Richard B. Gaffin. Phillipsburg, NJ: Presbyterian and Reformed, 1980.
Waldron, Samuel E. *Biblical Baptism: A Reformed Defense of Believers' Baptism*. Grand Rapids: Truth For Eternity Ministries, 1998.
Walker, Michael J. "The Relation of Infants to Church, Baptism and Gospel in Seventeenth Century Baptist Theology." *The Baptist Quarterly* 21.6 (1966) 242–62.
Weir, David. *The Origins of the Federal Theology in Sixteenth-Century Reformation Thought*. Oxford: Clarendon, 1990.
Wells, Tom, and Fred G. Zaspel. *New Covenant Theology: Description, Definition, Defense*. Frederick, MD: New Covenant Media, 2002.
Wellum, Stephen J. "Baptism and the Relationship between the Covenants." In *Believer's Baptism: Sign of the New Covenant in Christ*, edited by Thomas R. Schreiner and Shawn D. Wright, 97–161. NAC Studies in Bible and Theology. Nashville: B&H Academic, 2006.
West, W. M. S. "The Child and the Church: A Baptist Perspective." In *Pilgrim Pathways: Essays in Baptist History in Honour of B. R. White*, edited by William H. Brackney, Paul S. Fiddes, and John H. Y. Briggs, 75–110. Macon, GA: Mercer University Press, 1999.
Whiston, Joseph. *Energiea Planes: or a brief discourse concerning man's natural; romeness to, and tenaciousness of errour. Whereunto is added some arguments to prove that that covenant entred with Abraham, Gen. 17.7 is the covenant of grace*. London: J. D., 1682.
———. *Infant-Baptism Plainly Proved. A discourse wherein certain arguments for infant-baptism, formerly syllogistically handled, are now reviewed, abbreviated, and reduced to a plain method, for the benefit, of the unlearned, and persons of weaker capacity*. London: for Jonathan Robinson, 1678

Bibliography

Whitaker, E. C. *Documents of the Baptismal Liturgy*. Revised and expanded by Maxwell E. Johnson. 3rd ed. London: SPCK, 2003.

White, B. R. *The English Baptists of the Seventeenth Century*. A History of English Baptists 1. London: The Baptist Historical Society, 1983.

———. *The English Separatist Tradition: From the Marian Martyrs to the Pilgrim Fathers*. Oxford: Oxford University Press, 1971.

White, R. E. O. *The Biblical Doctrine of Initiation: A Theology of Baptism and Evangelism*. Grand Rapids: Eerdmans, 1960.

———. *Christian Baptism: A Dialogue*. London: Pickering & Inglis, 1977.

Wikenhauser, Alfred. *Pauline Mysticism: Christ in the Mystical Teaching of St. Paul*. Translated by Joseph Cunningham. New York: Herder and Herder, 1960.

Wink, Walter. *Engaging the Powers: Discernment and Resistance in a World of Domination*. Vol. 3 of The Powers. Minneapolis: Fortress, 1992.

———. *Naming the Powers: The Language of Power in the New Testament*. Vol. 1 of The Powers. Philadelphia: Fortress, 1984.

———. *Unmasking the Powers: The Invisible Forces That Determine Human Existence*. Vol. 2 of The Powers. Philadelphia: Fortress, 1986.

Wright, Nigel. "Covenant and Covenanting." *The Baptist Quarterly* 39, no. 6 (2002) 287–90.

Wright, Stephen. *The Early English Baptists, 1603–1649*. Rochester, NY: Boydell, 2006.

Yoder, John Howard. "A Non-Baptist View of Southern Baptists." *Review and Expositor* 67, no. 2 (1970) 219–28.

———. *The Politics of Jesus: Vicit Agnus Noster*. 2nd ed. Grand Rapids: Eerdmans, 1972, 1994.

Many Christians who practice believer baptism struggle answering basic questions about it:

What does it mean to be baptized? How does baptism relate to faith? What does God do through baptism?

In *Waters of Promise* Brandon Jones seeks to answer these questions by drawing from Scripture, theology, history, and church practice. The resulting recovery of the link between covenant theology and believer baptism may change not only how you think about baptism but also how your church practices it.

"Historically, Baptists have been quite adroit in their defense of why only believers should be baptized and exactly how this ordinance should be carried out. What they have often forgotten is to explain what baptism means. This new study by Jones addresses this forgotten question. A careful reading of his work promises to broaden our understanding of baptism's biblical meaning."

MICHAEL A. G. HAYKIN
The Southern Baptist Theological Seminary

"When I was writing my doctoral thesis on British Baptist baptismal theology, I found almost no engagement with the British material on this side of the ocean. Over the last decade, that has begun to change, and *Waters of Promise* both narrates and advances that process. Jones's suggestion of a Baptist sacramental theology rooted in covenant theology adds a new (or perhaps old!) idea worth considering."

STANLEY K. FOWLER
Heritage Theological Seminary

"*Waters of Promise* is a significant contribution that advocates the rediscovery of covenant theology, seeing in believers' baptism the Spirit's gracious work as a confirming sign and seal of initiation into the new covenant with God and his people. Jones's study is thought-provoking and a challenging contribution to an important subject."

ANTHONY R. CROSS
University of Oxford

BRANDON C. JONES (PhD, Calvin Theological Seminary) is pastor of Herreid Baptist Church in Herreid, South Dakota.

RELIGION / Theology

Cover Design by Matthew Stock

PICKWICK Publications
An imprint of *Wipf and Stock Publishers*

www.wipfandstock.com

ISBN 978-1-61097-628-2

ARIANA HUNTER

40 SUPER FOOD & SUPER SMOOTHIE RECIPES FOR BETTER HEALTH

Feel Amazing, Lose Weight, and Gain Unlimited Energy